The Royal Commission
on Environmental Pollution

CHAIRMAN: SIR JOHN LAWTON CBE, FRS

Twenty-eighth Report

Adapting Institutions to Climate Change

Presented to Parliament by Command of Her Majesty
March 2010

Cm 7843

£34.55

The cover image of an adaptation snakes and ladders board depicts some of the risks and opportunities presented by climate change.

A key to the images is provided below:

2:   Elderly lady warm at home in the winter

6:   New crop opportunities – vines

15: Cracked soil as a result of drought

17: Increased UK tourism

18: Extreme weather

21: Increased risk of flooding

22: New species in UK – dragonfly

24: New crops – sunflowers

29: Increased winter temperatures

31: Loss of species – purple saxifrage

34: Increased UK tourism – more cars on the road

39: Increased average temperatures

45: People queuing for drinking water

47: Species loss – dotterel

The cover image was drawn for the RCEP by Guy Allen.

PREVIOUS REPORTS BY THE ROYAL COMMISSION ON ENVIRONMENTAL POLLUTION

Special report	Artificial Light in the Environment	November 2009
27th report	Novel Materials in the Environment: The case of nanotechnology	Cm 7468, November 2008
26th report	The Urban Environment	Cm 7009, March 2007
Special report	Crop Spraying and the Health of Residents and Bystanders	September 2005
25th report	Turning the Tide – Addressing the Impact of Fisheries on the Marine Environment	Cm 6392, December 2004
Special report	Biomass as a Renewable Energy Source	April 2004
24th report	Chemicals in Products – Safeguarding the Environment and Human Health	Cm 5827, June 2003
Special report	The Environmental Effects of Civil Aircraft in Flight	September 2002
23rd report	Environmental Planning	Cm 5459, March 2002
22nd report	Energy – The Changing Climate	Cm 4749, June 2000
21st report	Setting Environmental Standards	Cm 4053, October 1998
20th report	Transport and the Environment – Developments since 1994	Cm 3752, September 1997
19th report	Sustainable Use of Soil	Cm 3165, February 1996
18th report	Transport and the Environment	Cm 2674, October 1994
17th report	Incineration of Waste	Cm 2181, May 1993
16th report	Freshwater Quality	Cm 1966, June 1992
15th report	Emissions from Heavy Duty Diesel Vehicles	Cm 1631, September 1991
14th report	GENHAZ – A system for the critical appraisal of proposals to release genetically modified organisms into the environment	Cm 1557, June 1991
13th report	The Release of Genetically Engineered Organisms to the Environment	Cm 720, July 1989
12th report	Best Practicable Environmental Option	Cm 310, February 1988
11th report	Managing Waste: The Duty of Care	Cm 9675, December 1985
10th report	Tackling Pollution – Experience and Prospects	Cm 9149, February 1984
9th report	Lead in the Environment	Cm 8852, April 1983
8th report	Oil Pollution of the Sea	Cm 8358, October 1981
7th report	Agriculture and Pollution	Cm 7644, September 1979
6th report	Nuclear Power and the Environment	Cm 6618, September 1976
5th report	Air Pollution Control: An Integrated Approach	Cm 6371, January 1976
4th report	Pollution Control: Progress and Problems	Cm 5780, December 1974
3rd report	Pollution in Some British Estuaries and Coastal Waters	Cm 5054, September 1972
2nd report	Three Issues in Industrial Pollution	Cm 4894, March 1972
	First report	Cm 4585, February 1971

Royal Commission on Environmental Pollution

Twenty-eighth Report

To the Queen's Most Excellent Majesty

MAY IT PLEASE YOUR MAJESTY

We, the undersigned Commissioners, having been appointed 'to advise on matters, both national and international, concerning the pollution of the environment; on the adequacy of research in this field; and the future possibilities of danger to the environment';

And to enquire into any such matters referred to us by one of Your Majesty's Secretaries of State or by one of Your Majesty's Ministers, or any other such matters on which we ourselves shall deem it expedient to advise:

HUMBLY SUBMIT TO YOUR MAJESTY THE FOLLOWING REPORT.

"Adapt or perish, now as ever, is nature's inexorable imperative."

H.G. Wells (1866-1946)

More information about the current work of the Royal Commission can be obtained from its website at http://www.rcep.org.uk or from the Secretariat at Room 108, 55 Whitehall, London SW1A 2EY.

Contents

	Paragraph	Page
Chapter 1		1
INTRODUCTION		
Adaptation	1.8	2
Mitigation and adaptation	1.11	3
The scale of the challenge	1.14	4
Conclusion	1.23	5
Chapter 2		6
SETTING THE SCENE		
Introduction	2.1	6
Impacts of current UK weather	2.5	6
Global climate change	2.8	7
The changing UK climate	2.16	9
Forecasting future change	2.19	10
Future UK climate	2.21	11
Possible effects of UK climate change on the exemplars, and implications for institutional arrangements	2.38	18
Freshwater	2.39	18
Demand for water	2.44	19
Water quality	2.49	20
Drought	2.58	21
Flooding	2.61	22
The impact on water management planning	2.67	23
The coastal zone	2.68	23
Coastal squeeze	2.74	25
Coastal erosion and flooding	2.75	26
Addressing threats to the coastline	2.80	27
Biodiversity		29
Climate envelopes and their consequences	2.83	29
Alien species	2.92	31
Changes in timing of life cycles	2.95	31
Unravelling species assemblages	2.97	31
Change and loss of habitats	2.99	32
Ecosystem services	2.102	33
Maintaining the *status quo* will be impossible	2.103	33
Chapter 3		34
INSTITUTIONAL ARRANGEMENTS		
Introduction	3.1	34
Policies and programmes for climate change	3.5	34
Reporting	3.20	41
Planning regimes	3.29	44
Institutions for water, coastal erosion and nature conservation	3.45	48

Management of water	3.48	49
Water quality	3.50	49
Water supply and wastewater treatment	3.55	52
Flooding	3.61	54
Managing coastal erosion and the risk of inundation	3.72	56
Institutional arrangements for nature conservation and biodiversity	3.95	61
Conclusion	3.109	64

Chapter 4   65

ADAPTING TO CLIMATE CHANGE: DEVELOPING INSTITUTIONAL RESPONSES

Introduction	4.1	65
What are the challenges of climate change adaptation?	4.5	65
Uncertainty	4.6	66
Complexity	4.15	68
Path dependency	4.18	69
Equity and efficiency	4.28	71
Equity	4.29	71
Efficiency	4.36	73
Addressing the challenges	4.43	74
Framing	4.50	76
The role of climate in relation to the key missions of an institution	4.54	78
The role of other relevant actors in partnerships	4.56	80
Competition with other goals	4.59	81
The tendency to 'short-termism' in decision making	4.64	82
The existence of different values and interests	4.66	82
Implementation	4.71	83
Up-scaling local and small-scale initiatives	4.73	83
Enabling mechanisms for adaptation goals	4.75	84
Engaging public support	4.79	85
Co-ordination between actors	4.86	86
Resources – people, skills and finance	4.90	87
Distribution of costs	4.92	88
Learning	4.100	90
The generation and sharing of information	4.106	91
Use of information and knowledge	4.113	93
Strategic memory and social learning	4.115	93
Innovative (non-standard) approaches	4.117	93
The circles of adaptive capacity	4.119	94

Chapter 5   95

DEVELOPING ADAPTIVE CAPACITY

Introduction	5.1	95
The policy framework	5.12	97
Policy appraisal	5.13	97
Investment appraisal	5.15	97
An adaptation duty	5.19	98
Reporting and monitoring	5.22	98
Indicators of adaptive capacity	5.25	99

Specific institutional arrangements   5.29   100
    The land use planning system   5.33   100
    Lessons from the exemplars   5.38   101
Resources to build capacity   5.47   103
    The importance of leadership and cultural change   5.48   103
    Increasing knowledge and skills   5.53   104
    Ensuring resources are available   5.58   105
Equity   5.60   105
Public engagement   5.71   107
The Adaptation Sub-Committee   5.80   109
Conclusion   5.82   110

References

113

Appendices

A: Announcement of the study and invitation to submit evidence   128
B: Conduct of the study   141
C: Seminars and workshops held in support of the study   148
D: Members of the Royal Commission on Environmental Pollution   151

Abbreviations

157

Index

160

Figures

Figure 2-I   Global average near-surface temperatures 1850-2006   7
Figure 2-II   Projected changes to winter and summer seasonal mean temperature for the 2080s   15
Figure 2-III   Projected changes to annual, winter and summer mean precipitation for the 2080s   16
Figure 2-IV   Change in observed temperature over Western Europe over a 200-year period   19
Figure 2-V   Aerial views of Hesketh Out Marsh before and after managed realignment   28
Figure 3-I   Governance structure for the Adapting to Climate Change (ACC) Programme   37
Figure 3-II   Work streams in the Adapting to Climate Change (ACC) Programme   38
Figure 3-III   Climate change impacts and risks identified by Government departments   39
Figure 3-IV   Summary of Defra's findings for selecting who will be asked to report on progress towards adaptation under the Climate Change Act 2008   42
Figure 3-V   Network diagram illustrating the complexity of the current organisation of institutions relevant to the water sector for England and Wales   53
Figure 3-VI   The Thames Barrier – one of the largest movable flood barriers in the world   55
Figure 3-VII   Evidence of cliff erosion at the site of the old lifeboat launch along the coast from Happisburgh   59
Figure 3-VIII Overview of institutional arrangements for delivering conservation management in the UK   62
Figure 4-I   Schematic representation of the different levels of understanding of risk, and example of approaches for decision making with different dimensions of uncertainty   67

Figure 4-II   Schematic illustrating framing, implementing and learning   76
Figure 4-III   The circles of adaptive capacity   94

Tables

Table 2.1   Examples of projected seasonal and annual changes in weather variables
                   for different regions of the UK   13

Information boxes

Box 1A   Definitions of different types of adaptation   2
Box 2A   Recent changes and trends in the UK climate   9
Box 2B   United Kingdom Climate Projections (UKCP09)   10
Box 2C   Uncertainties in global models and input data   12
Box 2D   Factors affecting the character and shape of coastlines   25
Box 3A   The Climate Change Act 2008 and the Climate Change (Scotland) Act 2009   35
Box 3B   ESPACE (European Spatial Planning: Adapting to Climate Events)   47
Box 3C   The EU Water Framework Directive   49
Box 3D   Case study: The River Glaven and catchment sensitive farming   51
Box 3E   The Thames Estuary 2100 project (TE2100)   56
Box 4A   The River InVertebrate Prediction And Classification System (RIVPACS)   70
Box 4B   Framing the problem: UKCIP's impacts and vulnerabilities approach   77
Box 4C   Hampshire County Council   78
Box 4D   The EU Birds and Habitats Directives   79
Box 4E   The Exmoor Mire Restoration Project   84
Box 4F   The hot-spot approach: An example from the Netherlands   86
Box 4G   Legal aspects of coastal protection   89
Box 5A   An indicative list of ten questions on adaptation   111

Chapter 1

Introduction

1.1 The compelling and growing body of evidence on climate change points to the need for drastic and urgent action. The requirement to reduce emissions of greenhouse gases is well recognised, but this alone will not suffice: substantial changes to our climate are already unavoidable. Despite the magnitude of this challenge and the powerful evidence now available, there is still a lack of understanding about what a changed climate really means for society, or what institutions should be doing to prepare for it. This report sets out some of the implications of a changing climate for the UK, addresses the challenges which institutions will face and considers ways in which we can prepare for inevitable climate change.

1.2 The main political and scientific response to climate change has, so far, been to develop mitigation measures to reduce the level of greenhouse gas emissions (a subject that the Commission addressed in its 22nd report *Energy – The Changing Climate*).[1] The UK is committed to reducing emissions by 80% from 1990 levels by 2050.[2]

1.3 But the evidence we have received has convinced us that society and governments are underestimating the challenge of climate change. The Commission supports the findings of the recent International Scientific Congress on Climate Change (March 2009, Copenhagen) which concluded:[3]

> "Recent observations confirm that, given high rates of observed emissions, the worst-case IPCC[i] scenario trajectories (or even worse) are being realised. For many key parameters, the climate system is already moving beyond the patterns of natural variability within which our society and economy have developed and thrived."

1.4 This stark warning stresses that 'business as usual' will be insufficient. To a certain extent, society adapts reactively to changing climate. Human societies have developed a wide range of socio-technological capabilities to deal with natural phenomena which they already understand. Adaptive capacity develops as events (such as heatwaves or major floods) are experienced. In the natural environment, plants and animals may adapt with time but do not have the human capacity of intervention, although humans may intervene to support and protect species and habitats. However, we are now faced with unprecedented changes in our environment. Anticipatory or forward planning rather than simple reaction is essential.

1.5 In these circumstances, the need to address adaptation – the process of adjusting to the changes in our climate – is especially important. These changes will have profound effects on many aspects of our lives in the UK. For example, there is a greater threat of both drought and floods, with extreme weather events becoming more frequent. Sea levels will rise, some familiar species will disappear and new alien species will arrive – for better or worse. These changes will only emerge erratically over the coming years and decades, but they require action now if society is to be prepared. There is an urgent need to address difficult questions about the design of infrastructure,

---

i   Intergovernmental Panel on Climate Change

for example, or appropriate policies for nature conservation in a changing world. Further, and whilst not a focus of this report, we should note that the UK will need to adapt to the effects of climate change elsewhere in the world.

1.6   Recent legislation and government policy does indeed require adaptation to climate change to be addressed, but little detailed attention has been given to the central issue of this study, which focuses on capabilities of institutions – on the organisations and the institutional frameworks which regulate the activities or determine the policies which will be affected by a changing climate. In particular we focus on how institutions can develop the capacity to deliver adaptation, including taking advantage of the possibilities of achieving multiple benefits.[ii] Responding to climate change is a particularly difficult problem, and many institutions will be challenged unless there is a deep understanding of the nature of the issue and of the responses it requires.

1.7   We received a great deal of helpful evidence. Whilst we have attempted to paint a picture of the impacts of climate change, our aim has not been to write a definitive text on climate change science, but to provide sufficient understanding of the nature of the challenges so as to set the context for our conclusions and recommendations.

ADAPTATION

1.8   The individual streams of analysis in this report build on important work done by others. The United Kingdom Climate Projections, updated in 2009 (UKCP09), have already set out the best currently available projections of climate change for different parts of the UK. And there is a rich literature in many areas, including business management, on how organisations can approach the demands of dealing with an uncertain and challenging future. But our strong conviction is that these different and often independent threads need to be woven together – the implications of climate change need to be more widely appreciated, and organisations need to address them more systematically in a way that recognises the scale and uncertainty of the challenge. Equally, there needs to be a deep and broad public discourse on climate change adaptation, so that political choices can be made in an informed and considered way. This report addresses those needs.

> ### BOX 1A DEFINITIONS OF DIFFERENT TYPES OF ADAPTATION[4]
>
> The Intergovernmental Panel on Climate Change (IPCC) recognises three types of adaptation:
>
> **Autonomous adaptation** – Adaptation that does not constitute a conscious response to climatic stimuli but is triggered by ecological changes in natural systems and by market or welfare changes in human systems. Also referred to as spontaneous adaptation.
>
> **Planned adaptation** – Adaptation that is the result of a deliberate policy decision, based on an awareness that conditions have changed or are about to change and that action is required to return to, maintain, or achieve a desired state.
>
> **Anticipatory adaptation** – Adaptation that takes place before impacts of climate change are observed. Also referred to as proactive adaptation.

---

ii   The cover of this report symbolises both the potential benefits (ladders) and problems (snakes) posed by climate change, both for the UK's natural environment and for society as a whole.

1.9 What is adaptation? The Intergovernmental Panel on Climate Change (IPCC) Third Assessment Report[5] defines adaptation as having three possible objectives: to reduce exposure to the risk of damage; to develop the capacity to cope with unavoidable damages; and to take advantage of new opportunities. IPCC definitions of different kinds of adaptation are provided in Box 1A.

1.10 Our report focuses on institutions and we take a broad view of the definition of an 'institution'. An institution can be an organisation, for example a government department, a company, a local authority or a statutory agency; it can be the practical arrangements for implementing policies, such as local partnerships between agencies to manage flood risk; or it can be a legal, regulatory or policy framework, such as the EU Habitats Directive which defines the objectives and measures required to achieve some aspects of nature conservation. For the purposes of this report, we will use the term 'organisation' to mean Government departments, authorities, companies and agencies, and 'institutional arrangements' to mean the legal, regulatory and administrative frameworks within which policies and programmes are delivered.

MITIGATION AND ADAPTATION

1.11 Mitigation and adaptation are not alternatives. The need for urgent and deep cuts in global greenhouse gas emissions cannot be overstated. But even if it were possible to secure significant, rapid reductions in future emissions, past and current greenhouse gas emissions mean that the climate will continue to change for several decades to come. Indeed, even if all anthropogenic greenhouse gas emissions ceased today the science suggests the planet is already locked into a temperature increase of more than 1.4°C.[6] One of the aims of the Copenhagen Accord is to limit global warming rises to 2°C.[7] Even if temperature increases can be limited to this amount, which is far from certain, the impacts for some societies and ecosystems will be significant.[8]

1.12 In other words, we face the challenge of having to adapt even if mitigation is successful. This may be an unpopular political message given the global imperative to reduce emissions. And if mitigation efforts are not successful or are too feeble, societies face the risk of dangerous[iii] climate change[9,10] which could have catastrophic consequences. Adaptation is therefore not only essential but an urgent imperative.

1.13 Mitigation and adaptation are different. Whilst a big reduction in UK emissions is necessary, this country alone cannot solve the problem of climate change, since it is the global total of emissions which will determine the trajectory of the global climate: future UK weather, for instance, depends on the success of global efforts at mitigation. Conversely, adaptation is primarily local: the effects of weather are felt in particular places. Whilst we shall feel the effect of certain climate impacts elsewhere in the world, adaptation measures need to be adopted within domestic policies and programmes and will be specific to UK circumstances. And while for mitigation what needs to be achieved is reasonably clear (despite the technical and political challenges of doing it), for adaptation a myriad of different responses will be required according to circumstance. Hence, the UK has significant responsibilities for putting its own adaptation policies in place, and their success or failure is in the hands of national and local government, UK businesses, and communities — from major cities and conurbations to the smallest village.

iii 'Dangerous' climate change is well defined in the literature, including by the IPCC. It is normally taken to include both the climate system passing one or more 'tipping points', leading to runaway climate change (the release of methane from permafrost, for example), and threats to society from the collapse of key components of the economy and social structures (a catastrophic decline in food production or a breakdown in healthcare provision, for example) because of the intolerable strains of climate change.

THE SCALE OF THE CHALLENGE

1.14   The Commission undertook this study because we believed that the challenge of adapting to climate change was not appreciated sufficiently widely. Nor is it being addressed with anything like sufficient urgency. Indeed, it is clear from recent events that UK infrastructure is not sufficiently well adapted even to our current climate – the floods in recent summers have exposed gaps in both planning and infrastructure resilience.[11] These are now being addressed, and in ways which begin to prepare and provide capacity to respond to the greater threats we will face in future years.

1.15   The Government and Devolved Administrations have introduced legislation and set up programmes to begin to plan climate change adaptation more systematically; this is welcome. But the implications of climate change reach into many aspects of our lives, and the Commission believes that the scale and breadth of the challenge has not been sufficiently widely articulated and recognised. The current response therefore falls short of what is necessary.

1.16   In Chapter 2 we outline how the UK climate may change, and we illustrate how these changes are likely to affect three issues relating to areas which we have selected as exemplars. These are: water (in terms of the increased risks of both flooding and drought, and the implications for water supply and water quality); the coastline, including the risk of erosion because of sea level rise and coastal flooding; and biodiversity and nature conservation.[iv] The effects of climate change on these exemplars are likely to be no more nor less than in other areas, but they provide valuable lessons which we believe are of general policy application. Chapter 3 describes the institutions and policies which are in place to deal with adaptation and also, more specifically, within the exemplar policy areas. It discusses some of the limitations of the institutional frameworks in responding to climate change. We are aware that in some cases the policy framework is changing; this report takes account of developments up to December 2009.

1.17   One thing is clear from the exemplars: the *status quo* cannot be maintained. There will be changes in natural systems which cannot be ignored. Some of the policies explored in this report will have to be revisited, because they are likely to become unachievable (or in some cases unaffordable) in a world of a different and more variable climate.

1.18   The challenge of adaptation is particularly difficult for several reasons. Firstly, although it is certain that the climate of the UK will change, it is not possible to say with certainty exactly how great or how fast those changes will be and what the implications will be. The UK's capacity for climate modelling is world class, but even so there are profound and possibly irreducible levels of uncertainty in the projections which have been published. These arise from uncertainty in the science and modelling of climate, and in understanding the scale of future greenhouse gas emissions, and because other major social and technological changes will be taking place at the same time. Climate change does not occur in a static world. Changes in society, nationally and globally, and changes in technology will each have an impact just as significant as, if not more significant than, climate change. Adaptive capacity needs to be responsive and flexible. A further complication is that adaptation in one sector could have significant impacts on another.

---

iv   These three exemplars were chosen pragmatically, because they fall within our Terms of Reference and focus on the natural (rather than the built) environment. Early in its investigation the Commission realised that a more comprehensive analysis of all the issues surrounding climate change adaptation was impossible on any realistic timescale. The Commission believes these exemplars and their interconnections are particularly challenging, and that they help to illustrate the complexity of adapting the UK to climate change.

1.19   Secondly, much decision making is focused on the relatively short term and is often constrained by traditional ways of thinking and working. But the full extent of changes to the climate will emerge only in the longer term (over several decades). The opportunity to be proactive has to be taken, in order to begin to build adaptation capacity into policies and as future infrastructure is planned. But a longer-term perspective may not fit easily with shorter-term electoral and budgeting cycles. The challenge is: how much should the UK and local communities invest now to solve a problem that future generations will face?

1.20   Thirdly, there will be difficult issues of equity. The impact on some places or groups will be more severe than others. This is perhaps most starkly seen in the case of coastal erosion, where higher sea levels and more frequent storms will mean some homes will be at increased risk of destruction. This issue relates not only to who should bear the costs and consequences of climate change but also to considerations of fairness in governance processes and substantive decisions.

1.21   We examine these challenges in Chapter 4, and suggest how organisations should approach capacity building to cope with climate change. Finally, in Chapter 5 we set out our recommendations to help institutions to prepare for adaptation.

1.22   This report cannot be a blueprint for adaptation, for the reasons just described; but we do know that anticipatory and flexible approaches will be essential to cope with an uncertain climate future. The report is intended to shape attitudes and practices and we therefore concentrate on the challenges faced by the institutions responsible for essential adaptation policies. The Commission believes that many institutions are ill-prepared for the changes that will confront them, and that society as a whole is remarkably and worryingly complacent about the challenges posed by adaptation to climate change.

CONCLUSION

1.23   This report is about moving institutions towards anticipatory, planned but flexible adaptation responses. We hope that it will stimulate a wide range of organisations to consider urgently and more thoroughly the potential implications of a changing climate for their work and the importance of building adaptive capacity. We repeat our conviction that the scale of the challenge has not yet been sufficiently appreciated. The potential costs of ignoring adaptation have not been sufficiently considered, and the potential benefits of adaptation have not been sufficiently explored. If institutions at all levels now address the need to build adaptive capacity, there is still time for the UK to be well positioned to cope with a future climate which will be considerably more challenging and disruptive.

Chapter 2

SETTING THE SCENE

INTRODUCTION

2.1 To appreciate the scale of the challenge of adaptation, the Commission found it helpful to consider first how the UK climate is likely to change and the effects of such changes. This chapter describes the changes to our climate that have already taken place and the changes expected over the next few decades.

2.2 We also found it helpful to consider briefly how well UK society is capable of dealing with the current climate, in particular with extreme weather events.

2.3 The chapter therefore begins by examining the impacts of current extreme weather in the UK. We then focus on how the global climate has already changed and recognise that the UK too has already undergone significant changes. A section on future climate projections for the UK examines the models and techniques used by climate scientists to make these projections, and it includes comments on various aspects of uncertainty.

2.4 We then examine the three exemplar areas of water, the coastal zone, and biodiversity and nature conservation in order to build up a picture of the implications of projected changes in the climate. This work forms the basis of the examination in Chapter 3 of the institutions involved in adaptation. We also consider in Chapter 3 relevant current institutional arrangements that may constrain or even prevent effective adaptation to climate change in the UK, again looking in particular at the three exemplars.

IMPACTS OF CURRENT UK WEATHER

2.5 The climate in the UK is usually described as temperate. It is not too warm, generally with mild winters and neither too wet nor too dry. The UK weather is greatly influenced by the ocean (a temperate maritime climate) and is naturally variable. However, this seemingly benign situation is frequently punctuated by extreme weather events.

2.6 Recent extreme weather events in the UK (for instance, floods, heatwaves and extreme winter weather) highlight the scale of the challenges facing our society. The heatwave of 2003 not only impacted detrimentally on the health of individuals but also caused problems for water supplies, agriculture (death of livestock and crops) and transport (buckled train tracks and melting road surfaces). There have been examples of flooding, caused both by rivers breaking their banks and by flash floods during summer and winter downpours, which have caused loss of life as well as widespread and serious social and economic disruption. The floods that followed a period of heavy rain during 18-20 November 2009 caused widespread flooding across Northern Ireland, Cumbria and south-west Scotland, and illustrates the degree of disruption that can follow such events.

2.7 The level of disruption caused by extreme weather indicates how well the UK is, or is not, prepared to cope with such events. We would not expect the UK to be perfectly prepared for every weather-related eventuality, especially as it may not be economically viable to prepare for every circumstance. However, the Commission is concerned that if today's extreme events become more frequent, as the modelled climate projections suggest, so too will the level of disruption that it causes if appropriate action is not taken. Not only will today's extreme weather events become more commonplace, but it is also likely that the events themselves will become more extreme.

GLOBAL CLIMATE CHANGE

2.8   Scientists have a range of tools that they can call upon for informing policy-makers about climate change – both changes that have already occurred and projections for the future. These include weather measurements from a variety of sources and climate simulations from computerised Global Circulation Models (GCMs). GCMs are used to provide the basis from which future climate projections are made, and the boundary conditions that enable more regional and local-scale projections, through a process of regional climate downscaling, to be made.

2.9   Globally, data from land-based weather stations and ships as well as from satellites confirm that, although there are regional variations in temperature, the planet is warming (see Figure 2-I and the more recent literature cited).[1,2] Generally, the warming trend is observed in both maximum and minimum recorded temperatures, with air masses over land warming faster than those over oceans, and winter months warming faster than summer. The number of days with temperatures below freezing declined during the second half of the 20th century in most land areas of the Northern hemisphere. In the Arctic region, temperatures have increased at almost twice the average global rate in the last century.[3]

FIGURE 2-I
Global average near-surface temperatures 1850-2006[4]

The deviation of annual average global mean near-surface temperature (red bars) from the average over the 1961-1990 baseline.[5] The blue line shows the data smoothed to emphasise decadal variations.

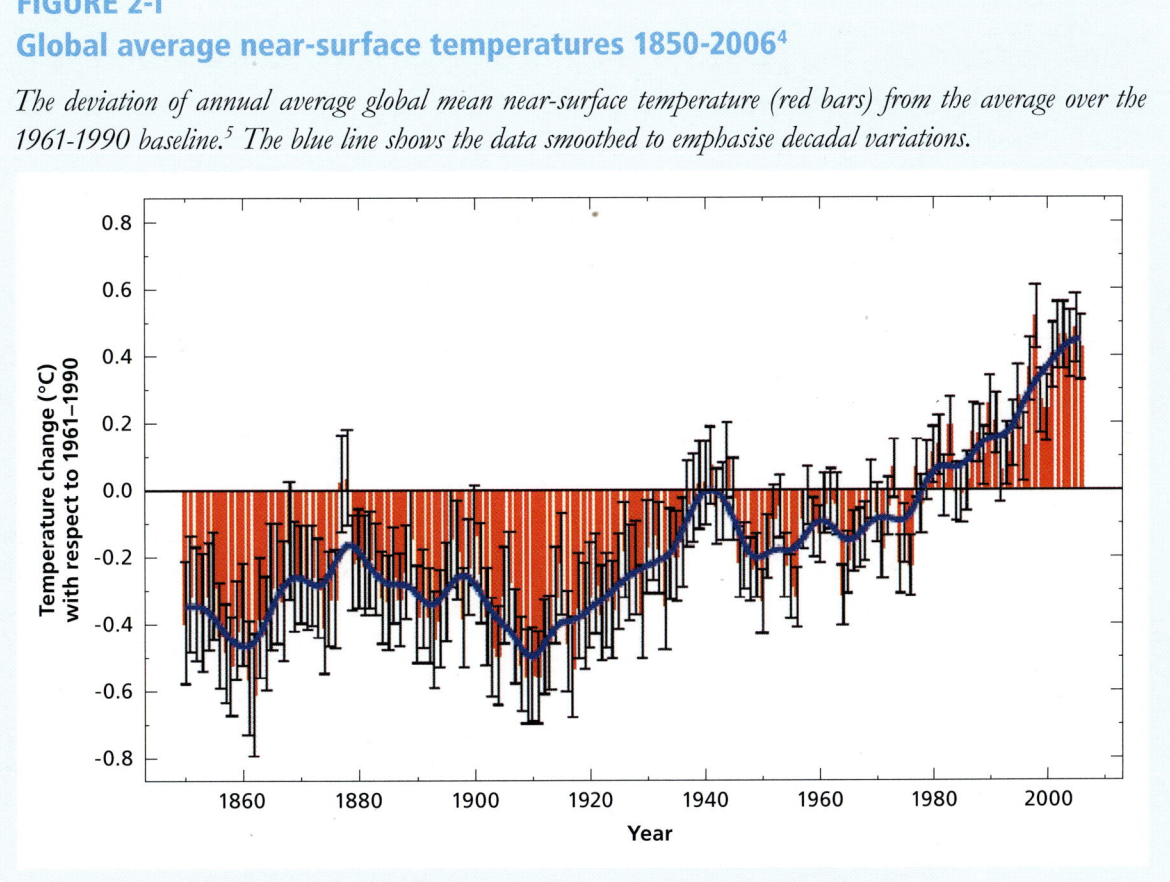

2.10 Since the late 19th century to the present day, global average temperatures have risen by 0.8°C. But the rate of warming is accelerating and in the last 25 years global average temperatures have risen at a rate of 0.2°C per decade. According to the Met Office, the 17 warmest years on record have all occurred in the last 20 years, and the warmest year so far has been 1998,[6] due in part to the global effects of a strong El Niño ocean-warming event.[i] The Intergovernmental Panel on Climate Change (IPCC) has concluded that it is 'very likely'[ii] that man-made greenhouse gas (GHG) emissions have caused most of the observed temperature rise since the mid-20th century.[7] This view is widely shared by the leading scientific institutions throughout the world.

2.11 As the climate warms, snow cover, the extent of sea ice and some land-based ice sheets and glaciers are declining worldwide. Recorded observations show that global average sea levels have been rising since at least 1870; the rise is accelerating. Global average sea levels have risen since 1961 at an average rate of 1.8 mm per year and since 1993 at about 3 mm per year, with contributions from ocean thermal expansion and melting glaciers, ice caps and polar ice sheets.[8] Variations in the geological movement in land will mean that local rates of sea level rise will themselves vary. For example, net sea level rise will be greatest in south-east England, where the land is sinking, and least in Scotland, where it is rising (2.72).

2.12 In 2005, the atmospheric carbon dioxide level was 379 ppm and rising at approximately 2 ppm per year.[9] The IPCC predicts that if atmospheric carbon dioxide levels continue to rise, and double from a pre-industrial concentration of 280 ppm, increases in the equilibrium global mean surface air temperature are 'likely' (see footnote vi) to be in the range 2.0-4.5°C, with a most likely value of about 3°C. However, temperature increases substantially higher than 4.5°C still cannot be excluded (although this carries a lower probability).[10] Increasing global average temperatures will have a pronounced impact on local weather. Commenting on future extremes of temperature, the IPCC stated it is 'very likely' that heatwaves will become more intense, more frequent and longer lasting.[11]

2.13 Heatwaves are prolonged periods of excessively hot weather which may be accompanied by high humidity that can cause serious health problems. As part of the Heat-Health Watch system operating in England and Wales from 1 June to 15 September each year,[12] heatwave alerts are issued when temperatures reach a certain threshold and are sustained over two days and the intervening night, with a forecast of higher temperatures to come. The temperature threshold will vary according to region – for example, in London the daytime threshold is 32°C and 18°C at night, whereas for the north-west of England the thresholds are 30°C and 15°C respectively.

2.14 Precipitation patterns (rain and snowfall) are also changing so that at tropical and higher latitudes, both average precipitation and the intensity of rainstorms are predicted to increase because of a general intensification of the global hydrological cycle. An increased risk of fluvial and urban flooding is one consequence of more frequent and more intense rainfall.

---

i   The El Niño phenomenon is a warm phase of a natural oscillation in the Earth's climate system. Involving both ocean and atmosphere, it occurs when the tropical surface waters of the Pacific Ocean warm, the westward trade winds slacken and the region of strongest rainfall moves eastwards from Indonesia out into the Pacific Ocean. Although not totally predictable, it tends to occur on average every four years, lasting for about 12-18 months.

ii   IPCC terminology expresses likelihoods thus: 'very likely' = >90% probability; 'likely' = >66% probability.

2.15 Average global sea levels are predicted to increase further, by between roughly 0.18 m and 0.59 m by the end of the 21st century, depending upon the GHG emission scenarios and other assumptions used in the projections.[13] Importantly, the IPCC sea level projections do not include potential contributions from melting ice sheets currently over Greenland and West Antarctica, potentially making these projections conservative in the long term.

THE CHANGING UK CLIMATE

2.16 The UK's climate is changing, reflecting the changes observed at the global scale. Observations (not model projections) show that average temperatures in central England have risen by about 1°C since the 1970s, whilst those in Scotland and Northern Ireland have risen by roughly 0.8°C since 1980. As an example of these changes and other aspects of how the climate has changed, see Box 2A.

BOX 2A RECENT CHANGES AND TRENDS IN THE UK CLIMATE

Temperature	Mean temperatures for both the summer and winter periods have increased for the majority of the UK. Two main periods of warming have occurred: 1914-1950 and 1970 to date. Increases in the daily maximum temperatures have been observed more for winter months, while daily minimum temperatures have increased more in summer months. The south-east of England, along with the Midlands and East Anglia, has experienced the greatest increase in mean monthly temperature.
Precipitation	UK monthly precipitation shows a high degree of variability and no overall annual trend. However, winter precipitation has shown significant increases since 1961 for all regions of the UK. Increases have been greatest in north and west Scotland (since 1914), and north-west England has experienced a decrease.
Snow cover	Since 1961 the number of days with snow cover (at 09:00GMT) has shown a strong downward trend. This trend is most pronounced in southern England (currently 75% fewer days with snow cover, compared with 1961).
Sunshine	In north Scotland, Northern Ireland, south-west England and south Wales, sunshine levels have on average decreased (though not significantly).
Days of frost	Since 1961, all regions of the UK have experienced a strong downward trend in the number of days with air frost (a reduction of between 25% and 35%).

2.17 Sea surface temperatures around the UK coast have risen over the past three decades by about 0.7°C. Interestingly, while annual mean precipitation over England and Wales has not changed significantly since records began in 1766, the seasonal distribution of rainfall has. All regions of the UK have experienced an increase over the past 45 years in the contribution to winter rainfall from heavy precipitation events, whilst in summer all regions except north-east England and northern Scotland show precipitation decreases. Sea levels around the UK rose by about 1 mm per year in the 20th century, corrected for land movement. The rate for the 1990s and 2000s has been higher than this.[14]

2.18 It is quite common for extreme weather events such as the floods of 2007 or the summer heatwave of 2003 to be linked to climate change by commentators. However, evidence of change is usually evaluated over periods of 30 years or longer; this means that it is not possible to link any single extreme weather event to climate change. It is, however, reasonable to regard increasingly extreme weather events as being consistent with the climate model projections. Furthermore, some believe that historical emissions of GHGs have already doubled the risk of this type of extreme event.[15]

FORECASTING FUTURE CHANGE

2.19 The UK has significant, world-class capacity for analysing the nature and impacts of future global and regional climate change, through the Met Office Hadley Centre[16] (which conducts work on global climate change), the Tyndall Centre for Climate Change Research[17] (which focuses on developing sustainable multidisciplinary responses to climate change in all parts of the world), the UK Climate Impacts Programme[18] (UKCIP, which looks at what the impacts of climate change might be for all regions and sectors of the UK and offers tools and advice to stakeholders on how to adapt) and numerous other research centres and academic groups throughout the country.

2.20 The UK Climate Projections (UKCP09) present new cutting-edge science in the development of local climate change projections (Box 2B).[19] These are designed to inform policy-makers and decision-makers about the possible changes to the climate at scales useful for different regions of the UK. The Commission welcomes these pioneering projections. But the inevitable uncertainties that surround the projections in UKCP09 pose considerable challenges for institutions intending to use them to guide policies and decisions about adaptation.[20] We return to this issue later in the chapter (2.25 and 2.31).

BOX 2B UNITED KINGDOM CLIMATE PROJECTIONS (UKCP09)

Climate science and information has improved continually over the last 30 years and the latest advance, the 2009 UK Climate Projections (UKCP09), constitutes the fifth generation of climate scenarios that have been produced for the UK. The latest projections are a result of seven years' work by the Met Office and a range of other organisations in which greater account is taken of the large uncertainties in climate modelling. This has occurred as a result of improvements in knowledge of climate science and in computing resources. The form of the projections themselves has evolved as a result of the expressed needs of those who use climate data. UKCP09 offers information on possible future climates for the UK projected to the end of the 21st century. The intention is that the projections will provide a valuable tool for those planning how society and the environment might change in the future. UKCP09 has been funded by the Department for Environment, Food and Rural Affairs (Defra), the Department of Energy and Climate Change (DECC) and the Devolved Administrations.

The projections use three different potential future emission scenarios representing low (IPCC B1), medium (A1B) and high (A1F1) GHG emission scenarios.[21] The scenarios are based on different potential pathways indicating how a range of factors, such as population, economic growth and energy use might change with time. The projections have been divided into seven overlapping 30-year time slots encompassing a period from 2010 to the end of the century, and they use a spatial resolution of 25 km.

The information in UKCP09 can be categorised into three main sections:

- Observed climate data and trends (20th and 21st century historical information on temperature, precipitation, storminess, sea surface temperature and sea level).

- Probabilistic projections for a future climate (for temperature, precipitation, air pressure, clouds and humidity).

- Marine and coastal projections (including sea level rise, storm surges, sea surface and sub-surface temperature, salinity, currents and waves).

UKCP09 projections differ from those of its predecessor (UKCIP02) in that the methodology developed by the Met Office Hadley Centre to create them attempts for the first time to provide probabilistic projections based on quantification of the known sources of uncertainty. At the request of those who will use the data, attempts have been made to make the uncertainties clearer by providing a range of potential outcomes along with a probability illustrating the strength of evidence for each outcome. The methodology involved is technically demanding and involves the use of Bayesian statistics.[22] It allows for the interrogation of the major known uncertainties in the physical, chemical and biological processes simulated in the modelling, and the use of expert judgement. The final results are based on projections of hundreds of different variants of the Met Office Hadley Centre climate model integrated with results from 12 of the world's other leading climate models. Information about past climate observations is also used.

All of this information has been made available to users over the web.[iii] Users can also gain access to an integrated 'weather generator' tool, allowing them to explore implications of plausible daily and hourly time series at spatial resolutions of 5 km. The methodology used in the development of UKCP09 has been peer reviewed in the scientific literature and by a panel of international experts.[iv,23] Because the nature of the projections is so very different from previous climate data tools, there is a risk that the application of the projections will be very challenging for some potential users, as UKCP09 acknowledges: "The methodologies used and the outputs available, particularly the probabilistic projections, are both complex and potentially powerful when used correctly. As such, to use UKCP09, users will also need to take a large step beyond UKCIP02 and this will be challenging for many."

FUTURE UK CLIMATE

2.21 To understand past climate variations, scientists can use a range of measurements, including monitored observations and ice core analyses. To project into the future, scientists rely on GCMs. Although the GCMs that underpin the projections of UKCP09 are without doubt state of the art and represent a significant advancement in our understanding of climate, it is not yet possible to represent all the relevant processes in the climate system. There are limitations to our knowledge and to the computing resources needed to make use of this information. Consequently, information from climate model analyses and projections of future climates, such as UKCP09, contain inherent uncertainties (see Box 2C) and "stretch the ability of current climate science".[24] These challenges mean that the regional and local projections that are derived from global-scale models, to which we now turn, inevitably contain uncertainties.

2.22 We present some examples from UKCP09 below (in Table 2.1 and Figures 2-II and 2-III). The projections illustrate summer, winter and annual mean changes in the climate out to the 2080s relative to a 1961-1990 baseline average. It is worth reiterating that the probabilities[25,26] given in the projections are not like those expected in a game of chance (such as rolling dice); they are Bayesian probabilities based on quantification of the known sources of uncertainty in the models and expert judgement. This means that if at some point in the future the available evidence changes, so too will the probabilities.

---

iii   See http://ukclimateprojections.defra.gov.uk.

iv   The Department for Environment, Food and Rural Affairs (Defra) undertook an international peer review in
         January 2009. See http://ukclimateprojections.defra.gov.uk/content/view/1140/664/.

BOX 2C UNCERTAINTIES IN GLOBAL MODELS AND INPUT DATA

Large-scale projections of future climate utilise GCMs to describe the physical circulation of the coupled atmosphere/ocean/land system. Although there are some uncertainties in the dynamic processes driving GCMs, they are by no means the only sources of uncertainty in such models, some of which are outlined below:

- Future changes in cloudiness and rainfall are subject to considerable uncertainties in current models, the physics of clouds being arguably the most uncertain of the atmospheric processes. Because clouds are important controls on albedo (reflectivity), this introduces significant uncertainty in climate models. Predicting how rainfall, snow, etc., may change is also difficult.

- Modelling future ocean circulation changes is less certain than for atmospheric circulation. For example, models show considerable differences in predicted changes in the circulation of the North Atlantic, which presents considerable problems in predicting the effect of such changes on the climate of Western Europe.

- Ice and snow cover are changing significantly (e.g. the extent of Arctic sea ice). Modelling future changes is difficult but of great importance since altered ice/snow cover has profound implications for albedo, because their reflectivity is considerably more than that of sea or land without such cover. In addition, predicting melting of grounded ice has large implications for estimating future sea level rise, as well as for ocean circulation, due to increased amounts of fresh (less dense) water entering the oceans.

- Climate models at the outset have to specify the amounts of greenhouse gases (GHGs) and particles expected in the future. This depends in part on the emission scenario adopted but also on the strength of any changes in sinks or sources of gases and particles arising from natural or human-induced processes.

Most of these uncertainties are either hard to predict (e.g. future man-made emissions) or poorly understood (e.g. how land and ocean sinks of GHGs will change). In addition, many of them are highly interactive with both positive (destabilising) and negative (stabilising) effects operating simultaneously.

Confidence in regional projections is generally lower than in global averages, as regional changes are dependent on particular changes in atmospheric circulation that are largely averaged out at global scales. The models consequently seem to be more realistic in some regions than others. Much depends on local climate processes, particularly the strength of links between ocean temperatures and atmospheric processes.

Although climate models are highly sophisticated, and the best tools presently available, some of the many uncertainties outlined above will be irreducible and indicate that the projections have to be applied with care.[v]

2.23   Table 2.1 summarises a range of outcomes for the projected climate of different parts of the UK. They include the central estimate of change (i.e. there is an equal chance that outcomes could be greater or less than the central tendency – the so-called 50% probability level). And they show, as outer bounds, levels very likely to be exceeded nine out of ten times (the 10% or lower probability

---

v   A more detailed description of the uncertainties in climate projections can be found in Chapter 2 of the UKCP09 Projections Science report at: http://ukclimateprojections.defra.gov.uk/content/view/824/517/. Accessed 20 January 2010.

level) and those which are only likely to be exceeded one out of ten times (the 90% or upper probability level). The estimates are projections for the 2080s with a medium emission scenario (see Box 2B).[vi]

TABLE 2.1
Examples of projected seasonal and annual changes in weather variables for different regions of the UK[27]

Weather variable	Projected change in weather variable	Central estimates for different regions of the UK (50% probability level)	Outer bounds probability ranges (10% & 90% probability levels)
Temperature	• All areas in the UK may warm by the 2080s		
Mean temperature	• Summer warming more than winter • Greatest summer mean temperature changes in southern England • Smallest changes in Scottish islands	Greatest change: 4.2°C Smallest change: 2.5°C	2.2°C and 6.8°C 1.2°C and 4.1°C
Mean daily minimum temperature	• Mean daily minimum temperature expected to increase • Greatest summer increase to occur in southern Britain • Smallest summer increase to occur in northern Scotland	Mean daily min. temp. increases: Summer: 2.7°C to 4.1°C Winter: 2.1°C to 3.5°C	Summer: 1.3°C and 4.5°C 2.0°C and 7.1°C Winter: 0.6°C and 3.7°C 1.5°C and 5.9°C
Warmest summer day	• Projections dependent on location • No clear geographical pattern has emerged	Changes lie in range +2.4°C to +4.8°C	-2.4°C and +6.8°C +0.2°C and +12.3°C
Annual precipitation	• Central estimates show little change for UK • No clear pattern has emerged	Very little change for central estimate	Range of changes: -16% (lower) to +14% (upper)
Winter precipitation	• Greatest increase expected along western side of UK • Parts of Scottish Highlands may see a decrease	Biggest increases: 33% Some decreases of a few %	Increases: +9% to +70%. Decreases: -11% to +7%
Summer precipitation	• Parts of the far south of England may undergo a decrease	Decreases of: -40%	-65% to -6%
Wettest day (winter)	• Central estimates of the change may range from zero in Scotland to increases in parts of southern England	Central estimate change: zero to +25%	-12% to +13% +7% to +56%
Wettest day (summer)	• Parts of southern England may experience the smallest increases whilst parts of Scotland the greatest	Central estimate range: -12% to +12%	-38% to +9% -1% to +51%

vi   The IPCC emission scenario used to represent medium emissions for the UKCP09 analyses is the A1B scenario. This scenario assumes a balanced mix of energy sources and conversion technologies, such that no single source of energy is overly dominant.

2.24 Results from the UKCP09 projections suggest a broad trend of warmer, drier summers and warmer, wetter winters throughout the UK by the end of this century. The projections also suggest that local variations in climate will see average summer temperatures in the least affected areas of the UK rise by 2.5°C and by about 4.5°C in those areas most affected.

2.25 Table 2.1 illustrates the considerable variability and uncertainty in some of the projected weather variables. These uncertainties mean that, for some variables, we cannot even be confident about the direction of change let alone the size of the change. For example, the 50% probability level for central estimates of annual precipitation shows little change throughout the UK. However, potential changes range from -16% for the 10% probability level at some locations, to +14% in some places for the 90% probability level.

2.26 Another way to summarise the projections is to use maps. Temperature projections are shown in Figure 2-II for a medium emissions scenario. For winter, the central estimates of change (50% probability level) range between 2°C and 3°C for most of the UK. Slightly larger changes can be seen in the south-east and slightly smaller in the north-west of Britain. For the summer months a more straightforward north–south gradient exists, with projected changes in parts of southern England being a little over 4°C and in parts of northern Scotland about 2.5°C.

2.27 Central estimates for changes in annual mean precipitation are projected to stay within a few percentage points of zero throughout the UK (Figure 2-III). But there are projected seasonal shifts in rainfall, with a 10-30% increase over most of the UK, and the possibility of much drier summers. Even so, as the bottom-right panel of Figure 2-III shows, UK summers could actually get wetter.

2.28 The projected long-term trend for the UK winters to be warmer will not mean that cold winters will be a phenomenon of the past. Instead, cold winters such as that of 2009-10 will just become less frequent. Inter-annual variability will always be a feature of our climate system and institutions will have to continue to expect such variations.

FIGURE 2-II

Projected changes to winter and summer seasonal mean temperature for the 2080s[28]

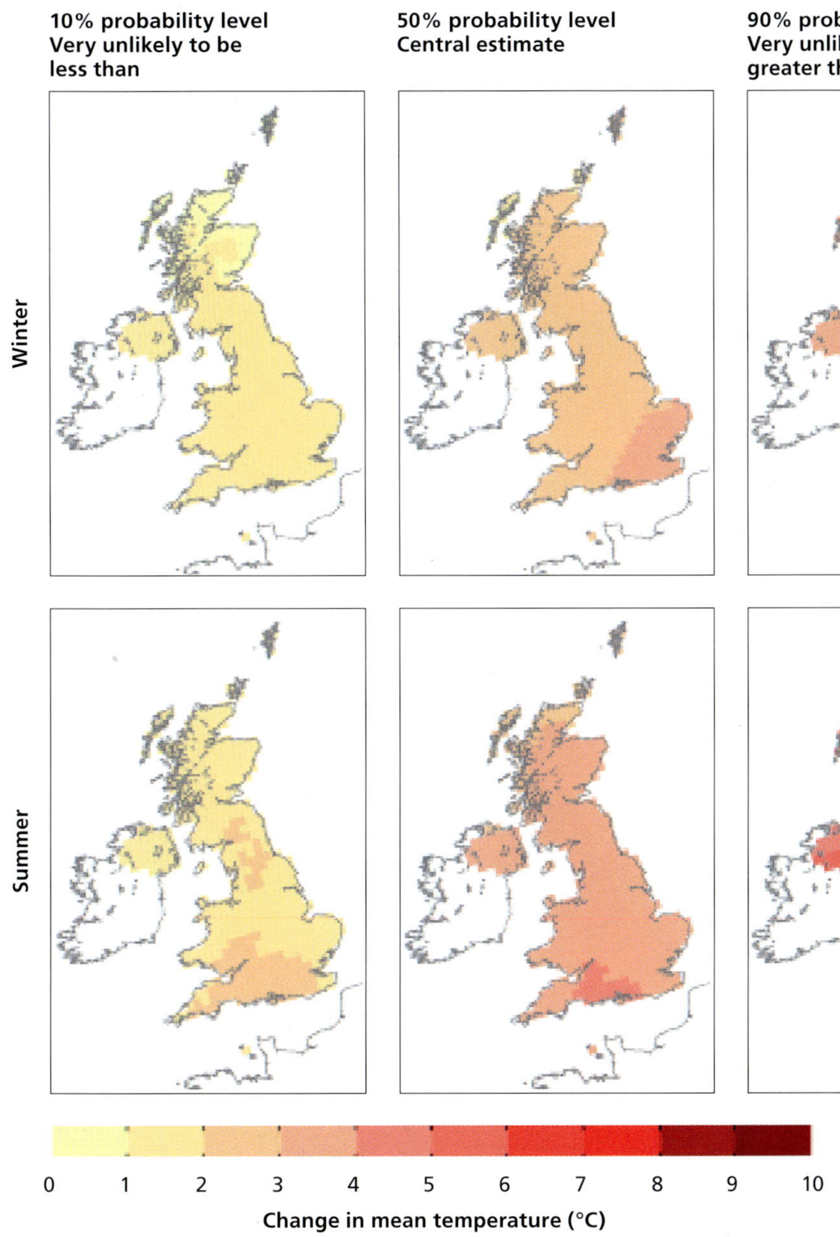

15

FIGURE 2-III

Projected changes to annual, winter and summer mean precipitation for the 2080s[29]

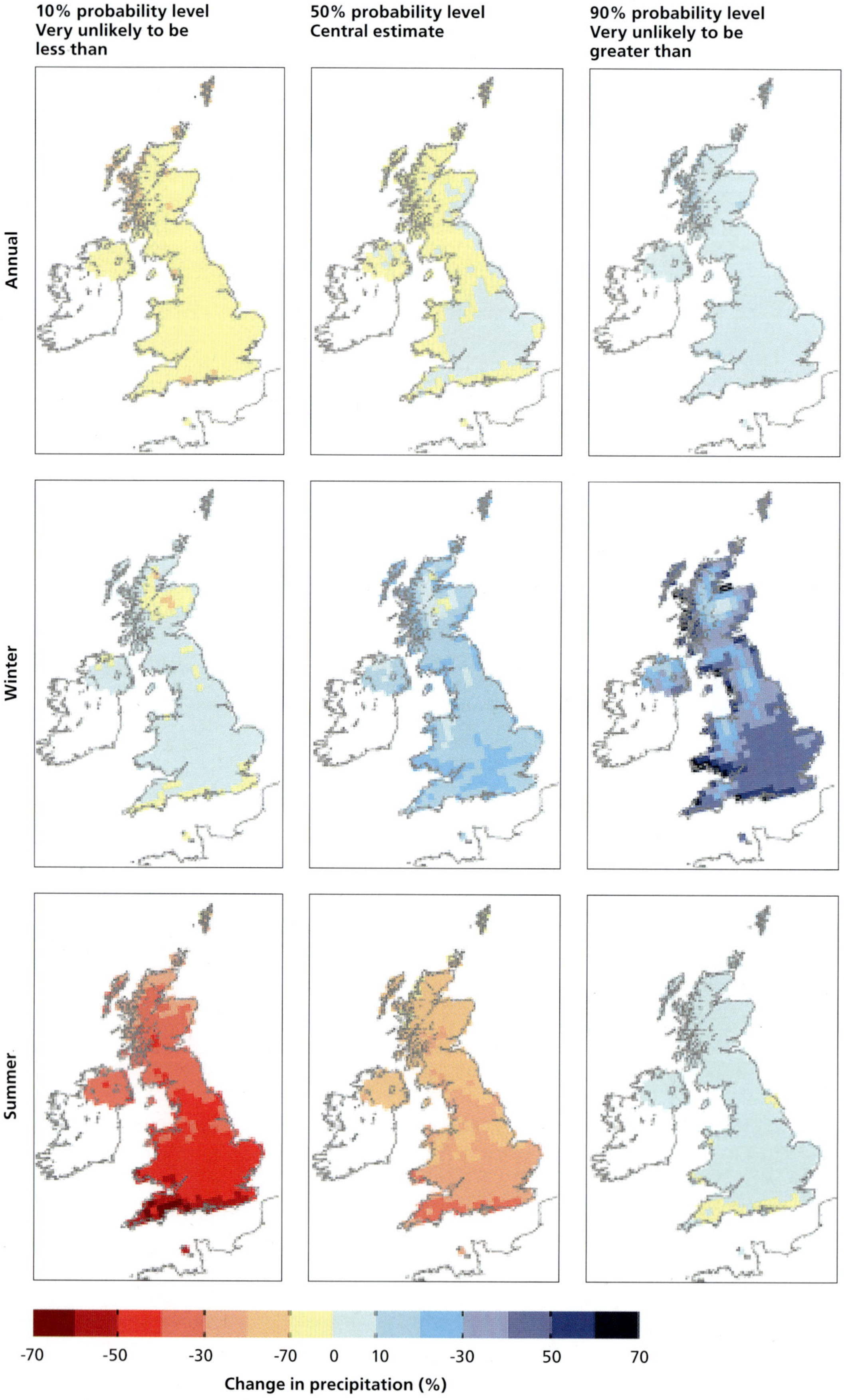
10% probability level
Very unlikely to be
less than
50% probability level
Central estimate
90% probability level
Very unlikely to be
greater than
Annual
Winter
Summer
-70
-50
-30
-70
0
10
-30
50
70
Change in precipitation (%)

2.29 Some of the projected temperature changes shown in Table 2.1 and Figure 2-II may not at first appear to be very large. But even a 2-3°C increase in average temperatures is far from trivial if it is compared with a global mean temperature change of 4°C to 7°C between a full-blown ice age and the peak warmth of an inter-glacial period. In the past these changes occurred very gradually (over 5,000 years or so) and with much smaller human populations; the concern nowadays is that recent observed and projected changes in global temperatures are more rapid, and hence are unusual in the context of past changes.[30] In other words, projected increases of the order of 2-3°C are sufficient to have profound impacts on society and the natural world.

2.30 But average increases in temperatures could be larger than this. In September 2009 the Met Office Hadley Centre reported that there was a real potential for the global average temperature to warm by as much as 4°C by the end of the 21st century, with a risk of some extreme regional variations.[31] The modelling work that led to this conclusion assumed a 'business as usual' emissions scenario that did not include the impact of any mitigation policies (IPCC A1B scenario). It also concluded that if the feedback processes between the carbon cycle and the climate are strong, this could bring forward the time the Earth reaches a 4°C rise in average temperature by as much as 10 or 20 years. The Department for Environment, Food and Rural Affairs' (Defra's) Chief Scientific Adviser, Professor Robert Watson, is quoted in mid-2008 as saying that the UK should strive to mitigate for a global average temperature rise of 2°C but plan to adapt to a rise of 4°C.[32] An increase of 4°C in global average temperatures would present huge challenges for society: "[I]n effect there is no science on how we are going to adapt to 4°C warming."[33]

2.31 How should people use the UK Climate Projections (UKCP09)? Whilst they are the best tool available at present for predicting future climate, as UKCP09 itself makes clear and as Table 2.1 and Figures 2-II and 2-III illustrate, there is considerable uncertainty about the exact nature and degree of the change that the UK is likely to experience. Recognising and accepting this uncertainty is itself an advance. Being 'uncertain' should not be a reason for not taking action on adaptation by developing flexible responses.

2.32 Climate is not the only change we can expect. Other important areas of rapid change in society include globalisation, technology, demography, the economy, regulation and cultural preferences, all of which are uncertain. Uncertainty in the science of climate change is matched by uncertainty in the way other drivers may impact on the UK and hence on the manner in which we adapt to changes in our weather that will result from climate change.

2.33 As a first step in responding to the challenges posed by uncertainty, some organisations are already considering how well they manage current extremes in the weather. A clearer understanding of the manner in which we currently cope with extreme weather will indicate how a changing climate may impact on day-to-day business.

2.34 Discussion of climate change often concentrates on detrimental effects. But, in the UK, climate change may also offer opportunities – for example, there may be an expansion in the tourism industry because the weather is warmer, and milder winters may provide medical benefits including a reduction in excess winter mortality. The cover of this report reflects both the possible benefits, as well as the hazards, to society from climate change. Both opportunities and risks require adaptation.

2.35 Examples of both beneficial and detrimental effects are numerous. Within the water industry, higher water temperatures may enhance biological processes for water and wastewater treatment. But reduced summer rainfall will result in lower river flows, leading to less water dilution and higher pollutant concentrations below point discharges. An increase in the frequency of heavy rain showers may increase the frequency of stormwater discharges from sewers, thus challenging any benefits to water quality gained from higher water temperatures. The potential opportunity to grow more exotic food in the agricultural sector may be tempered by the advent of new and different diseases and pests that survive the milder winters, and so on.

2.36 Adaptation is not a 'one-off' event. The way in which we adapt will need to be continual, rather than a single action designed to solve a predicted or actual problem at a point in time. A key theme of this report is that adaptation is an open-ended process, not an action that 'solves' a single problem. Given the uncertainties about future climates, adaptation will be impossible to achieve by single, simple 'solutions'.

2.37 Recent extreme weather events in the UK illustrate the scale of the challenge. Although the summer heatwave of 2003 was considered at the time to be an extreme weather event, evidence emerging from climate projections suggests that such events may become more frequent (Figure 2-IV). A fundamental part of society's response to a changing climate is not only the provision of more resilient physical infrastructure (important as this is) but also the development of robust and flexible institutional arrangements to deal with substantial changes to our weather.

POSSIBLE EFFECTS OF UK CLIMATE CHANGE ON THE EXEMPLARS, AND IMPLICATIONS FOR INSTITUTIONAL ARRANGEMENTS

2.38 In this next section we examine some of the possible consequences of climate change with reference to the three exemplars. As explained in Chapter 1, we have focused on the three areas of water, coastlines and nature conservation, but the general lessons we draw apply to many institutions and institutional arrangements well beyond the three exemplars (1.16).

FRESHWATER

2.39 Water is central to life, both for society and for organisms and ecosystems. Too little water poses a big problem but, equally, too much water and/or water in the wrong place can cause loss of life and considerable economic and social disruption.

2.40 As described in 2.27, current climate change projections suggest that patterns of precipitation in the UK are likely to change over the coming years. There is likely to be change to the seasonal distribution of precipitation, leading to drier summers and wetter winters with more extreme weather such as storms.

2.41 However, predicting the effect of climate change is not simple. Apart from the inherent uncertainty in the climate change projections themselves, which means, for example, that we cannot be certain about the amount of rainfall, the natural hydrological cycle is heavily affected by other factors, particularly those that are anthropogenic (2.44 and 2.47). How we choose to manage land or water demand and use will impact on the hydrological cycle, so that the effects of climate change may either be intensified or reduced by human interventions.

FIGURE 2-IV
Change in observed temperature over Western Europe over a 200-year period[34]

The black-line graph shows the change in observed temperatures from 1900, including the unusual 2003 temperature (see 2003 arrow). Superimposed in red are the modelled temperature changes extended to 2100. The projections suggest that the unusual temperature experienced over Western Europe in 2003 could be considered normal by 2040 and cool by 2060. Temperature change is illustrated as a change from the 1961-1990 baseline.

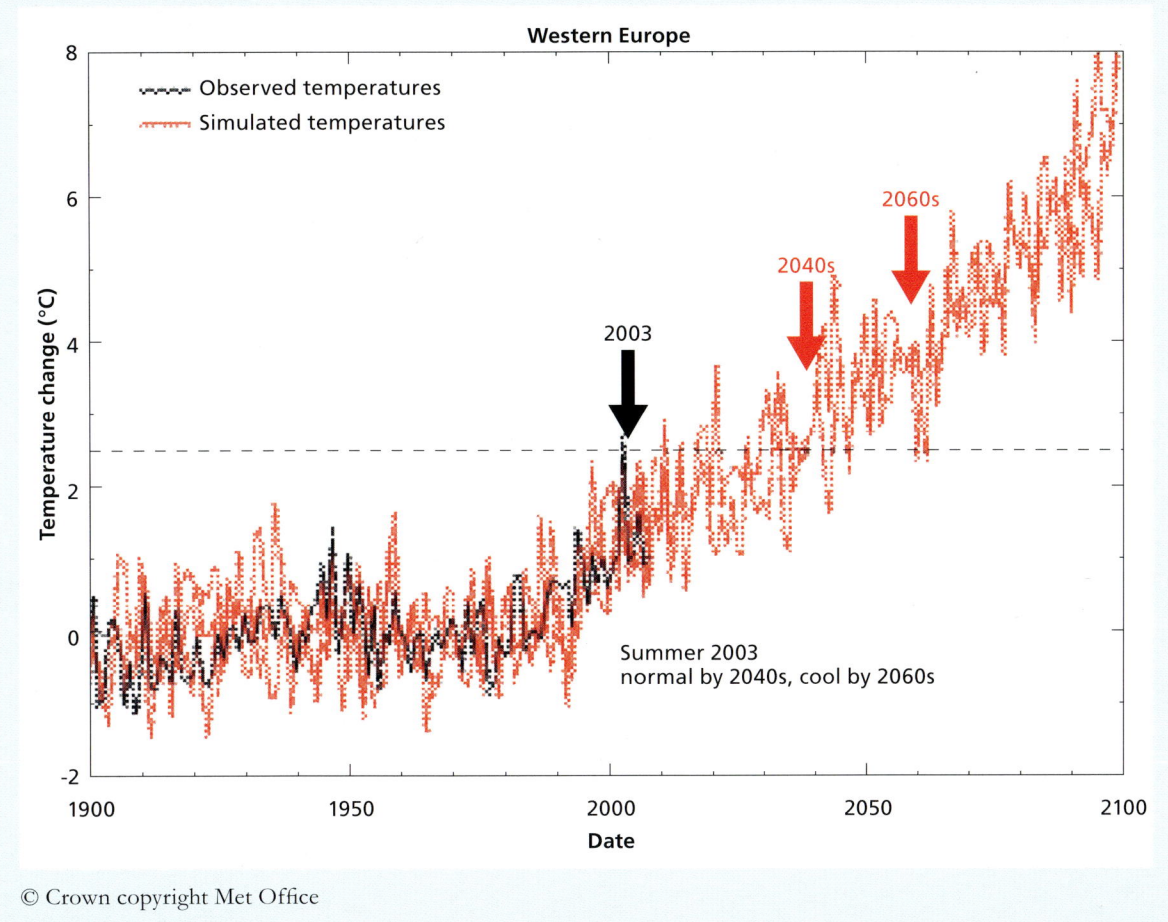

© Crown copyright Met Office

2.42 Because of these complex interactions, the hydrological system is non-linear; small changes in precipitation may cause disproportionate changes in other factors such as the environmental quality of rivers and streams, for example, if abstraction rates increase to meet the needs for water. And changes in demand for water as a result of policy, technology or behavioural changes may mitigate some of the impact of drier summers.

2.43 In this section we shall illustrate the likely impact of climate change on demand for water, water quality and the risks of drought or flooding.

Demand for water

2.44 Climate change is unlikely to be the most significant influence on the demand for water. People may use slightly more water for showering or for domestic gardening, for example, during hot periods (which will become more common) and industrial use may also change. Other factors such as demographic change and greater use of domestic appliances are more significant drivers for higher demand. Other influences, such as policies to reduce demand (for example to charge according to metering or to promote water efficiency), will offset some of these upward pressures.

19

2.45 The demand for water for the irrigation of crops in the UK may increase because of climate change, but irrigation currently accounts for only about 1% of water abstraction.[35] This demand is not evenly distributed; at certain times of the year and in certain parts of the UK our water resources will be stretched, and even small changes in the availability of and demand for water for irrigation could have profound implications for river water quality and ecosystems.

2.46 The Environment Agency forecasts a 5% increase in demand for water by 2020 in England and Wales.[36] What is significant is that the growth in demand will vary regionally, along with population; the southern and eastern parts of the UK will have the highest growth in demand. If a greater demand for water coincides with a decrease in precipitation (as the projections in Table 2.1 suggest could happen), this will lead to considerable challenges for the future management of water. The south and east are the regions in which water resources are currently under the greatest pressure. For example, rainfall in eastern England is often less than 600 mm per year[37] (which is lower than in parts of the world we already regard as very dry, for example Jerusalem, Provence or Melbourne). And, with climate change, the seasonal distribution of rainfall will alter, and more rain will fall in intense bursts, which means that less will find its way into usable resources.

2.47 The amount of water available will of course be influenced by other factors, such as changes in land use (urbanisation and some forms of afforestation are of particular concern), water leakage in the supply system, and technological advances leading to improvements in water efficiency.

2.48 In summary, however, it seems likely that the challenge of meeting the demand for water in some parts of the UK will become greater as a result of climate change. This will have implications for the institutions that can influence demand: the need for effective policies to best use what water is available will become all the greater.

Water quality

2.49 A changing climate will affect water quality in several ways. A rise in water temperature will affect the rate of the many biogeochemical processes affecting water quality, and so perturb ecosystem balance.

2.50 Water quality is defined by the chemical characteristics of water as well as properties such as temperature, colour and sediment concentration. The quality, flow and depth of water affect ecological quality. These factors are brought together in the EU Water Framework Directive, described in the next chapter (Box 3C), which uses the concept of good ecological status and the regulation of prescribed uses. Different water systems have different characteristics; for example, streams in upland areas tend to be generally faster flowing and oligotrophic[vii] with a high dissolved oxygen content and generally high quality, while in lower-lying regions, which tend to be more heavily utilised (e.g. for agriculture) and have larger urban populations, streams will tend to have unnaturally high nutrient content which promotes algal growth. High concentrations of algae can be problematic due to toxicity, and when they die and decompose they can cause de-oxygenation.

2.51 Dissolved oxygen is crucial to water quality. The breakdown of organic matter consumes oxygen and hence there is a 'sag' in dissolved oxygen levels downstream of discharges containing organic matter. The magnitude depends on the organic burden (described as biochemical or chemical

---

vii   Oligotrophic systems lack plant nutrients and are well oxygenated. Eutrophic systems contain high levels of nutrients.

oxygen demand), dilution and temperature. These relationships were recognised at the beginning of the 20th century by the Royal Commission on Sewage Disposal. Warmer waters brought on by climate change will have a lower capacity for dissolved oxygen, and biochemical activity will be greater. This means that more restrictions will have to be placed on the organic material present in discharges.

2.52   Warmer lowland waters, enriched with nitrate and phosphate, are more prone in sunny conditions to algal blooms, which have potential health and aesthetic implications, and can cause problems for aquatic ecosystems. Water supply reservoirs are particularly prone to this phenomenon, which is likely to become a more frequent event in the future. Treatment costs to produce drinking water may rise as a result.

2.53   Another important factor is the presence of nitrogen compounds. Ammonia in untreated sewage and from farm waste run-off is noxious, particularly to fish, and affects the dissolved oxygen regime through nitrification. Again, changes to temperature and flow, and the sudden discharge of untreated sewage during storms, will need even greater attention as climate changes.

2.54   Nitrates present in, or produced from, discharges of untreated sewage and farm waste add to that present in the diffuse run-off from agricultural land and in discharges of treated sewage effluent from sewage works. Agricultural nitrate arises from nitrification of organic nitrogen in the soil and from fertiliser application; it will be washed into water bodies by rainfall and some will find its way into groundwater as well as rivers. The interface between soil and water is a major factor in water quality control, and climate change will affect this complex interface. Biochemical processes of denitrification, in which nitrates can be reduced to nitrogen in anoxic environments, will be just one of the processes affected. The Commission was provided with evidence of the operational challenges of nitrate in groundwater in North Norfolk.

2.55   Reduced aquifer levels and freshwater flows, coupled with rising sea levels, may allow the ingress of salt water upstream in estuaries, potentially affecting freshwater environments where excess salt concentrations can affect the usability of water for irrigation and for potable water supplies. Rising salt concentrations will also impact on the biodiversity of affected freshwater ecosystems.

2.56   Sediment can also be a major problem; it may be washed off land during intense rainfall. It can reduce the clarity of water, blanket organisms that live in the bottom of water bodies, smother plants, congest the gills of fish and smother the gravel-based spawning grounds of fish such as salmon and trout. The Commission saw efforts in the River Glaven catchment sensitive farming management project to reduce the sediment burden (Box 3D).

2.57   If agricultural practices change as a result of climate change, the types and amounts of fertilisers or pesticides which find their way into water through run-off could also change, with implications for river chemistry and biology.

Drought

2.58   The climate projections suggest drier summers, and so droughts may become more prevalent. The implications for water supply for the natural environment and for domestic, agricultural, industrial and recreational use will be significant.

2.59   Long periods of abnormally dry weather – and dry winters coupled with warm, dry summers in particular – result in reduced winter replenishment of water resources and increased demand for water use. So aquifer levels fall, springs stop, wetlands dry out, and river levels and flows decrease. Less water in rivers provides less dilution for discharges and for any polluted run-off which might occur. Prolonged hot weather can also affect the treatability of sewage because of reduced flows and high temperatures; smells from sewerage systems may also increase. Reduced water flows will also have a significant impact on ecosystems (see 2.101). Prolonged dry weather can result in increased flood risks as very dry soils in most of the UK absorb water more slowly than when they are partially moist. Prolonged dry weather followed by rain may also lead to increased risk of erosion and increased sedimentation of rivers and lakes, affecting drinking water supplies as well as aquatic biodiversity.

2.60   There are several potential technical and management responses to the challenge of summer drought. These include short-term responses, such as restrictions on abstraction and on use by domestic and business consumers – for instance, hosepipe bans. So called 'compensation boreholes' may be used to provide water to drying wetlands, and farmers may be allowed to irrigate more if water is available. There may also need to be tighter restrictions on all discharges to rivers from sewage treatment works. Medium- to longer-term responses to drought include the development of new sources of water. These in turn include: recycling or, where appropriate, the use of saline water; investment in new reservoirs; promoting mechanisms that reduce consumer demand; the construction of more resilient pipework systems to reduce leakage; the reduction of nitrate and phosphate inputs to watercourses by controlling farming practices and discharges; and more investment in the capacities and capabilities of water distribution systems, and sewage and water treatment works.

Flooding

2.61   Paradoxically, drought and summer flooding from intense storms can occur together. In the Mediterranean region, large storm drains have been constructed to cope with sudden large volumes of surface run-off. In the UK, where such sudden downpours are unusual, there are no comparable structures. Intense summer rainstorms deluge drainage systems, which then cannot cope; and if land is dry and temporarily impermeable, 'flash' surface flooding can result. Under these circumstances there is an increased risk of soil erosion and increased sedimentation of rivers and lakes, leading to potential effects on drinking water supplies as well as water biodiversity. Flooding may also originate from overloaded rivers that cannot suddenly drain very large increases in flows. The drought of 1976, which was broken by storms in the August of that year, and the floods at Boscastle in the summer of 2004 are good examples of this phenomenon.

2.62   The drainage of surface water is a major issue. In many places, surface water is combined with foul-water drainage and when there are excessive stormwater flows, the overflows, called storm sewage, can cause pollution. Combined sewers are designed for specified return periods of storms, which will alter with climate change. Sewers may 'back up' and cause internal flooding of property, the most distressing being homes. Surface water may also be drained by separate systems which can also be overwhelmed by high flows. It has not been practical to continually upsize sewers to cope with increasing flows. The issue of surface water drainage has been addressed in more recent times by the development of sustainable drainage systems,[38] in which as much drainage water as possible is kept out of the sewerage systems.

2.63   Not only are habitats damaged but recreational uses of water can be threatened by these sudden floods. Angling, boating and swimming may be restricted. Sudden storms within a dry period are also a pollution threat as contaminated water may run off roads, and stormwater discharged from sewers (combining drainage of both foul and surface water) enters watercourses and may spill on to land. The failure of some designated bathing waters to meet prescribed EU standards has been attributed to this cause.[39]

2.64   The risk of flooding in winter, which may rise if winter rainfall increases, results from steady heavy rain, or rapidly melting snow, both of which can present an unrelenting demand on drainage systems that are eventually overwhelmed. Property, domestic and commercial life can be severely damaged and disrupted and utility assets can be inundated, with further threats to society, such as loss of water and energy supplies. The stormy weather that affected north-west Britain in November 2009 led to record amounts of rainfall for a 24-hour period of 314.4 mm.[40] In Cumbria more than 1,300 homes were affected by the floods and many more were left without power and water. A number of bridges were swept away and others were closed pending inspection. The Pitt Review on the floods of summer 2007 presents a comprehensive analysis of the problems.[41]

2.65   As with summer floods, the most significant source of increased pollution is from polluted storm surface waters and from stormwater discharge of sewage. In winter, surface water can also be contaminated in other ways, for instance from salt used for road de-icing.

2.66   Again, there are both short- and longer-term responses available to deal with flood risk – particularly, greater investment in infrastructure to manage stormwater but also changes in land management to recreate 'natural sponges' (for example, projects observed during the Commission's visit to the Exmoor Mire Restoration project in Devon, see Box 4E), more sustainable lowland natural drainage systems including sustainable drainage systems, and the restoration of river flood plains.

The impact on water management planning

2.67   The models and practices on which water management is based rely on perspectives from the past being projected into the future. This is true for concepts such as resource replenishment, water demand, river flows, urban sewage flows, the ecology of healthy river communities, and so on. Changes to the climate will impact on all of these. For example, the concept of what constitutes 'undisturbed river communities' (see 4.22 and Box 4A) is affected by temperature and water availability. The models used in water management are based on historic data and perspectives from the past. They rely typically on records of water demand, river flows and urban sewage flows, and on judgements about the ecology of healthy river communities. They are used, for example, to inform decisions on acceptable levels of discharges from sewage treatment works, which are calculated with reference to expected river flows in periods of dry weather based on historical records. As the climate changes, models based on such records, or historical assumptions about what the ecology of an undisturbed river should be, will become less reliable. We return to these issues in Chapter 5 (5.43).

THE COASTAL ZONE

2.68   Coastal locations have always been attractive places for people to live and plans for increased accommodation will increase the number of people living there. Many industries are also sited by preference in a coastal location and some, such as ports and power stations, require it. Any changes to the coastline resulting from climate change are likely, therefore, to have considerable socio-economic as well as environmental impacts. The potential impacts on coastal habitats and ecosystems are considered in the next section.

2.69   Because there are so many sectoral interests operating in the coastal zone, governance is extremely complicated. The urgent need for some form of holistic management of sectoral interests across the land–sea boundary has been raised on numerous occasions over the last 20 years; see, for example, the 1992 report of the House of Commons Environment Committee on Coastal Protection and Planning.[42] Interest in integrated coastal zone management (ICZM) has been promoted by the EU and governments have produced ICZM strategies. Although the Marine and Coastal Access Act 2009 does not address ICZM directly, the provisions for marine spatial planning are at least an important step in addressing the maritime side.

2.70   The rest of this section is concerned with the landward side of the boundary, and it outlines the challenges that local authorities and other public and private bodies are likely to face in the future.

2.71   Coastal zones are complex and dynamic regions. The coastline is continually changing due to the dynamic interaction between land and sea, resulting in some stretches of coastline being eroded while others accrete. Changes at one point on the coastline may affect what happens further along the coast, for example by providing sediment which is then carried by longshore drift or by creating new configurations of coastline and altering the wave patterns. Under natural conditions these changes go on all the time altering the shape, extent and nature of the coastal strip of land and usually in a gradual way that happens very slowly on a human timescale. Box 2D lists the main factors determining the character and shape of the coastline.

2.72   A huge weight of ice disappeared from northern and western Britain at the end of the last glaciation. Land to the north and west of a line roughly from the Severn to the Humber is still slowly 'bouncing back' (isostatic readjustment) after removal of the ice sheet, and land to the south and east is sinking. In the 6,000 years since sea levels became relatively stable after the last ice age, erosion has predominated over accretion in the UK, although within a human lifetime the coastline has appeared to be broadly stable. However, increases in the frequency and magnitude of winter storms can have a major impact on the form of the coastline, especially where this occurs alongside sea level rise. Cliffs can become weakened or be made heavier by water saturation, and they are therefore more likely to collapse. The number of cliff landslides happening on the east coast of England in the winter of 2000-01 was much higher than usual and this coincided with increased periods of storminess and heavy rain.

BOX 2D FACTORS AFFECTING THE CHARACTER AND SHAPE OF COASTLINES[43]

Geology

- Nature of rocks/sediments onshore and offshore

- Rock structure – bedding, joints, faults

- Position of water-table in coastal cliffs

- Rate of sediment supply to coastal areas

- Changes in the Earth's crust

Physical processes

- Waves – largely influenced by wind and water depth

- Tides

- Rates of relative sea level change

- Rainfall

- Frequency and intensity of storms

Human interference

- Coastal construction

- Aggregate extraction

- Flood and coastal defences against erosion

- Coastal reclamation

- Agricultural land drainage

2.73 There can be no doubt, therefore, that climate change will have a profound impact on the shape of the coastline just through the operation of natural forces. Coastal infrastructure, including coastal defences, ports and harbours, not only alters the appearance of the coastline but also has an influence on natural processes. More than 40% of the coastline of England and Wales has some form of coastal defence. Our present suite of coastal protection structures will be stretched to its full capacity under the conditions predicted for climate change and many may no longer be effective. The Commission saw evidence in south Wales from the National Trust on the scale and extent of the challenges confronting that organisation as it attempts to defend coastal sites and properties under its jurisdiction.[44] Adapting to the changed conditions presents a major institutional challenge.

Coastal squeeze

2.74 Low-lying coastlines with sandy or muddy seashores result from the gradual accretion of sediment deposited by tidal action. Because the slope of the seashore is so shallow, the extent of the intertidal zone can vary considerably with changes in sea level. Under natural conditions this can result in the coastline retreating inland as sea levels rise or moving further offshore where sea levels fall. Coastal development tends to form a barrier to this dynamic repositioning of the coastline so that there is no possibility of the coastline retreating inland. As a consequence, coastal habitats such as saltmarshes get squeezed and may eventually be lost altogether. This in turn means that there is no natural resilience in the system to absorb occasional bursts of high energy. As a result, in the absence of artificial defences there can be considerable storm damage to coastal properties as well as tidal inundation.

Coastal erosion and flooding

2.75   Coastal erosion occurs where the rate of sediment deposition is insufficient to balance the loss of land through wave action. In soft sediment environments this sort of erosion is less noticeable, although the scouring of beach sediments during a severe storm can have rapid and highly visible effects. Where sediment is removed from the system, for example by offshore marine aggregate dredging, the nature of a beach may change fundamentally. In extreme cases, holiday resorts may suffer because their once sandy beaches are scoured down to hard bedrock because of sediment starvation.

2.76   Coastal erosion is more evident where there are sea cliffs, especially if these are of relatively soft rocks such as the sandstone cliffs on the east coast of England and in south Wales. Where these cliffs are on the tideline, it is inevitable that there will be some erosion and such erosion naturally releases sediment, which feeds intertidal habitats elsewhere. If the wave energy is increased because of changes in coastal configuration elsewhere along the coast, the rate of erosion is likely to increase. Sea level rise as a result of climate change is therefore likely to have both direct and indirect effects on the erosion of coastal cliffs. Increased storminess will exacerbate the impact of higher sea levels and contribute to cliff erosion. Any coastal protection infrastructure installed to protect vulnerable parts of the coastline may result in further deflection of wave energy to more vulnerable unprotected parts of the coastline. The Commission saw dramatic evidence of this in the erosion of a bay along the coast from Happisburgh, Norfolk.[45]

2.77   Rising average sea levels are a threat, but they are exacerbated by other weather-related factors. During storms the action of the wind on the sea surface coupled with barometric pressure changes can result in tidal surges, particularly in the restricted areas of the southern North Sea. When pressure drops by about one millibar (mb) the sea level may rise by as much as one centimetre. During a deep depression where atmospheric pressures may fall to about 960 mb, the sea level may rise by half a metre above that expected during average pressures of about 1013 mb.

2.78   Concerns about coastal flooding are greatest when there is a severe storm surge combined with high tides, resulting in a significant rise in high-water levels combined with very energetic waves. The vulnerability of coastal regions of eastern England under these conditions is always a concern and can result in terrible loss of life and damage to property, as in January 1953 when the sea surge height reached 2.74 m at Southend in Essex and 2.97 m at King's Lynn in Norfolk. The resulting floods across south-east England killed more than 300 people, damaged 24,000 houses and affected 70,000 hectares of land; even more damage was caused in the Netherlands. It remains the greatest storm surge on record for the North Sea.[46] The last major threat to this part of the English coast bordering the southern North Sea was in November 2007, but there have been near misses since then – for example in March 2008. If winter storms increase in frequency or intensity because of climate change, such threats will only increase.

2.79   In addition to the effects of storms on the erosive potential of the sea, heavy rain may cause problems with drainage – for example, seepage of water is softening the clays of the Norfolk coastline, causing cliffs to slump and making them more vulnerable to erosion. The Commission saw evidence of this during its visit to Norfolk. Many of these erosive effects may be exacerbated by the changing climate as sea levels rise and more extreme storm events occur. Coupled with this is the realisation that many of the UK's coastal defence structures are nearing the end of their viable lifespans or may require considerable maintenance.

Addressing threats to the coastline

2.80　There are four groups of threats arising from rising sea levels and increased incidence and violence of storms:

- erosion of land above the tidal range;

- flooding of low-lying coastal land;

- damage to marine structures; and

- changes to coastal habitats.

2.81　In the past, the technical and management response to threats to the coastline has tended to be the construction of hard coastal defences such as sea walls and groynes,[47] although there has been an increasing use of soft protection and the use of beach nourishment and sediment management. The emphasis nowadays is on an approach based on coastal and estuarial flood risk management, and investment has focused on measures to provide reduced risk from and increased resilience to defined events. Measures to improve the drainage of coastal lands, especially following storm events, fall into this category.[48]

2.82　There have been some initiatives aiming to restore or recreate coastal habitats by breaching established defences and allowing natural processes to take over. An example of this can be seen in Figure 2-V. This so-called 'coastal realignment' has, to date, been carried out with the voluntary agreement of affected landowners who agree, in effect, to abandon their land. Coastal realignment has the potential to act as a safety valve, whereby some coastal land is sacrificed in order to reduce the threats of coastal erosion and flooding along the coast. However, the process is not without controversy, not least because of concerns about the loss of productive land at a time of increasing food insecurity.

FIGURE 2-V
Aerial views of Hesketh Out Marsh before and after managed realignment[49]

Before the Royal Society for the Protection of Birds (RSPB) purchased Hesketh Out Marsh (the Ribble Coast, Lancashire) the land was used for growing crops. This was possible because an outer wall separated the land from the estuary. It was acknowledged that the wall would not last due to the rise in sea level. After purchasing the land, the RSPB and the Environment Agency created a stronger sea defence and a new saltmarsh habitat through a process of 'managed realignment'.[viii]

Before:

After:

Images kindly reproduced from RSPB Reserves 2009. Before – courtesy of Sefton MBC, after – courtesy of www.commissionair.co.uk

---

viii   For more information on the Hesketh Out Marsh saltmarsh habitat see: http://www.rspb.org.uk/reserves/guide/h/heskethoutmarsh/about.asp. Accessed 19 January 2010.

BIODIVERSITY

SUMMARY OF THE IMPACTS OF CLIMATE CHANGE ON ECOSYSTEMS FROM THE STERN REVIEW[50]

"Ecosystems will be highly sensitive to climate change. For many species, the rate of warming will be too rapid to withstand. Many species will have to migrate across fragmented landscapes to stay within their 'climate envelope' (at rates that many will not be able to achieve). Migration becomes more difficult with faster rates of warming. In some cases, the 'climate envelope' of a species may move beyond reach, for example moving above the tops of mountains or beyond coastlines. Conservation reserves may find their local climate becoming less amenable to the native species."

Climate envelopes and their consequences

2.83   A 'climate envelope' describes the range of climatic conditions within which an organism can survive and reproduce. Climate envelopes are conceptual, multidimensional spaces, with axes defined by the key climatic variables directly or indirectly influencing survival or reproduction in a particular species – for example average, winter minimum and summer maximum temperatures, frost-free days, rainfall patterns and so on. The concept applies equally to terrestrial, freshwater and marine organisms, although the key climatic variables may be very different.

2.84   The geographic range of any particular species will be strongly, but not uniquely, determined by its climate envelope. Whereas no species can survive for long in a hostile environment, a species may not occur everywhere across geographic areas with a suitable climate.[51] For example, barriers to dispersal (mountain chains or open ocean) may prevent a species reaching all potentially suitable areas; competition with other species may exclude them, as may diseases or natural enemies; and overexploitation by humans may eliminate species from climatically suitable regions. Still others may be absent because important habitat features are missing or otherwise unsuitable – for instance, the underlying geology might be wrong or a key food species might be absent. Nevertheless, climate envelopes are an important, but by no means the sole, determinant of species' distributions.[52]

2.85   As the Earth's climate changes, so each species' characteristic climate envelope will shift geographically. Studies on European breeding birds[53] and on a sample of 32 European species (including breeding birds, insects, bats and plants) from a variety of different habitats[54] analysed shifts in the geographic distributions of species' climate envelopes in Britain and Europe under various climate change scenarios in the late 21st century. For example, the centroids of the current and potential (based on their climate envelope) breeding distributions of 430 species of breeding birds are predicted to move an average of 545 km north-eastwards across Europe, but with huge variations in both direction and distance; the largest movement is nearly 2,500 km, and the climate envelopes of individual species settle across all points of the compass.[55] The climate envelopes of some species, both birds and plants, may disappear completely from the UK, or even Europe, whereas those for other species are projected to increase in size.[56] In general, the climate envelopes of most species of birds are likely to be smaller than now by about 20%.[57]

2.86   If climate change makes parts (or all) of a species' current geographic distribution increasingly inhospitable and ultimately uninhabitable, there are three things that might result: the species might evolve to keep pace with the change, it might move (migrate) to stay within its climatic envelope, or it might die out, either locally or globally. At the moment ecologists are unable to predict with any accuracy what the balance of these three possibilities will be across the thousands of species that make up the UK's flora and fauna.[58]

2.87　The potential evolutionary responses to rapid climate change are poorly understood.[59] There are examples of species evolving in response to climate change – for example, the inherited shift in the direction of migration in blackcaps (*Sylvia atricapilla*) to winter in Britain as our winters have become milder[60,61] – although circumstantial evidence points to adaptive changes in other organisms. However, although for the great majority of larger, longer-lived organisms with generation times measured in years or decades, *in situ* evolution (adaptation in the Darwinian sense) to cope with climate change seems unlikely, too little is known about the range of genetic variation already present across the geographic ranges of most species to rule out rapid selection and/or migration of better adapted genotypes.

2.88　Shifts in species' ranges are much more certain. Some species are already expanding their geographic ranges northwards or to higher ground, apparently in response to climate change that has already happened, both within the UK (several species of birds, mammals, butterflies, dragonflies, other insects from several groups, some intertidal invertebrates, and marine fish and plankton) or into the UK from the near-continent (some birds, butterflies, dragonflies and other insects, and marine invertebrates). At the same time, species with southern range limits in the UK are retreating northwards.[62] These patterns are being repeated worldwide.[63] Nevertheless, there is no comprehensive analysis of the likely numbers and nature of new species that will arrive and establish themselves in the UK over the next 50-80 years because of climate change, nor of those that may be lost, if indeed such an analysis is even possible with current levels of knowledge.

2.89　Although shifts in geographic ranges are an obvious response of organisms to climate change, a major problem is that in the highly fragmented terrestrial landscapes of the UK, criss-crossed by hostile barriers to dispersal in the form of urban areas, roads and other built infrastructure, and intensive agriculture, many less mobile species may be unable to disperse effectively.[64] Some species of butterfly, for example, are unable (or unwilling) to fly even a few kilometres from one suitable habitat patch to another across farmland.[65,66]

2.90　Other species may be able in principle to migrate, but fail to keep pace with their climatic envelope because they cannot move fast enough, or because other critical living components of their habitat (food organisms, for example) fail to move with them. Alternatively their prey species may disappear, leaving them to starve, as could be happening with some sea bird species in the North Sea, and the disappearance of their main prey, sand eels (*Ammodytes*), from warming waters.[67] For such species, extinction threatens and, for those whose climate envelope disappears completely, is inevitable. Globally, one (admittedly contested) estimate suggests that 15-37% of a sample of 1,103 terrestrial plant and animal species are threatened with extinction by 2050 as their habitats shift and shrink under climate change.[68] No similar estimates are available for the UK's flora and fauna.

2.91　What is clear is that climate change poses a challenge to current networks of protected areas (nature reserves of various kinds) because they will become increasingly unsuitable for the species that now occupy them; or even if they remain suitable, migratory species may simply cease to utilise them because they can find suitable conditions closer to home.[69] However, "[designated] areas of natural habitat will remain important valuable areas, even if circumstances change. For example these sites support the movement and changing distribution of species, as they respond to climate change".[70] The new species that will inevitably migrate into them may either be welcomed and seen as a benefit of climate change (even though they are not the species for which the reserve was designated) or regarded as undesirable invaders, particularly if they are aliens.

Alien species

2.92   The terminology surrounding alien species can be confusing[71] but, in general terms and unlike species that have reached or will reach the UK unaided by humans (directly or indirectly), aliens are deemed those that arrive here accidentally via human means or are deliberately released here by humans. The changing climate may exacerbate the problem, either by providing climate envelopes that will allow species already established in small numbers (and possibly not breeding successfully) to spread rapidly, or by creating climate envelopes for entirely new alien taxa to invade. Red-eared terrapins have been released or escaped into the wild in the UK, but as yet do not breed because summers are not warm enough; they could become a threat to native aquatic species if warmer summers enable them to reproduce.[72] Marine organisms are carried round the world in ships' ballast water, and several such species that are not yet present in the UK could pose a serious threat to marine ecosystems as seas warm.[73]

2.93   On the other hand, the Commission received evidence that the deliberate introduction of some species – for instance, drought-tolerant tree species from Europe – might be desirable in the future, although there could also be potential disbenefits for native wildlife that would have to be very carefully evaluated.[74]

2.94   What is clear is that the potential for deliberately or accidentally introduced species to establish in the UK because of climate change adds another layer of complexity for the institutional arrangements underpinning conservation strategies and policies in this country, particularly if those alien species come to be considered invasive because of some kind of harm that they cause.

Changes in timing of life cycles

2.95   Phenology is the study of the timing of events in species' life histories, and for many taxa within the UK there has been a general (but not universal) trend towards spring and summer events taking place earlier in the year, along with somewhat more variable trends towards later responses in autumn.[75]

2.96   The timing of events in the life cycle of a species is crucial to survival; such events are triggered by various environmental cues, most often temperature and photoperiod (day length), with the role of a particular cue varying from species to species. If a bird's breeding cycle is set by photoperiod (which is unaffected by climate change) but the abundance of caterpillar prey for its young responds to temperature (which will change as climate changes), there is potential for serious disruption to breeding attempts. Such a process seems to be causing breeding failures and hence population declines in pied flycatchers (*Ficedula hypoleuca*) in the Netherlands,[76] and widespread population declines in a number of other European summer-visiting birds.[77] Again, at the very least local extinction threatens.

Unravelling species assemblages

2.97   A significant consequence of the shifts in species' geographic ranges and the local extinctions that are already happening, or that are predicted within the next 50-80 years, is the unravelling of extant assemblages of species. This is because in general each species responds differently (as can be seen, for example in the staggeringly diverse predicted shifts in the climate envelopes of European breeding birds already referred to). Such 'idiosyncratic' or 'individualistic' species' responses (in the sense that ecologists currently have no way of predicting them) characterise the behaviour of many species to a wide range of environmental changes.[78] One consequence is that many extant assemblages of species that we think of as characteristic of a particular region have no antecedents in previous inter-glacials; assemblages that have existed in the past have no modern equivalents; and future assemblages will not be like the present.[79]

2.98 There are consequences here for the designation of protected sites for nature conservation, many of which are based on the existence of particular species and combinations of species. There are also practical considerations when defined species assemblages are used in a regulatory framework – to measure water quality, for example. We return to these issues in Chapters 3 and 4.

Change and loss of habitats

2.99 Some indications of the impacts of climate change on UK habitats (rather than individual species) are provided by several research projects funded by Defra and the Devolved Administrations based on UKCIP02, the predecessor to UKCP09. There are currently no equivalent analyses for the more recent UKCP09 projections. These early studies were based upon an estimate of warming of 1.5–2.5°C by 2050, significant changes in precipitation (a 30-40% decrease in the south-east of the UK in summer and a 15-20% increase in winter) and a sea level rise of 36 cm over the same period.[80] The studies concluded that, of the 32 Priority Habitats in the UK Biodiversity Action Plan, eight were assessed to be at high risk from direct impacts of climate change based on 'good to moderate evidence'. The habitats were in three main categories: montane habitats; freshwater habitats (standing waters, flood plain forests and grazing marsh); and maritime habitats (saltmarsh, coastal cliffs and slopes, saline lagoons and open seas). The studies have informed the development of UK guidance on climate change adaptation for conservation practitioners, published in 2007 under the aegis of the UK Biodiversity Action Partnership,[81] and also of guidance to policy-makers on climate change, published in 2008 under the title *Climate Change Adaptation Principles* in support of the cross-sectoral England Biodiversity Strategy.[82]

2.100 Sea level rise driven by global climate change also threatens direct destruction of other habitats – particularly saltmarshes, saline and freshwater lagoons, sand dune systems and shingle banks – especially where these coastal habitats are backed by hard, engineered defences or other infrastructure that prevent natural coastal processes taking place.[83] When the sea comes in, for example in a tidal storm surge, the habitats are destroyed and have nowhere else to reform. Clearly, populations of their associated organisms, many of high conservation value, also disappear. It is estimated that 1,200 hectares of intertidal habitats with designated conservation status in the Thames estuary will be lost to sea level rise towards the end of this century.[84] Nationally, 4,000 hectares of freshwater and brackish coastal habitats could disappear in the next 50 years.[85] There are consequences for the operation of legal regimes for protected areas, some of which may be unintended. The focus of the Habitats Directive is to maintain at, or restore to, favourable conservation status the natural habitats and species of wild fauna and flora of European Community interest. Part of the regime involves protection of designated special areas of conservation for certain species and habitats and physical compensation elsewhere for loss of those areas in very limited circumstances. Damage to these designated sites could potentially lead to inappropriate recreation of habitats, which may not then stand the test of time as climate change proceeds.

2.101 As already discussed, changes in the hydrological regime will have significant direct impacts on wetland species and wetland habitats – such as peatlands, marshes, mires, bogs, wet grassland and flood plain forests. Wetlands provide several key ecosystem services, including flood reduction, low flow augmentation, water quality improvement, carbon sequestration and habitats for species assemblages of conservation importance. Climate change will alter the water supply to wetlands through changes in river flows, groundwater recharge and flooding frequency. The frequency of droughts will increase if rainfall declines and the rate of evapotranspiration increases (currently considered particularly likely in southern England). In addition, increased frequency of wildfires – particularly in heathlands and peatlands – would have significant impacts on the conservation value of these areas.

Ecosystem services

2.102 Formal consideration of the services provided by ecosystems has only entered discussions about conservation priorities relatively recently, inspired by the 2005 Millennium Ecosystem Assessment.[86] More recently the European Commission has emphasised the importance of protecting ecosystems in its White Paper *Adapting to Climate Change: Towards a European Framework for Action*.[87] The first action listed is "to promote strategies which increase the resilience to climate change of health, property and the productive functions of land, inter alia by improving the management of water resources and ecosystems". Only one recent spatial analysis of ecosystem services delivered by existing conservation strategies has been attempted across the human-dominated landscapes of England, and this for a very restricted range of services.[88] Mapping the spatial distribution of ecosystem services is extremely difficult or currently impossible because of a lack of data, and there are currently no studies that attempt to predict how such services may change under climate change, as the species composition of protected (and other) areas changes. A recent study gloomily predicts that some key ecosystem services may be severely impaired or lost altogether from human-dominated landscapes because of climate change.[89] Yet the protection of ecosystem services is not part of the remit of most conservation bodies. Natural England, for instance, has no explicit mandate to conserve ecosystem services,[90] although its representatives told the Commission that its existing powers do not prevent it from taking such actions.

Maintaining the status quo *will be impossible*

2.103 This summary points to one simple conclusion on the future state of UK biodiversity: trying to maintain the *status quo*, i.e. 'keeping things as they are', will be increasingly difficult and ultimately impossible. Virtually all the evidence we received accepts that change is inevitable,[91] whilst advocating conservation practices that will hold the line for as long as possible. New species will arrive in the UK and other species will disappear from our shores. 'How many?', 'When?' and 'Where?' are questions to which it is currently impossible to predict the answers. But these changes are already happening and will do so with increasing rapidity. They pose considerable challenges for the legal and regulatory frameworks that exist to protect UK biodiversity, and the statutory and voluntary bodies charged with its delivery.

Chapter 3

INSTITUTIONAL ARRANGEMENTS

INTRODUCTION

3.1 We described in the previous chapter how the climate in the United Kingdom may change as the global climate warms, and discussed the implications for three exemplars. In this chapter, we describe the governance arrangements for these issues – both those which have been put in place to deal specifically with adaptation and those for the exemplars of water, coastal issues, and nature conservation and biodiversity. Given the importance of land use planning, we also describe the institutional arrangements for spatial planning. As introduced in Chapter 1, when referring to institutions we are concerned with both organisations and institutional arrangements.

3.2 We have not attempted to give a comprehensive description of the institutions. This would be lengthy, not to say tedious (not least because the arrangements are complex, involve many institutions and vary in the different parts of the United Kingdom). Furthermore, a full description is not necessary for our purpose. Rather, we have sought to describe a number of specific cases which we believe illustrate more general considerations. In the next chapter we shall identify the generic challenges and the approaches which will be necessary if the UK is to build the capacity needed to respond and adapt to climate change.

3.3 We recognise that adaptation is local – it happens in specific places, albeit sometimes in response to impacts elsewhere. This is in marked contrast to mitigation where, although every local action contributes, it is the global aggregation of actions to reduce emissions which matters. But it is important that local actors can operate within EU, national and regional strategic policy and regulatory frameworks which take account of the need for, and indeed encourage and co-ordinate, action aimed at adaptation. We therefore address all levels of governance.

3.4 Here and in later chapters, by 'Government' we mean the UK Government, responsible for all matters in England and for reserved matters elsewhere. Most issues concerned with adaptation are, however, devolved, and the Scottish Government, Welsh Assembly Government and the Northern Ireland Executive therefore have significant responsibilities. When we refer to all four bodies collectively, we do so as 'government' or 'the governments'.

POLICIES AND PROGRAMMES FOR CLIMATE CHANGE

3.5 Since we began this study, there has been growing recognition of the need for adaptation, and new policies and institutions have been developed to deal specifically with adaptation.

3.6 UK initiatives to combat climate change must be viewed against the backdrop of a growing commitment to act at a European and global level. For example, the 1992 United Nations Framework Convention on Climate Change acts as a unifying global framework. Within Europe, the European Commission's White Paper *Adapting to Climate Change: Towards a European framework for action*[1] encourages Member States and EU institutions to take a more strategic approach to climate adaptation that will foster good communication and the sharing of best practice. Commission President Barroso recently announced that he would launch an initiative to enable the EU to anticipate the changes which need to be made to cope with climate change and he has asked the new Commissioner-designate for Climate Change to ensure adaptation is addressed in all Community policies.[2]

3.7 In 2007 a duty to adapt to climate change was placed on the Mayor of London and the London Assembly. This amendment to the Greater London Authority Act 1999 imposes a duty on them to "address climate change". That duty is spelled out further by requiring the Mayor and London Assembly to "take action" with a view to mitigation of, or adaptation to, climate change. In exercising that duty, the Mayor and London Assembly are each required to take into account Government policies on those subjects, and to have regard to any guidance published by the Secretary of State. The Mayor is also required to prepare and publish an Adaptation to Climate Change Strategy for London.

3.8 In the UK more generally, the Climate Change Act 2008 and the Climate Change (Scotland) Act 2009 provide a statutory framework for planning and implementing adaptation. Box 3A describes the main provisions of these Acts. A key provision of the 2008 Act was the establishment of the Adaptation Sub-Committee (ASC) of the Committee on Climate Change. The ASC has interpreted its statutory remit broadly, and describes its role as "to advise on the development of a UK Climate Change Risk Assessment,[i] to assess the preparedness of the UK to meet the risks and opportunities arising from climate change, and to promote effective actions to adapt to climate change by society as a whole".[3]

> ## BOX 3A THE CLIMATE CHANGE ACT 2008 AND THE CLIMATE CHANGE (SCOTLAND) ACT 2009
>
> The Climate Change Act 2008 (the UK Act) received Royal Assent on 26 November 2008. The Climate Change (Scotland) Act 2009 (the Scottish Act) received Royal Assent on 4 August 2009. Both Acts contain provisions on climate change adaptation.[4]
>
> The UK Act provides for the establishment of an Adaptation Sub-Committee (ASC) of the Committee on Climate Change to provide advice to the Government, and upon request to UK national authorities, on adaptation to climate change. The ASC is chaired by Lord Krebs and consists of nine members.[5] The Scottish Act provides for the possible establishment of a Scottish equivalent to the UK Committee on Climate Change, which would be known as the Scottish Committee on Climate Change.
>
> The Government is to conduct a Climate Change Risk Assessment for the whole of the UK, with the first assessment due in January 2012 and subsequent assessments to be published every five years after that. Both the UK and Scottish governments, as well as the relevant Northern Ireland department, are required to prepare programmes setting out their objectives, proposals and policies in relation to adaptation. The Scottish Act also provides that Scotland's adaptation programme must set out arrangements for involving employers, trade unions and other stakeholders in meeting programme objectives, as well as the mechanisms for ensuring public engagement in the process.

i   The Climate Change Risk Assessment is "the report on the impact of climate change" referred to in Section 56 of the Climate Change Act 2008.

Different arrangements are in place in different parts of the UK for assessing progress towards attaining the objectives laid down in these adaptation programmes. The Committee on Climate Change is charged with regularly assessing progress in respect of the UK adaptation programme. Similarly, in Scotland the UK Committee on Climate Change or its Scottish counterpart will perform this function. In Northern Ireland, by contrast, it will be for the relevant department preparing the adaptation programme to assess its own progress over time.

One key element of the climate change legislation in relation to adaptation concerns the duties of public bodies. This is most striking under the Scottish Act, which imposes a duty on public bodies to exercise their functions in a way best calculated to deliver on the Scottish adaptation programme, and which allows the Scottish Government to issue directions requiring these bodies to report on compliance.[6] The Scottish Government may establish a body to monitor compliance by public bodies with their climate change obligations.

Under the UK Act, the Secretary of State or the Welsh Ministers may issue guidance to 'reporting authorities' (statutory undertakers or bodies with functions of a public nature) or direct them to produce adaptation reports, including an assessment of the impact of climate change in relation to that authority's functions, together with proposals and policies for adaptation. Joint reporting by more than one authority may also be required. No equivalent powers to issue guidance and directions to public bodies are laid down for Northern Ireland.

In accordance with the terms of the UK Act, the Secretary of State has laid a statutory report before Parliament setting out the Government's strategy for using the reporting power and a list of priority reporting authorities.[7] As more than 100,000 authorities are eligible for direction under the reporting power, the Government has identified about 90 authorities that will be required to report in the first round.

3.9 In 2008 the Government set up the cross-departmental Adapting to Climate Change (ACC) Programme to co-ordinate work from all areas of government and the wider public sector in England and the UK for reserved matters. Figure 3-I illustrates the governance structure of the programme.

3.10 Government departments are represented at senior level on a Programme Board, which oversees the work of the ACC Programme (and is part of that Programme in terms of Figure 3-I). This Board aims to ensure engagement across Whitehall and determine priorities for the ACC Programme, including the initiation of joint projects across departments. The Programme reports upwards to the Climate Change and Energy Delivery and Strategy High-level Board (the DASH Board), which is responsible for the delivery of the Government's climate change and energy objectives. The DASH Board reports to the Cabinet Sub-Committee on Environment and Energy (ED(EE)). As adapting to climate change forms one of the Department for Environment, Food and Rural Affairs' (Defra's) Departmental Strategic Objectives, Defra is also responsible for providing the ACC Programme delivery team.

3.11 After its formation in 2008, the ACC Programme established a Local and Regional Adaptation Partnership (LRAP) Board, which acts as a focal point for bringing together representatives from local and regional government with key institutions such as the UK Climate Impacts Programme (UKCIP) and the Environment Agency. In addition to LRAP the ACC Programme also established a Partnership Board to engage with wider stakeholder groups from across the private and public sectors and to ensure external advice is incorporated. Finally, the UK Adaptation Group supports collaboration across national efforts on adaptation and addresses any shared issues by linking with representatives from the Devolved Administrations of Scotland, Wales and Northern Ireland.

FIGURE 3-I

Governance structure for the Adapting to Climate Change (ACC) Programme[8]

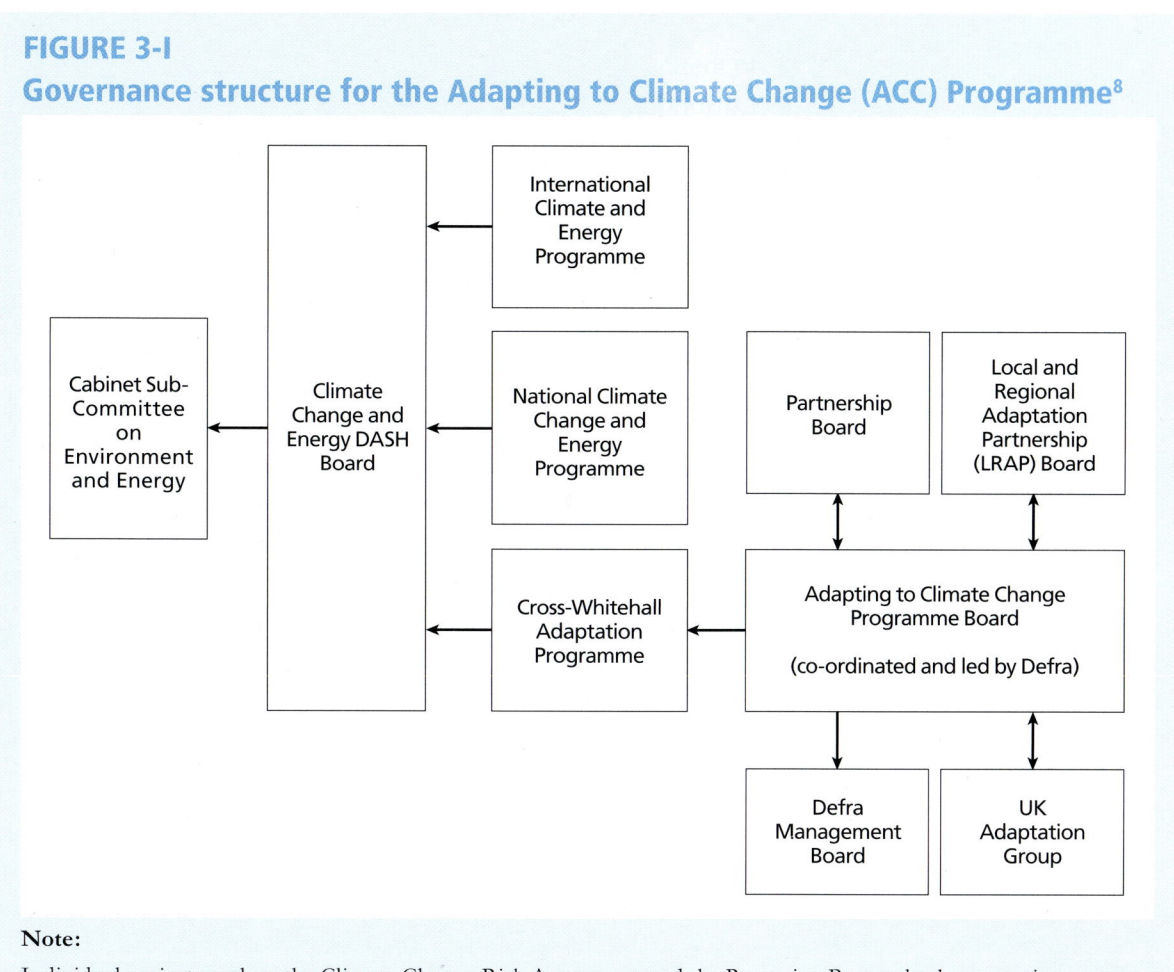

Note:

Individual projects such as the Climate Change Risk Assessment and the Reporting Power also have steering groups made up of Government departments and other stakeholders as appropriate, which are not shown.

3.12 The ACC Programme has developed a structured approach, prioritising its work projects across four work streams:

- providing evidence;

- raising awareness and taking action;

- ensuring and measuring progress; and

- government policy and process.

Figure 3-II illustrates the main underlying elements of each work stream.

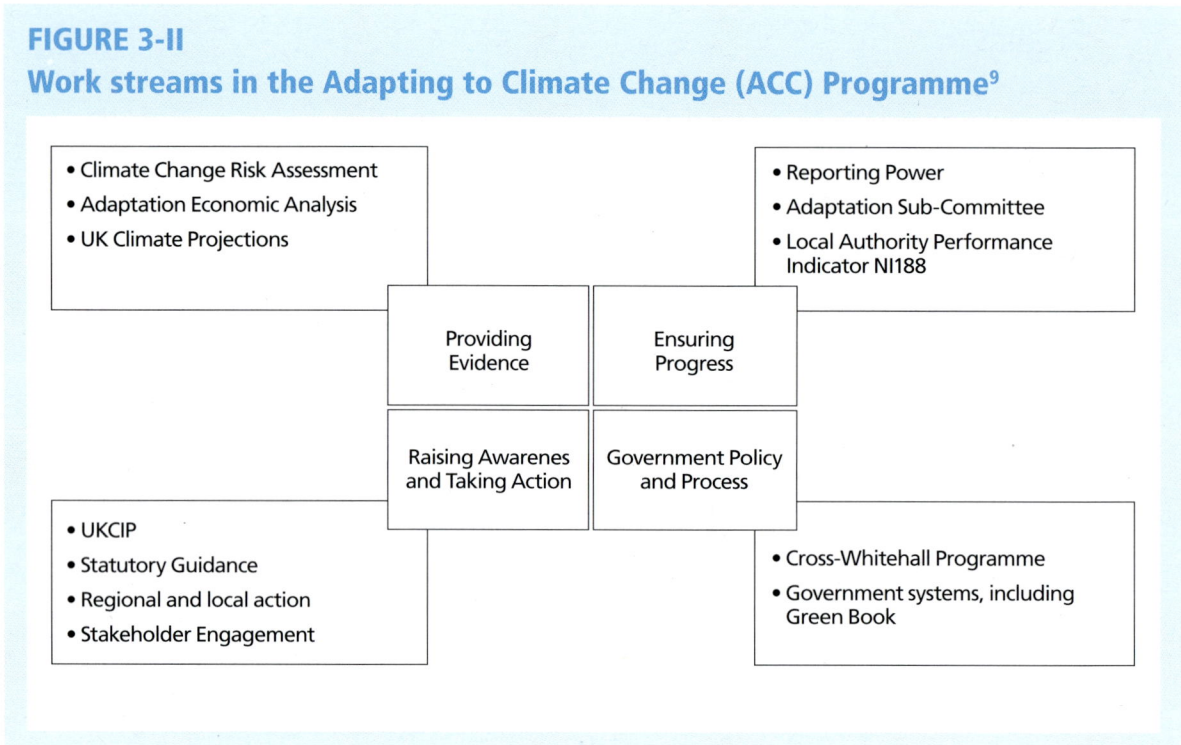

FIGURE 3-II
Work streams in the Adapting to Climate Change (ACC) Programme[9]

- Climate Change Risk Assessment
- Adaptation Economic Analysis
- UK Climate Projections

- Reporting Power
- Adaptation Sub-Committee
- Local Authority Performance Indicator NI188

Providing Evidence

Ensuring Progress

Raising Awarenes and Taking Action

Government Policy and Process

- UKCIP
- Statutory Guidance
- Regional and local action
- Stakeholder Engagement

- Cross-Whitehall Programme
- Government systems, including Green Book

3.13   Although Defra has lead responsibility for adaptation for England, many other Government departments will need to address adaptation in their own areas of responsibility (Figure 3-III). We welcome the fact that they will be publishing adaptation plans in spring 2010, following guidance issued by Defra. No department can avoid the need to adapt to climate change.

FIGURE 3-III
Climate change impacts and risks identified by Government departments[10]

Infrastructure

- **Critical national infrastructure**
  - **Energy generation** (e.g. flooding, heat and subsidence affecting generating capacity, sub-stations and demand)
  - **Transport** (e.g. flooding, heat and subsidence affecting roads, railways, airports and sea ports)
  - Water supply and wastewater treatment (e.g. increased precipitation in winter increasing demand for wastewater treatment, summer droughts changing clean water treatment processes and increasing water scarcity)
- **Large-scale sports facilities** (e.g. suitability of the legacy of the 2012 Olympics infrastructure)

Business and the economy

- **Economic growth** (e.g. impact on UK economic growth from future climate change impacts)
- **Business risks** (e.g. businesses not planning for changing climate adequately)
- **Costs to consumers** (e.g. fluctuations in global commodity prices)
- **Costs of defences** (e.g. sources of funding for flood defences)
- **Changing immigration patterns** (e.g. increased pressures on employment, public services, provision of benefits and housing)

Risks to departmental objectives arising from climate change impacts

Public health

- **Strategy** (e.g. uncertainty of climate predictions may make strategic healthcare planning challenging)
- **Changes in demand for services** (e.g. weather patterns altering demand for services)
- **Changes in health** (e.g. fewer cold-related deaths in winter, more heat-related deaths in summer)
- **Changing immigration patterns** (e.g. increased pressure on NHS resources)
- **Vulnerable groups**

Homes and buildings

- **Social cost**s (e.g. damage from flooding, failure/inability of householders to obtain adequate flood risk insurance leading to increased demand for crisis loans)
- **Comfort and safety** (e.g. Urban Heat Island effect, excessive summer heat following insulation and water shortages)
- **Damage** (e.g. as a result of floods, storms, or subsidence)
- **Public buildings** (e.g. excessive heat in summer in hospitals, schools, government offices, and prisons)
- **Building contents** (e.g. damage to collections with cultural and financial value)
- **Communities** (e.g. coastal erosion leading to necessary relocation of coastal communities, and increased fluvial and surface water flood risks in urban areas)

Government estate

- **Provision of services** (e.g. disruption of court proceedings due to flooding or storm damage)
- **Training** (e.g. increased flooding making terrain unsuitable for armed forces training)

Agriculture, food security and the natural environment

- **Biodiversity** (e.g. loss of native species, introduction of new species)
- **Pests and diseases** (e.g. increased prevalence of existing pests and diseases, introduction of new pests and diseases)
- **Forests and woodland** (e.g. higher risk of forest fires, and new commercial opportunities following introduction of new species)
- **Crop yields** (e.g. changing weather patterns may alter crop yields negatively or positively, and changes in yields leading to fluctuations in availability and prices)
- **Livestock** (e.g. impact of exotic animal diseases and heat stress)

3.14 The recent review prepared for the House of Commons Environmental Audit Committee by the National Audit Office, *Adapting to Climate Change*, provides a fuller overview of Government policy on adapting to climate change.[11]

3.15 The Scottish Government recently published *Scotland's Climate Change Adaptation Framework*,[12] which consists of an overarching national framework for climate change adaptation as well as sector summaries. The overarching framework comprises three 'pillars' which are concerned with building the evidence base, with equipping decision-makers with appropriate skills and tools, and with integrating adaptation into regulation and public policy. The 12 accompanying sectoral summaries seek to identify the key consequences and challenges for the relevant sector, to identify existing initiatives in planning for climate change, and to provide a summary of future actions. A Climate Change Delivery Board, consisting of senior cross-government officials, will provide oversight and strategic direction, and provide a forum to co-ordinate sectoral responses.

3.16 The Climate Change (Scotland) Act 2009 requires that the Scottish Government publish a public engagement strategy and ensure that this is regularly reviewed.[ii] This strategy is intended to inform people of the steps being taken to achieve the targets laid down in the Scottish Act, and to encourage them to contribute to the attainment of these targets. The reference to targets invokes the concept of emission reduction targets in the first part of the Act, and hence this public engagement strategy appears to focus on mitigation not adaptation. Nonetheless, the Scottish Adaptation Framework suggests that the government's public engagement strategy will extend to adaptation as well.[13,iii] For this to be so, the concept of public engagement needs to be more fluid. In the Scottish Act, the public engagement strategy is presented as a top-down process concerned with informing people of actions being taken to achieve settled objectives and of garnering their support for these. As we suggest in more detail in Chapters 4 and 5, public engagement strategies in relation to adaptation must be about more than how we achieve an objective which is settled in advance, and should seek to generate debate about a range of different possible outcomes as well as about their consequences for individuals and groups.

3.17 The Commission also recognises initiatives which aim to build on the UK's capacity for analysing the nature and impacts of the future climate. Initiatives, such as Living With Environmental Change (LWEC), bring together research councils, Government departments, Devolved Administrations and delivery agencies to draw on a wide range of research (from the fields of engineering, economics, social science, medical science, culture, arts and the humanities) to provide the best possible evidence base for environmental policy.[14] While it is at an early stage in its ten-year programme (2007 to 2017), LWEC has the potential to provide decision-makers within government with the information needed to protect vital ecosystem services and to address the uncertainties associated with climate change impacts. LWEC aims to achieve this goal through a process of extensive research, knowledge transfer and training.

3.18 We were also encouraged by the extent to which – in advance of work on adaptation – the Government is working to enhance societal resilience to current risks. Government, public bodies and some businesses are already responding to the challenges in the National Risk Register[15] – which describes the risks of civil emergencies including those posed by extreme weather – for example in the Department of Health's *Heatwave Plan for England*,[16] the Welsh Assembly Government's *Heatwave Plan for Wales*[17] and the Government's response to the Pitt Review.[18] The Cabinet Office Civil Contingencies Secretariat is working with Defra to ensure that the national risk assessment for climate change,[19] due in 2012, is co-ordinated with the National Risk Register. The Commission explored the conclusion in the Government's response to the Pitt Review that Government, regulators and operators need to work together to drive up resilience to flooding by reducing the most substantial risks and improving the national capacity for emergency response and business continuity. The Cabinet Office Civil Contingencies Secretariat has a remit to mitigate impacts from a wide range of hazards, and has been given a wider remit in regard to critical infrastructure in the near term. The Infrastructure Planning Commission (see 3.43) will have a

---

ii   The first strategy is to be published by the end of 2010.

iii   Note also that the Scottish Government's adaptation programme must specify the mechanisms for ensuring public engagement in meeting the adaptation objectives it lays down.

significant role in determining major developments over the longer term and the Commission heard evidence that its capacity to incorporate climate change impacts will be critical to the delivery of effective adaptation strategies in relation to the national infrastructure network.

3.19 These are important and welcome developments which, in our view, provide a good start in addressing the challenge of adaptation. Nevertheless, the Commission feels that much greater efforts will be required in the future to build the adaptive capacity of UK institutions. The Adaptation Sub-Committee will have a vital role to play in advising Government on appropriate actions.

REPORTING

3.20 There are arrangements in place in a number of areas to require organisations to report on progress towards adaptation. The UK Climate Change Act 2008 establishes a reporting power, under which the Secretary of State can direct public bodies and statutory undertakers[iv] to produce reports on their assessment of the potential impacts of climate change on them, their proposals and policies for adaptation, and the progress they have made. Following a public consultation, Defra set out in November 2009 the Government's plans for using this power.[20] It proposed that around 90 priority organisations should be asked to report in 2010 (out of 100,000 organisations potentially covered within the terms of the Act).

3.21 Figure 3-IV shows these organisations categorised by Defra according to their vulnerability to climate change, responsibility for national infrastructure, and whether they have comprehensive regulations already in place relating to climate change. The 'priority reporting authorities' are those which fall within the first two categories and have no existing reporting responsibilies.

3.22 It is notable that there are bodies which satisfy Defra's criteria as priority reporting authorities but which do not meet the definition of a reporting authority for the purpose of the UK Climate Change Act 2008 (petroleum and electronic communications companies in particular). Defra is proposing to ask these bodies to report on a voluntary basis.

---

iv   That is, bodies with a statutory responsibility for delivering services such as energy and water.

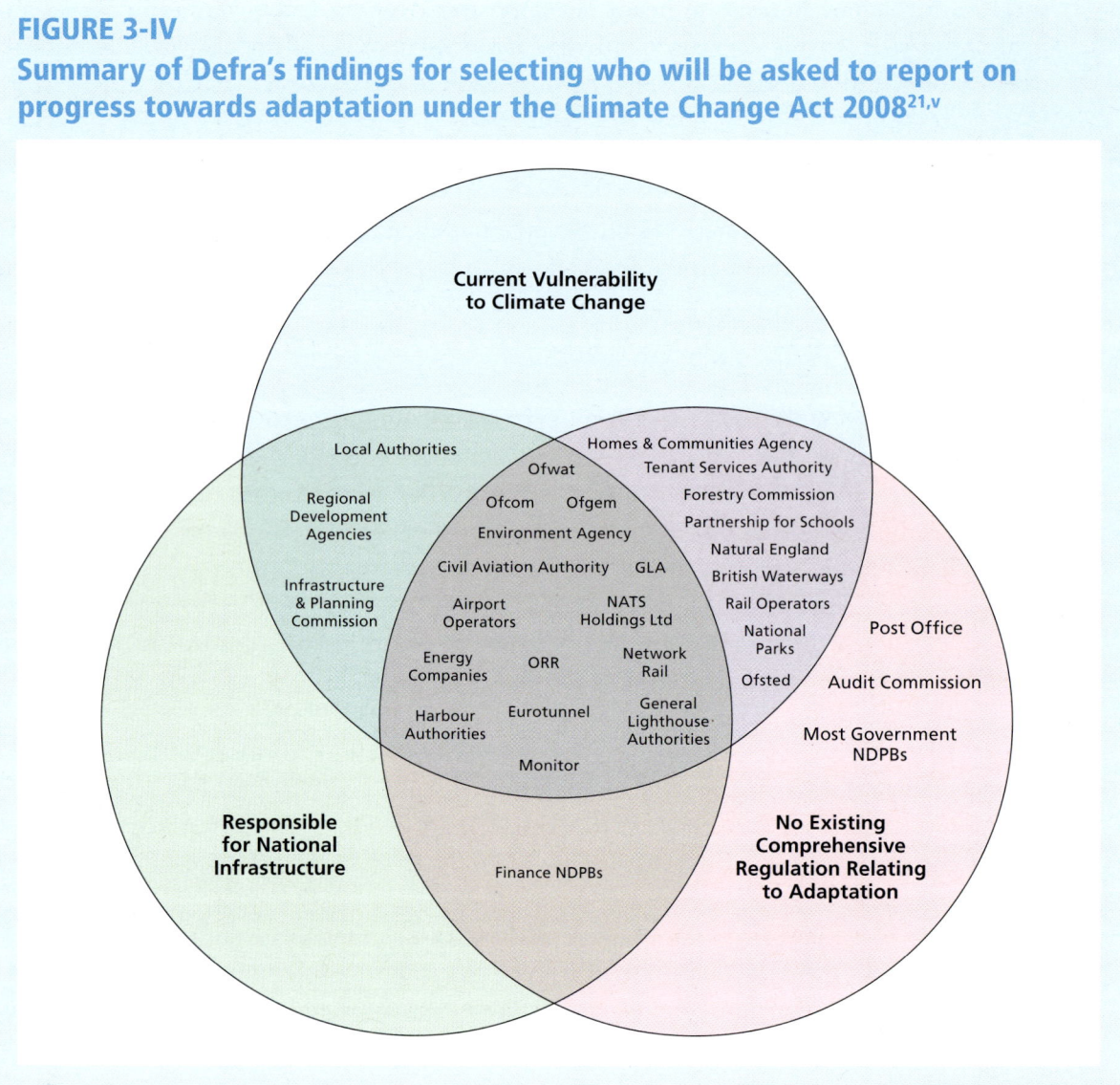

FIGURE 3-IV

Summary of Defra's findings for selecting who will be asked to report on progress towards adaptation under the Climate Change Act 2008[21,v]

3.23   Local authorities are not required by Defra to report in this round, as they already report through a system set out in the 2006 Local Government White Paper[22] and implemented through the Local Government and Public Involvement in Health Act 2007. This mechanism offers potentially one of the most significant opportunities for tackling climate change at the sub-national level, if implemented robustly. Central to the reforms is a new performance framework which aims to improve social, economic and environmental wellbeing outcomes for local areas.

3.24   The Local Government and Public Involvement in Health Act 2007 requires all 150 single- and upper-tier authorities in England,[vi] to work alongside statutory and non-statutory agencies, and private and voluntary sector institutions in Local Strategic Partnerships to adopt three-year local area agreements (LAAs). The LAAs define outcomes, indicators and targets specifically aimed at improving the performance within a range of national and local cross-cutting priorities. The new framework introduces 198 national indicators (NIs) covering a wide range of Government priorities, which themselves were set out in Public Service Agreements and Departmental Strategic Objectives. Local authorities are expected to pool resources and expertise in order to achieve

---

v   For a list of abbreviations used, see page 157.

vi   That is, county councils, metropolitan borough councils, London borough councils and unitary authorities.

their LAA targets. Making use of qualitative, quantitative, contextual and comparative data, local authorities are asked to track and report performance on all NIs. The NIs replace all other existing sets of indicators such as the 'Best Value Performance Indicators' and the 'Performance Assessment Framework'. Performance against each of the indicators will be published annually by the Audit Commission as part of the Comprehensive Area Assessment process.

3.25 Local Strategic Partnerships (LSPs) have been given greater control over their priorities and targets, each being allowed to select up to 35 NIs as designated improvement targets for inclusion within their LAAs. Several of these indicators are related to progress on climate change, with NI188 relating specifically to planning for adaptation to climate change. Unlike the outcome-based indicators designed to cover climate mitigation actions (NI185 and NI186), where reporting on carbon dioxide emission reductions is required, NI188 is a process-driven indicator developed in consultation with the UK Climate Impacts Programme (UKCIP), the Local Government Association (LGA), the Environment Agency and the Audit Commission. NI188 was designed to measure progress in preparedness in assessing and addressing the risks and opportunities of a changing climate. The aim is to embed the management of climate risks and opportunities across all levels of services, plans and estates. It will gauge progress of a local area in:

- assessing the climate-related risks and opportunities comprehensively across the area;

- taking action in any identified priority areas;

- developing an adaptation strategy and action plan setting out the risk assessment, where the priority areas are (where necessary in consultation and exhibiting leadership of local partners), what action is being taken to address these, and how risks will be continually assessed and monitored in the future; and

- implementing, assessing and monitoring the actions on an ongoing basis.

3.26 All authorities are expected to make an assessment of their performance across all indicators, but they select only a number of indicators to report on as part of their LAAs. Only about 35% have to date chosen to include NI188 in their reporting; and although this puts it among the top third of indicators in terms of popularity for selection, it does raise questions about relying on NI188 as the central reporting mechanism on adaptation for local authorities.

3.27 Local authorities are required to report on progress against national indicators through a process of self-assessment; the Audit Commission audits the assessments made. Local authorities are required to grade progress against their targets according to a five-point scale. Level 0 is 'getting started'; Level 1 requires 'public commitment and impacts assessments'; Level 2 requires a 'comprehensive risk assessment'; Level 3 requires a 'comprehensive action plan'; and Level 4 requires 'implementation, monitoring and continuous review' to be in place. An analysis of the first round of reporting shows that 75% of those authority areas which adopted NI188 in their LAAs reported that they had achieved level 1 or higher.[vii] For all local authority areas, 49% reported being at Level 1 or above. However, there is little evidence of authorities reporting at Level 4. A revised indicator is being developed for the 2011-2014 period, in the light of experience in the first round.

3.28 Through Scotland's Climate Change Declaration, all of Scotland's local authorities have committed themselves to take action, in partnership with the Scottish Government, both to mitigate their impact on climate change and to adapt to predicted climate change impacts. Signatories also agree to issue an annual statement detailing the progress of their climate change response. The Declaration has been in place since January 2007, and 2008 was the first year that councils reported. In the recent round of reporting, roughly half of local authorities reported against commitments in the Declaration. Similar arrangements are in place in Wales.

PLANNING REGIMES

3.29 The land use planning regime has a crucial role to play in promoting adaptation to climate change in all parts of the UK. The first Town and Country Planning Act in 1947 focused largely on physical factors relating to land use and the development of the built environment. Over the years, the scope of planning has expanded to include socio-economic and, more recently, environmental factors. There is ample scope now for spatial planning and development control to address both the effects of development on an environment that is subject to a changing climate, and the effects of climate on development. Given the importance of the planning system, the Commission asked the Town and Country Planning Association to undertake a study on the institutional capacity of the planning system to deliver climate change adaptation. Its report, which covers all parts of the UK, comprehensively reviews the institutional arrangements and the powers and duties in planning legislation; this report has now been published.[23] Here we limit our discussion to the key elements of the system.

3.30 The town and country planning regime has two closely connected components: development planning and development control. The nature of development plans has changed several times to meet the prevailing policies of governments in power but the basic premise remains the same: a development plan is a forward look aimed at matching the predicted social and environmental needs for the area in question against the availability of suitable land. Plans are drawn up by local authorities; the geographical scale and the detail of coverage, including whether or not there is a hierarchy of plans at different geographical scales, has been a matter of government policy. One key feature of development plans is that they do not dictate what development will take place but, rather, encourage developments whilst placing limits on the uses to which land may be put. In this respect they are prospective but not prescriptive.

vii   Level 1 requires that the authority has made a public commitment to identify and manage climate-related risk. The authority will have undertaken a local risk-based assessment of significant vulnerabilities to, and opportunities arising from, weather and climate change, both now and in the future. It can demonstrate a sound understanding of those vulnerabilities not yet addressed in existing strategies and actions (e.g. in land use planning documents, service delivery plans, flood and coastal resilience plans, emergency planning, community risk registers/strategies, etc.). It will have communicated these potential vulnerabilities and opportunities to department/service heads and other local partners and will have set out the next steps in addressing them.

3.31 Anyone wishing to develop land has to apply for planning permission (unless permitted development rights apply). One of the most important functions of a development plan is to inform the planning authority's decisions on such applications. Planning decisions have to be in accordance with the development plan unless material considerations indicate otherwise. The need for adaptation to climate change is surely a material consideration.

3.32 There are a number of statutory obligations on plan-makers in respect of climate change adaptation. So regional spatial planning in England must include "policies designed to secure that the development and use of land in the region contribute to the mitigation of, and adaptation to, climate change";[24] the regional strategies proposed in the Local Democracy, Economic Development and Construction Act 2009 also demand policies "designed to contribute to the mitigation of, and adaptation to, climate change".[25] Local development plan documents in England and Wales similarly must "include policies designed to secure that the development and use of land in the local planning authority's area contribute to the mitigation of, and adaptation to, climate change".[26]

3.33 Scotland does not have England's explicit statutory duties in respect of planning in particular, although the Climate Change (Scotland) Act 2009 imposes a duty on all public bodies (including planning bodies) in the exercise of their functions to act in the way best calculated to help deliver the Scottish programme for adaptation to climate change.[27]

3.34 Planning authorities are further guided by national planning policy, issued by the Department for Communities and Local Government (CLG), the Scottish Government and the Welsh Assembly Government. Scotland and Wales each have national plans with supplementary technical guidance; in England there is a series of Planning Policy Statements (PPSs) and guidance documents. Relevant government policy is a material consideration in all decisions taken within the planning regime and, although this does not necessarily mean that policy will be followed in all cases, any departure must be justified. Specific guidance on climate change for England can be found in CLG's supplementary PPS on planning and climate change issued in 2007, which includes adaptation alongside mitigation.[28] We would expect adaptation to feature more strongly in the recast PPS on climate change to be issued later in 2010. The Scottish National Planning Framework requires development plans to include policies designed to "contribute to" adaptation. For Wales, the Welsh Assembly Government has published Technical Advice Notes (TANs) on development and flood risk,[29] and on design,[30] which are relevant. Northern Ireland as yet has no comprehensive spatial guidance on adaptation.

3.35 The second National Planning Framework (NPF2) is Scotland's strategy for the long-term development of its towns, cities and countryside.[31] NPF2 guides the spatial development of Scotland to 2030. It addresses critical elements of national infrastructure: transport, energy, waste management, water and drainage, flooding and water resource management, and communications technology. NPF2 specifically endorses the creation of national ecological networks to create better environments and new opportunities for local communities. In doing so, it supports both the delivery of greater resilience to a changing climate and sustainable economic growth. NPF2 must be taken into account by local authorities in the preparation of statutory strategic and local development plans, thereby promoting climate change adaptation into the land use planning system and investment decisions. In addition, the Climate Change (Scotland) Act 2009 placed a requirement on Scottish Ministers to lay before the Scottish Parliament a land use strategy by the end of March 2011. This strategy will set out the Scottish Ministers' objectives in relation to sustainable land use, which must contribute to adaptation to climate change as set out in the adaptation programme and other matters.

3.36 Planning authorities will also turn to more specific policy, on flooding or biodiversity for example, which may also make direct reference to climate change. For example, recently updated advice on nature conservation issued by the Welsh Assembly Government provides for: "plans to accommodate and reduce the effects of climate change by encouraging development that will reduce damaging emissions and energy consumption and that help habitats and species to respond to climate change".[32] General government policy (for example, Scotland's *Climate Change Adaptation Framework*)[33] is also relevant in the planning framework.

3.37 The introduction of strategies such as Defra's *Making Space for Water*[34] in England (3.64) has implications for land use planning, in particular the planned development of new property or business infrastructure, which is obliged to consider flood and coastal erosion risk. Planning policy was revised (in the form of Planning Policy Statement (PPS) 25 on development and flood risk)[35] to ensure a closer relationship between planning authorities and the Environment Agency, which was made a statutory consultee for planning applications involving major development in flood-prone areas. PPS25 further provides that, where the local planning authority is mindful to approve major developments despite maintained objections from the Environment Agency, the Secretary of State can be asked by the Agency to consider 'calling in' the application for his or her determination. Local planning authorities have to balance all material (including social and economic) considerations; thus if they approve developments despite advice from one agency, it is open to the Secretary of State to approve or not their balancing of different considerations. The Environment Agency's most recent assessment of flood risks for England[36] reports that, in 2007-08, where the Agency objected to the grant of planning consent on flood risk grounds, less than 4% of applications gained consent but 15 big developments gained approval against their advice. In Wales, equivalent guidance is available in Technical Advice Note 15.[37]

3.38 The formal legislative and policy arrangements for addressing climate change through the planning system are, whilst fragmented and convoluted, thoroughly embedded. High-level policy is rightly ambitious in terms of the contribution of spatial planning to adaptation, and there are emerging frameworks with the potential to take that even further. For example, CLG plans to revise the PPS1 supplement on planning and climate change and consolidate it with PPS22 on renewable energy; we would expect adaptation to feature more strongly in this recast PPS on climate change. PPS20 on coastal planning is to be replaced with an updated supplement to PPS25 on development and flood risk. *World Class Places*, the Government's strategy for improving the quality of place, identified the need for a step change in the provision of green infrastructure to help urban areas adapt to climate change, and committed the Government to updating planning policy to provide a clearer message to local authorities about what is expected of them.[38]

3.39 We are concerned that these high-level principles are not routinely part of planning practice. Development planning and, more particularly, the review and updating of plans can be slow relative to the developing science of climate change. Moreover, the importance of adaptation does not seem always to be recognised in development control decisions in practice. In its report for us, the Town and Country Planning Association concluded that even where strong guidance exists on adaptation to climate change, it appears to be limited by its enabling rather than prescriptive nature.[39] Other underlying problems also exist, not least the professional capacity of planners in terms of adaptation, and the training and awareness of politicians who are ultimately responsible for planning decisions. We discuss these issues further in Chapter 4.

3.40 Various appraisal obligations could reinforce the consideration of climate change adaptation in the planning process. Strategic environmental assessment (of plans and programmes) and environmental impact assessment (of projects) both focus on the impact of proposals *on* the environment, rather than *vice versa*. Whilst these assessments encompass the impact of proposals on, for example, water or biodiversity in a changing climate, they provide a somewhat indirect approach to adaptation. Nevertheless, the prospective, cross-sectoral and consultative approach of the environmental assessment legislation could prove to be a key tool in adapting to climate change. Environmental assessment obligations originate in EU law and so apply across the board (including to nationally significant infrastructure). Sustainability appraisal is also required of development planning at the regional and local level and of National Policy Statements under the Planning Act 2008.[40] CLG planning policy emphasises that adapting to the impacts of a changing climate should be a 'key part' of sustainability appraisal;[41] even without this policy guidance, that would be a reasonable expectation.

3.41 The ESPACE Project (European Spatial Planning: Adapting to Climate Events, Box 3B) demonstrates the way a number of planning authorities across north-west Europe have begun to approach these issues.

> ### BOX 3B ESPACE (EUROPEAN SPATIAL PLANNING: ADAPTING TO CLIMATE EVENTS)[42]
>
> Launched in 2003, ESPACE is a five-year project led by Hampshire County Council and funded by the European Commission's north-west Europe INTERREG IIIB Programme, the ESPACE Partnership and the Department for Communities and Local Government (CLG).
>
> ESPACE recommends how adaptation to climate change can be incorporated into spatial planning policies, processes and practices. Concentrating on water management issues, it was one of the first projects to focus on increasing awareness of the need for spatial planning systems to adapt to the impacts of climate change and to begin to provide some of the necessary policy guidance, tools and mechanisms to incorporate adaptation into planning systems and processes.
>
> ESPACE was founded by a transnational group of ten partners, also known as the 'ESPACE Partnership', spanning four north-west European countries and bringing together representatives from all levels of civic society. They include: Hampshire County Council (lead partner), the Environment Agency, South East Climate Change Partnership, South East England Regional Assembly, Surrey County Council and West Sussex County Council from the UK; Regional Landschap Zenne, Zuun en Zoniën from Belgium; Waterschap Rivierenland and Ministerie van VROM from the Netherlands; and the Bayerisches Landesamt für Umwelt from Germany.

3.42 Finally on planning, we should note the new approach in England (also Wales in respect of some non-devolved energy projects) to 'nationally significant infrastructure', in the fields of energy, transport, water, wastewater and hazardous waste, set out in the Planning Act 2008. This provides for National Policy Statements on nationally significant infrastructure to be drawn up by Government, subject to parliamentary scrutiny. The obligation on the Secretary of State to exercise his/her functions "with the objective of contributing to the achievement of sustainable development" embraces a further explicit obligation to "have regard to the desirability of … adapting to … climate change".[43] This rather weak (especially for such a recent statute) reference to adaptation is considerably strengthened by the requirement that National Policy Statements include "an explanation of how the policy set out in the statement takes account of Government policy relating to the mitigation of, and adaptation to, climate change".[44]

3.43   The new Infrastructure Planning Commission (IPC) is currently empowered to take final decisions on consent for nationally significant infrastructure, replacing the role of the local authority or Secretary of State (who would generally have called in such an application and made a decision following a public inquiry). The IPC has limited discretion: it must decide in accordance with the relevant National Policy Statement, unless to do so would lead to a breach of legal obligations, or where the IPC "is satisfied that the adverse impact of the proposed development would outweigh its benefits".[45] The operation of the IPC is, however, not yet clear. Whilst there is clearly an expectation from Government that the National Policy Statement will 'once and for all' consider infrastructure planning in the national interest, there is scope for the IPC to make full use of the 'adverse impact' provision of the statute. Nevertheless, we can conclude that getting the policy right is even more important than usual under the new regime.

3.44   The Department of Energy and Climate Change published several draft National Policy Statements relating to energy infrastructure for consultation on 9 November 2009.[46] The IPC is under no explicit duty to consider adaptation to climate change. However, the Draft Overarching National Policy Statement for Energy would require the IPC to be satisfied that any applicant has taken into account the potential impacts of climate change, using the current projections at the time, and that appropriate mitigation and adaptation measures have been identified. The guidance also suggests that if there are critical features of the design which would be seriously affected by more radical changes to the climate, the IPC should be satisfied that action can be taken to keep the infrastructure operational over its estimated lifetime. This is welcome. We assume that other departments will include similar requirements in their draft Statements when they are published in due course.

INSTITUTIONS FOR WATER, COASTAL EROSION AND NATURE CONSERVATION

3.45   The governance of each of the exemplars we have chosen, as for many issues, is complex. It is multilayered, involving both national governments and local bodies such as district or county councils, and it involves both democratic bodies with a broad range of responsibilities, such as local authorities, and specialist agencies such as the Environment Agency, the Countryside Council for Wales, and Scottish Natural Heritage. In addition to statutory agencies, the private sector and non-governmental organisations have important roles. And in many cases there are partnerships in place, where a number of these bodies come together to deliver shared objectives – a response to the need for co-ordinated and complementary actions in the face of complex organisational responsibilities.

3.46   In addition, for both water and nature conservation, national institutions operate within institutional arrangements laid down by the European Union, most significantly in the Water Framework Directive, the Birds Directive and the Habitats Directive. These lay down, with legal force, both the broad objectives to be achieved for water resources or for conservation, and some of the mechanisms and the processes to be followed by Member States to achieve those objectives.

3.47 For each of the exemplars, national governments have a major role in establishing regulatory frameworks and policy goals, and in providing financial resources for the agencies. This is taken for granted in the following descriptions.

MANAGEMENT OF WATER

3.48 The governance arrangements for water seek to achieve several aims, including:

- Protecting water quality – in particular the ecological and chemical quality of water bodies (covering surface water – lakes, rivers, reservoirs, coastal waters and the sea – and groundwater);

- Managing water as a resource – ensuring that there are adequate, wholesome supplies of water for domestic use and for industry, and proper management of wastewater, and (for domestic consumers) ensuring that monopoly suppliers do not exploit their position and that water is affordable. Water is also a resource for recreation, navigation and fishing; and

- Managing the threat of flooding, through land and surface water drainage, and flood protection works.

3.49 The Government's Water Resources Strategy for England was published in 2008 and covered objectives up to 2030.[47] This highlighted the need for adaptation to climate change, as well as mitigation, and recognised the need for regional and local approaches. The Environment Agency published its water resources strategy in 2009, and this sets out a number of adaptation objectives and a timetable for implementing its work.[48] The European Commission's White Paper on adaptation is also relevant.[49]

Water quality

3.50 The Environment Agency (for England and Wales), the Scottish Environment Protection Agency and the Northern Ireland Environment Agency have the key roles in environmental management. For example, they are the 'competent authorities' for ensuring that the requirements of the EU Water Framework Directive are met. This overarching European Directive (Box 3C) requires Member States to aim to achieve good status for water bodies and specifies processes – such as drawing up river basin management plans – to help to achieve this.

BOX 3C THE EU WATER FRAMEWORK DIRECTIVE

The EU Water Framework Directive (WFD) (2000/60/EC) was agreed in 2000. It sets out a framework for the protection of inland surface and coastal waters and groundwater. It aims to protect and enhance the status of aquatic ecosystems, to promote sustainable water use based on the long-term protection of water resources, and to reduce pollution and the threat from hazardous substances.

It requires Member States to characterise the current condition of surface water and groundwater bodies. They are first to ensure that there is no deterioration in the status of water bodies, and second to work to achieve good ecological and chemical status for surface waters and good quantitative and chemical status for groundwaters by 2015 (though there are some exceptions and derogations). The Directive focuses on river basin districts as the unit of management, and requires Member States to prepare for each river basin district an analysis of its characteristics and the impact of human activities on the status of water bodies, and an economic analysis of water use. A river basin management plan was to be produced for each river basin district by 22 December 2009. Member States must also prepare programmes of measures to achieve the objectives, and put in place monitoring arrangements to keep the status of water bodies under review.

Member States and the European Commission have worked together on a 'common implementation strategy' to ensure broad consistency in the interpretation of the Directive. The common implementation strategy has produced the guidance *River Basin Management in a Changing Climate* published in November 2009.[50] This broad guidance advises Member States on how to prepare for climate change through the second and third river basin management planning cycles.

Whilst not created specifically with climate change in mind, the Directive demonstrates a number of institutional innovations that may be helpful in the adaptation challenge, in particular by pointing towards flexibility, learning and collaboration (discussed further in Chapter 4).

Flexibility can be found most obviously in the relatively open-ended definitions (e.g. of 'good ecological status') and aspirational environmental objectives set by the Directive, and in the wide range of permissible exceptions and derogations. There is some concern that the reference point of 'undisturbed conditions', against which elements of 'good status' are assessed, posits an unchanging baseline. The language (and philosophy) of the WFD allows for a dynamic baseline, at least in the sense that what we understand as 'undisturbed conditions' are able to change to reflect the impact of climate change; the flexibility of the WFD depends, however, on the approach taken in implementation. There are more prescriptive standards in some specific cases, for example for bathing waters. Given its reliance on fixed quantitative measures that are difficult to amend, the definition of 'good chemical status' may be less amenable to flexible interpretation.

Flexibility raises questions of legal and political accountability. As with all legislation, the precise interpretation and requirements for proper implementation of the WFD will only finally be resolved by judicial interpretation. Legally, this flexible understanding of the WFD could be challenged in national courts (with reference to the European Court of Justice). Politically, the 'who' and 'how' of involvement in decision making will be scrutinised. In this respect, the role of 'river basin management planning' and the 'common implementation strategy' are especially significant. These key institutional innovations enhance the potential for a collaborative approach to water management, and provide opportunities for learning and further flexibility.

River basin management plans are drawn up with the involvement of interested parties, and subject to obligations of public engagement. The European Commission and other Member States provide peer review of these plans. The production of the plans demands the generation, collection and publication of information on every river basin district. The process is renewed every six years, an iterative process allowing the revisiting and reconsideration of policy.

The common implementation strategy is not found in the wording of the WFD, but it is crucial. Responsibility for implementation of the WFD rests in principle with each Member State, but the common implementation strategy provides for a joint approach to implementation, through networks of national regulators.

3.51 While the environment agencies themselves can do much to improve water quality, for example by regulating discharges through consents, for many other issues they have to work in partnership with others – for example by seeking to influence development control decisions taken by local authorities where development could have an impact on water quality, or by influencing farming practice through programmes such as that on catchment sensitive farming (see Box 3D on the

River Glaven). The agencies must also work with the nature conservation agencies to ensure that the decisions they take, for example on abstraction licences or discharge consents, do not have an adverse impact on nature conservation objectives. River basin panels serve to co-ordinate the activities of the main agencies, and catchment panels serve as a means of engaging with local stakeholders.

BOX 3D CASE STUDY: THE RIVER GLAVEN AND CATCHMENT SENSITIVE FARMING

A significant challenge for water purification in the future will be dealing with surges from sudden rainfall events. This increases the amount of pollutants and sediment that need to be removed from water; and it is a source of diffuse pollution, as opposed to pollution from a single, identifiable source.

In the North Norfolk region, one challenge is agricultural run-off. Catchment sensitive farming (CSF) is an initiative sponsored by Defra and co-managed by Natural England and the Environment Agency. They work with local farmers to tackle diffuse pollution by managing run-off, by promoting practices which enhance soil structure and reduce erosion, and by controlling the use of fertilisers and pesticides in a way that is sensitive to the ecological balance both of the immediate area and further downstream. One potential difficulty is that there is no security of long-term funding as CSF is a five-year programme, launched in 2007.

The Commission visited one such scheme in the River Glaven catchment in North Norfolk. The Commission also met the Glaven Conservation Group, a local volunteer organisation. The Group's work demonstrates the potential role of local, small-scale activists in driving adaptation behaviour, as they are able to bring different actors together. By removing banks to open up flood meadows, the Group has helped change the riverside to make it flood more naturally, thereby reducing the risks of more damaging floods downstream.

3.52   The water industry, with its statutory duties to meet discharge limits and drinking water standards, also has an important role to play, since both flooding and drought affect the ease with which it can achieve water quality standards. The balance is difficult even in environmental terms alone, as the standards for water quality carry with them a significant carbon cost – an example of where the trade-offs between mitigation and adaptation need to be considered. There are also many non-environmental factors.

3.53   The Water Framework Directive is a potentially effective lever to drive adaptation practice in the water industry and other sectors. This could be achieved through rigorous implementation of regularly updated river basin management plans, the first sets of which were published in December 2009.

3.54   There is, however, the potential for environment agencies and nature conservation agencies, each with their own mandates and priorities, to have different perspectives. For instance, the Environment Agency has statutory obligations, the fulfilment of which may sit uneasily with the nature conservation roles of Natural England and the voluntary local Wildlife Trusts. This has the capacity to generate day-to-day tensions. For example, the Agency will regulate abstraction for business and industry which has the potential to damage wildlife sites. But as the climate changes, and as the pattern of rainfall changes, it is likely that such potential tensions will occur more often.

Water supply and wastewater treatment

3.55   Water supply and wastewater collection and treatment are undertaken by diverse utilities in the UK: by private sector companies in England, by a company limited by guarantee in Wales,[viii] and by government-owned companies in Scotland and Northern Ireland. Water companies operate within a statutory framework which imposes a number of duties on them, e.g. to ensure that domestic customers are provided with wholesome water. Private sector companies must also reflect the requirements of their shareholders. Guaranteeing adequate supplies of freshwater requires investment in reservoirs and other infrastructure, as well as in measures to encourage efficiency of use.

3.56   The water utilities work within well established environmental and economic regulatory frameworks (Figure 3-V). For example, as mentioned in 3.49, the Environment Agency has prepared a water resources strategy for England and Wales[ix] which sets out medium- and long-term considerations for management. The Agency also issues consents both for the abstraction of water from rivers or groundwater and for the discharge of wastewater back into rivers or the sea.

3.57   Water companies are subject to regulation by economic regulators – the Water Services Regulation Authority (Ofwat) in England and Wales, the Water Industry Commission in Scotland and the Utility Regulator in Northern Ireland.[x] The focus of economic regulation is to further the interests of customers (both those of today and of tomorrow), to secure the financial sustainability of water and sewerage services, and to contribute to sustainable development. The emphasis has tended to be on customers and services, but there is a growing awareness of the need to address adaptation.[51]

3.58   Water resource management plans, which are now required on a statutory basis, allow each water company in England and Wales to set out how it will meet water demand up to 2035 and deal with factors such as changes in climate and population. Draft plans have been subject to consultation and will be finalised in 2009 and 2010. These plans will become vital to work on adaptation because they will include projections of current and future demand for water that are based on climate change and other considerations such as population and household size.

3.59   A balance has to be struck between the objectives of economic and environmental regulation. In England the Defra policy document *Future Water* sought to give guidance on this balance for the current review of water pricing.[52] In Wales, the Strategic Policy Position Statement on Water sets out the Assembly Government's priorities on water, including affordability.[53] However, a tension could well occur in future as the need to build in adaptation becomes more apparent, particularly as it becomes necessary to invest now for infrastructure which may be necessary to cope with a changed climate in decades to come.

viii   The situation is in practice more complicated, since water supply areas do not match national boundaries. For example, Dŵr Cymru Welsh Water provides services in parts of England, and Severn Trent Water provides services in parts of Wales.

ix   There is also a separate Water Resources Strategy for Wales. See http://grdp.org/research/library/publications/40731. aspx. Accessed 16 February 2010.

x   Declaration of Interest: A member of the Commission is the Chair of the Utility Regulator for Northern Ireland.

3.60 Planning future provision raises difficult issues over the attitude and appetite for risk – for example, in a situation of uncertainty is it more appropriate to build significant capacity at the outset to meet all foreseen needs, or to rely on modular approaches which allow incremental investment as the future unfolds but with the risk that there will be less time to respond? This also raises important issues about how the cost of meeting future needs should be spread across generations.

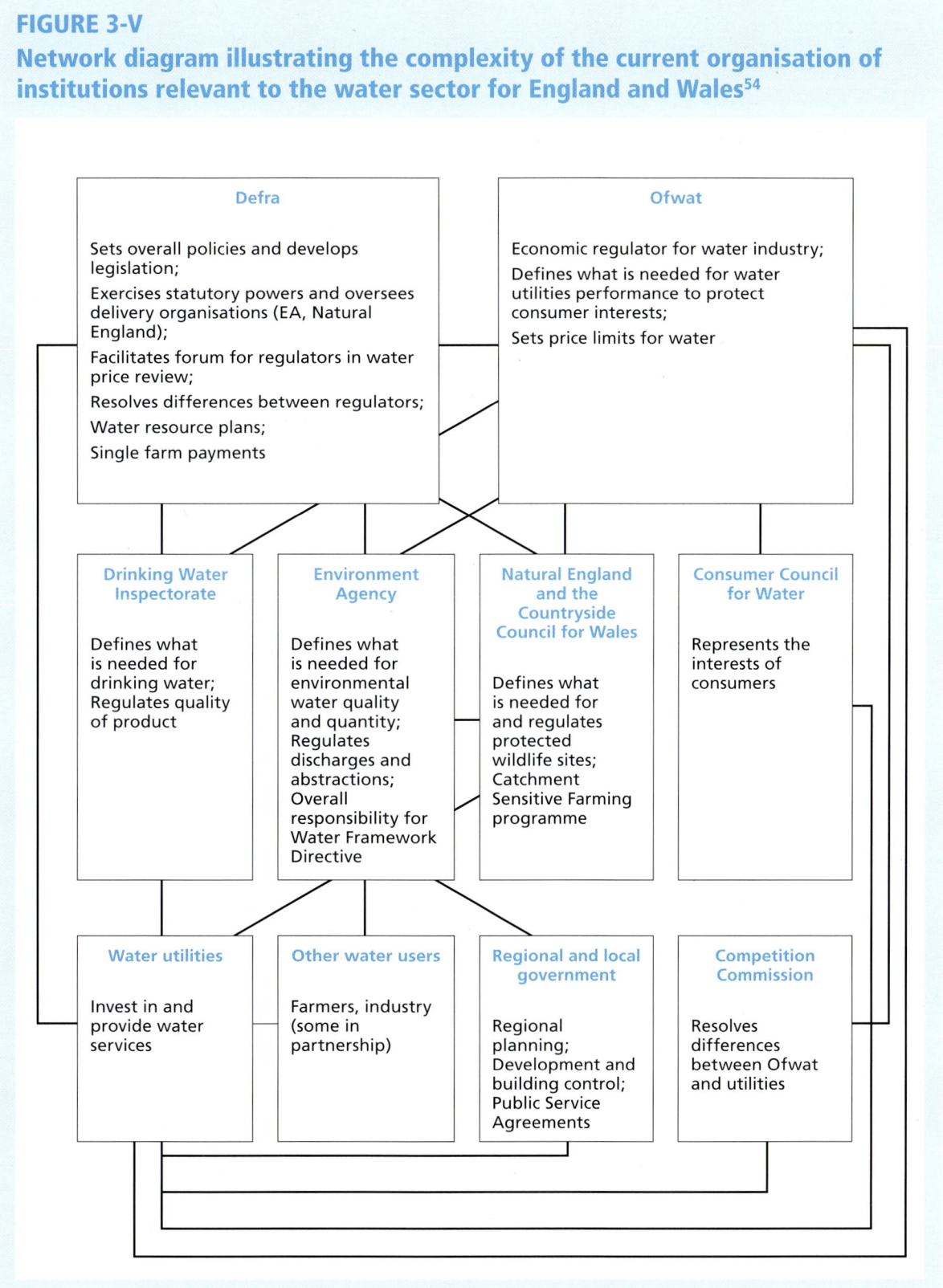

FIGURE 3-V

Network diagram illustrating the complexity of the current organisation of institutions relevant to the water sector for England and Wales[54]

Flooding

3.61   In England and Wales, responsibility for managing flood risk is shared between the Environment Agency, Welsh Assembly Ministers and local authorities. In Scotland, primary responsibility rests with local authorities. In Northern Ireland the Rivers Agency[xi] plays a key role. As we describe below, the Flood and Water Management Bill which is currently before Parliament will make some significant changes for England and Wales.

3.62   Flood abatement requires evaluation of how much society is willing to spend to reduce risk. Like all insurance investment, the costs may seem excessive until abatement measures fail. The risk management toolkit to deal with flooding also includes forecasting, early warning systems and flood risk mapping, for example by the Environment Agency.

3.63   Flood risk management requires co-operation on the part of a number of authorities. Decisions made to manage water to minimise flood risks may have implications for nature conservation, with potential for synergies and also tensions – and the latter are likely to become more rather than less acute as the climate changes.

3.64   *Making Space for Water,* published by Defra in 2005, sets out the Government's strategy for both flood management and coastal erosion.[55] It aims to set out a more holistic approach than previous strategies, taking account of the need for adaptation and based on the principles of sustainable development, with a greater emphasis on risk management and solutions incorporating economic, social and environmental factors.

3.65   Following widespread flooding in the summer of 2007, the Government commissioned an independent review of flood risk management and emergency response. The Pitt Review was published in June 2008.[56] The first recommendation was that adaptation to climate change, along with mitigation, should be a priority in Government programmes. Other recommendations dealt with (among other things) investment in infrastructure and how this should be integrated into the periodic reviews of water charges by Ofwat.

3.66   The Flood Risk Regulations 2009 in England and Wales[57] and, in part, the Flood Risk Management (Scotland) Act 2009[58] are designed to implement the EU Floods Directive (2007/60/EC).[59] The purpose of the Directive is to establish a framework for assessing and managing flood risks, and in England and Wales responsibilities for this are placed on both the Environment Agency and certain local authorities. The Scottish Flood Risk Management Act (which received Royal Assent in June 2009) seeks to streamline decision making and to ensure co-ordinated governance of flood risk, including the part played by local authorities and Scottish Water.

3.67   The Flood and Water Management Bill, which was published on 19 November 2009 and at the time of writing was before Parliament, seeks to implement a number of recommendations from the Pitt Review. It provides a statutory basis for the Environment Agency's strategic role in relation to floods, and also coastal erosion which we cover below, obliging the Agency to develop a national strategy for England. Welsh Ministers will prepare the strategy for Wales. The national strategies will have to consider the current and predicted impact of climate change, and specify how and when the strategies are to be reviewed. Local authorities in England and Wales will be required to develop local flood risk strategies, covering flood risk from surface water run-off and

---

xi   In Northern Ireland, the Rivers Agency is an Executive Agency of the Department of Agriculture and Rural Development.

ordinary watercourses. As with the national strategies these will be required to set out objectives for managing local flood risk as well as the measures to achieve them. In contrast to the national strategies, however, there would be no specific obligations on local authorities to consider the impact of climate change.

3.68 For our purposes, it is important to note that the Bill contains a broad definition of risk management which would provide additional flexibility for decision-makers. As well as hard engineering solutions, risk management measures might include, for example, "maintaining or restoring natural processes" or "making arrangements for forecasting".[60]

3.69 Local authorities are to be given responsibility under the Bill for surface water flooding, a major source of flooding in 2007. The central role of local authorities in surface water flooding reflects the growing need to manage flood risk through the use of sustainable drainage systems by soft engineering and effective management of the urban infrastructure, and not just through specific flood defence works. There is a need to clarify responsibilities for private surface sewers and public water sewers not owned by the water companies – we understand that a lack of clarity has caused problems in the past.

3.70 We were particularly interested in an approach to sea flood defences adopted by the Environment Agency with the Thames Estuary 2100 project. One of the prime functions of the Thames Barrier (Figure 3-VI) is to protect London and its estuary from tidal surges entering from the North Sea. The area under protection includes the Thames estuary, its tidal tributaries and the related flood plain. This area encompasses 500,000 homes and 40,000 non-residential buildings, including key government and financial centres in London. In addition the area is one of the five most important estuaries in Europe for birds.

FIGURE 3-VI
The Thames Barrier – one of the largest movable flood barriers in the world[61]

3.71 The original approach adopted to provide protection uses sea walls, embankments, barriers, gates and other flood defence structures designed to protect against a once-in-a-thousand-year flood up to 2030. Some of the original arrangements of defence structures are gradually deteriorating and are expected to reach the end of their design life over the next 20-30 years. The potential for an increased frequency of flooding due to this deterioration and to socio-economic and climate changes prompted the development of the Thames Estuary 2100 (TE2100) initiative. The initiative has been developed by the Anglian, Southern and Thames regions of the Environment Agency. In order to deal with the inherent uncertainty associated with climate change, the approach to flood defence had to incorporate a strong element of adaptive management (see Box 3E).

BOX 3E THE THAMES ESTUARY 2100 PROJECT (TE2100)[62]

With the TE2100 project, the Environment Agency has shifted efforts in the Thames estuary from reactive flood defence to proactive flood risk management – the first major British project to put climate change adaptation at its core.

Instead of extrapolating directly from specific scenarios (such as those provided by UK Climate Projections (UKCP09)), the TE2100 team used a 'scenario neutral analysis' approach, which has produced a more generic and flexible strategy. This will help avoid over-engineering too early and overspending, as options (such as new barriers or barrages) will only be deployed when needed and at a point when they are most useful. Scenario neutral analysis focuses on thresholds, allowing the team to develop decision pathways in order to identify adaptation options. TE2100 incorporates continuous monitoring, with links to the British Antarctic Survey (at the forefront of ice-melt science and hence data on sea level rise), which is essential for planned adaptation and to provide critical lead times.

Co-ordinated public engagement and participation have been a crucial feature of the project. The formal consultation period was just one part of this, and the team has worked closely with people living along the estuary since the project was first commissioned by Defra in 2002.

In developing the project, the team considered a range of socio-economic factors as well as projected future changes in climate; they employed multi-criteria analysis which enabled them to factor in intangible qualities, such as a local sense of community, as well as the location of existing and future infrastructure. The estuary was divided into five principal zones based on the character of the area and where flood water would flow.

The final plan lays out proposals for the short, medium and long term, which brings implementation forward to the point where decisions need to be taken. The team has considered the difficulty of planning so far into the future when decision-makers (for example politicians) operate on much shorter timescales, and the plan will be reviewed on a five-year rolling basis.

MANAGING COASTAL EROSION AND THE RISK OF INUNDATION

3.72 Many agencies are involved in the management of the coastal zone. An audit of coastal activity in the east of England by CoastNet found a wide range of stakeholders in possession of five sets of overlapping plans, 14 designations of coastal sites and landscapes, a mix of management bodies, many organisational cultures, unco-ordinated organisational activity at different scales, and overlapping jurisdictions, responsibilities and functions. Besides central Government departments, four regional bodies, five statutory agencies, four *ad hoc* groupings, 17 local authorities and five forums all shared an interest in coastline planning but did not necessarily work together. In addition, non-governmental organisations and lobby groups, service providers, insurers, businesses, members of the public, various partnerships and coastal fora were also involved, operating at different institutional scales, having different remits and interests, and spanning the public, private and civil sectors.[63]

3.73 More generally, coastal management is essentially a devolved responsibility and there are separate institutional arrangements in England, Wales, Scotland and Northern Ireland. In England, several Government departments, including Defra and CLG, have a direct involvement. There is a role for local authorities in each administration and revenue support grant from the Treasury is also important. As the primary planning bodies, local authorities have a vital role to play in planning for coastal protection, for which they also provide funding. Their wider roles in economic development and social wellbeing are also relevant. A number of public bodies are also involved in coastal management. The Environment Agency takes the lead on strategic coastal management, shoreline management plans and coastal risk management in England and Wales, and the nature conservation bodies in England, Wales and Scotland (Natural England, the Countryside Council for Wales and Scottish Natural Heritage) have the remit for wildlife and habitat conservation in both coastal and marine sites. Coastal sites often have important artefacts of historic and cultural heritage, which means that English Heritage, Cadw in Wales, and Historic Scotland may also be involved. In Northern Ireland, an Integrated Coastal Zone Management Plan was formulated in conjunction with a wide range of stakeholders and is being taken forward by the Northern Ireland Environment Department.[64]

3.74 Numerous partnerships, often local authority led, have been set up at various places around the coast, usually where many different sectors have an interest. Such arrangements include coastal and estuarine partnerships – such as the Severn Estuary Partnership, which brings together local government, business and the voluntary sector. Several non-governmental organisations, including, for example, the National Trust and the Royal Society for the Protection of Birds (RSPB), have a particular interest in coastal management and own significant stretches of coastal land for management as nature reserves.

3.75 It is not surprising, therefore, to learn that some think this situation leads to confusion, poor integration of policy and management activity, and a lack of decision making.[65]

3.76 Even for the more limited issue of managing coastal erosion and the risk of inundation by the sea, the responsibilities are complex. Both environment agencies and local authorities have been responsible for executing coastal defence works (with separate responsibilities for protection against erosion and protection against inundation), and the nature conservation agencies are also involved where protected areas – many of which are in coastal areas – are present. Policy on coastal defence has been changing in recent years, partly with the realisation that historic approaches might no longer be sustainable as the climate changes and the risks of erosion increase.

3.77 In 2004, the Office of Science and Technology published its Foresight report entitled *Future Flooding*, which reviewed flood and coastal erosion risks to 2100.[66] The report suggested that the future coastline in England and Wales could not be realistically protected to the current level. As a result, Defra reviewed the Government's coastal management policy and published the results in *Making Space for Water*.[67]

3.78 *Making Space for Water* outlined a strategic shift away from the use of hard coastal defence structures, which were becoming more expensive to maintain, to a more holistic, risk-driven strategy including managed realignment (see 2.82 for an example). It recognised the importance of economic factors in decisions on continued investment in coastal defences, a change likely to result in decisions for 'no active intervention' or 'managed realignment' in some cases where previously the decision had been to 'hold the line'. This means that low-lying, sparsely populated areas which once benefited from coastal defences cannot necessarily expect the same level of protection in the future. This gives rise to difficult issues about balancing efficiency in the use of public resources with the equity of changing arrangements on which local people have come to rely, as we discuss below.

3.79   *Making Space for Water* also committed the Government to work more closely with communities to help manage coastal risks. Up to £28 million of Defra's Comprehensive Spending Review settlement for the period 2008-11 was made available to support communities to adapt to flooding and coastal erosion.[68] Funding was made available for a variety of projects; for example, to improve the level of public information about risks, the Environment Agency published flood risk maps and shoreline management plans, and a £5 million grant scheme was established to help individual households introduce resistance and resilience measures to protect themselves from flood risks.[69] Planning Policy Statement 25 on development and flood risk incorporated a new risk-based approach to development in flood risk areas.[70]

3.80   The current Flood and Water Management Bill will require the Environment Agency (for England) and the Welsh Ministers (for Wales) to develop and apply an integrated flood risk and coastal erosion risk management strategy (see the discussion at 3.67 above). As noted previously, this will have to include specific consideration of the current and predicted impact of climate change on flood risk and coastal erosion risk management. In preparing its strategy, the Environment Agency would be obliged to consult with the public.

3.81   In Scotland, coastal erosion is not covered by the Flood Risk Management Act 2009. Matters pertaining to coastal erosion are therefore covered by the national framework (the Coast Protection Act 1949). Primary responsibility rests with the local authorities, subject sometimes to approval from the Scottish Government and the possibility of receiving grant aid in part.

3.82   The mechanism for guiding decisions about coastal protection is the shoreline management plan (SMP). We note that in practice SMPs are non-statutory strategic documents rather than operational management tools. SMPs are intended to provide an assessment of the risks involved with coastal processes and to develop a strategic and long-term policy framework within which the risks can be reduced in a sustainable manner. First-generation SMPs were introduced in the mid-1990s and their strategic and co-ordinated approach to coastal management was seen as a welcome change to the previous piecemeal system. Collectively they cover the entire 6,000 km of coast in England and Wales and are designed to be reviewed at five-yearly intervals to ensure advances in scientific research and alignment to national policy are taken into account. After a period of consultation with the relevant stakeholders, Defra published updated policy guidance for SMPs in 2001.[71] The guidance concluded that first-generation SMPs were excellent high-level strategic documents but additional research was required into how future coastlines would change.

3.83   Since SMPs were first introduced, several major studies have led to a re-examination of shoreline management (including Futurecoast,[72] the Foresight study[73] and strategic flood risk assessments carried out by local authorities and the UK Climate Impacts Programme). As a consequence, the second generation of SMPs are currently being formulated (SMP2s). It is hoped that SMP2s will offer decision-makers a 'route map' assisting them to progress from the current situation towards meeting short-term (0-20 years), medium-term (20-50 years) and long-term (50-100 years) needs.

3.84   SMPs have a prominent role in the proposed planning policy on development and coastal change.[74] It is proposed to encourage the use of an agreed evidence base, drawing primarily on SMPs, which will provide the means of identifying risks for a local area and offer proposals as to how to manage them. The SMP would then be a material consideration for decisions on planning applications.

3.85   The Commission nevertheless noted that there is some confusion concerning the precise function of SMPs and how they align with the planning system. As mentioned above, SMPs are not management plans (for example, they have no means of implementation[75] and they are not statutory documents). They are described as providing an information base but, at the same time, they contain management scenarios which may be difficult to distinguish from proposals for policy. That said, they potentially form a very important high-level document from which strategies for coastal flooding and erosion risk management can be developed.

3.86   During our study we received evidence from the Anglian Coastal Authorities Group concerning the draft SMP for the Kelling to Lowestoft coastline covering parts of Norfolk and Suffolk. First published in 2004, it recommended a policy of 'no active intervention' for some locations where it had previously been 'hold the line'. In some areas where knowledge of this decision became widespread, properties and businesses were financially blighted; additionally there was a perception among local communities that no further protection or compensation would ever be offered.[76]

3.87   An important step in development of an SMP is public consultation. The revised SMP for Kelling to Lowestoft was put to public consultation, but its initial preparation had lacked adequate or effective communication with the local communities. A particular concern of local communities was that in their view the SMP underestimated the social and economic value of property and activity in a given coastal location. Another issue concerned the lack of a mechanism to consider the social implications – such as disruption – and consequential losses for those whose homes would be lost. We return to this difficult issue in Chapter 5.

FIGURE 3-VII

Evidence of cliff erosion at the site of the old lifeboat launch along the coast from Happisburgh[77]

3.88   In some cases where the final recommendations of the SMP did not meet with local agreement, local action groups were formed. We met representatives of the Coastal Concern Action Group at Happisburgh in North Norfolk. Locally-raised funds (from residents, businesses and donations from visitors), supplemented by money set aside by North Norfolk District Council (NNDC), were used to protect parts of the coastline vulnerable to erosion (see for example Figure 3-VII). This course of action went directly against the SMP, which recommended 'no active intervention'. However, it was felt by the NNDC that once the decision of the SMP had been accepted there was a policy vacuum with no obvious adaptation mechanism or support to fulfil it.[78] The NNDC therefore intended to use the funds to 'buy time' until adaptation mechanisms could be developed and initiated. Coastal protection would therefore remain on a temporary basis (paid for by locally-raised funds). This action formed part of a much wider Coastal Management Plan, which involved the local community and made them feel part of the negotiations that would decide on the future of their homes and businesses.

3.89   We also note the potential for conflicts between policies for managing coastal risks and land use planning, and mechanisms for controlling development in future high-risk areas.[79] Generally, local planners will work to a time horizon of around 20 years, which may be short in relation to the longer timescale required for thinking about climate impacts. In addition, planners may also often come under considerable local political pressure to contribute to the regeneration of coastal economies through continued development of coastal areas. As a result, there are areas where businesses and homes have been built in locations which will be at risk of flooding or erosion in the future.

3.90   Additional sources of potential conflict arise where local communities witness investment in restored local habitats to comply with the EU Birds and Habitats Directives, while their own livelihoods remain neglected. As we saw when we visited Happisburgh, this can result in very real feelings of anger and tension.

3.91   We note that the challenges of managing the coast will become greater in future. We saw evidence that the current institutional arrangements for dealing with coastal communities affected by the threat of coastal erosion are not perceived to be working as well as arrangements for inland needs. So one of the key questions is whether or not the institutional arrangements are in place to enable communities to respond to these challenges, including the possibility of relocation, if coastal protection schemes are not a viable and sustainable long-term solution.

3.92   Under the terms of the Flood and Water Management Bill, the right of Regional Flood and Coastal Committees to consent to local levies for land drainage would be extended to coastal erosion risk management as well as inland flooding. This would permit money to be raised to support locally important coastal erosion work. In addition, the Government has expressed an interest in receiving views on whether, even with this, sufficient local discretion exists to invest in projects which are not centrally funded.[80]

3.93   In response to the challenge of coastal change, Defra launched a consultation in June 2009.[81] The consultation document set out Defra's ideas on how coastal communities can successfully adapt to a changing coastline. The document also described the new coastal change pathfinder programme. In addition, CLG consulted on new planning policies on coastal change which seek to provide a planning framework for the continuing economic and social viability of coastal communities and the planning tools that will be needed to help communities to adapt.[82] CLG aims to publish the final policy in spring 2010.

3.94 Defra announced on 1 December 2009 the 15 pathfinder local authorities which had been successful in bidding for resources under the coastal change pathfinder programme.[83] The programme will explore new approaches to planning for, and managing, adaptation to coastal change, and will run until spring 2011. The available funding, £11 million, will be used to help pathfinder authorities explore ways of engaging and supporting local communities as they adjust to the impacts brought on by coastal change. The projects being funded range from education to schemes for the purchase of property. The funding will also help with the design and implementation of local solutions as coastal communities adjust. Although no solutions are offered by the consultation, it does suggest what planning for and managing coastal change could look like in the future.

INSTITUTIONAL ARRANGEMENTS FOR NATURE CONSERVATION AND BIODIVERSITY

3.95 Nature conservation is the responsibility of several organisations operating under a number of different institutional arrangements. The legislative framework and the division of responsibilities have been largely shaped by previous policy imperatives which are not necessarily appropriate for addressing adaptation to climate change in the delivery of the UK's nature conservation agenda.

3.96 Institutional arrangements established in the era immediately after the Second World War made a clear distinction between scientific and aesthetic aspects of nature; different bodies were responsible for the designation and management of land for nature conservation and for the public enjoyment of the countryside. Organisational changes over the years have brought these two strands together but have also created geographical differences, so that there are now separate bodies in England, Northern Ireland, Scotland and Wales, each covering both nature conservation and recreation. The underlying legal framework has nonetheless remained largely intact.

3.97 The legal framework in relation to species developed separately from that for protected areas and it has a number of separate strands relating to the protection of rare and endangered species (nature conservation), and pest control and exploitation (hunting, shooting and fishing). Private bodies, including non-governmental organisations, have been instrumental in developing policy in this area.

3.98 The National Parks and Access to Countryside Act 1949 placed a duty on the then Nature Conservancy Council to notify planning authorities of the locations of Sites of Special Scientific Interest (SSSIs) and it also established powers to designate land as National Nature Reserves or Local Nature Reserves. These powers were used extensively over the following 30 years to protect natural habitats from land use change (such as intensive agriculture, forestry and urban development) by designating sites on the basis of specific geological features, species and habitats.

3.99 Subsequently, EU legislation has provided a broader framework for nature conservation. In 1979, the Birds Directive (79/409/EEC) provided the framework for the conservation and management of wild birds. In the UK, protection mechanisms were implemented through the Wildlife and Countryside Act 1981, the Wildlife (NI) Order 1985 and the Environment (NI) Order 2002, leading to the partial protection of a wider range of habitats through a strengthened SSSI designation (Area of Special Scientific Interest, ASSI, in Northern Ireland).

3.100 The 1992 Habitats Directive (92/43/EEC) subsequently required Member States to introduce a range of measures to maintain and restore natural habitats and certain wild species at "favourable conservation status". In Great Britain, the Directive was transposed into national laws by means of the Conservation (Natural Habitats, etc.) Regulations 1994 that provided for the designation of 'European Sites' and the protection of 'species of Community importance'. (The equivalent Northern Ireland regulations are the Conservation (Natural Habitats, etc.) Regulations (Northern Ireland) 1995.) Figure 3-VIII shows some of the bodies and legislative frameworks responsible for conservation management in England and Wales.

FIGURE 3-VIII

Overview of institutional arrangements for delivering conservation management in the UK[84]

The diagram illustrates the many different sectors that are involved in developing and delivering conservation objectives in the UK. Each box is an over-simplification because links between the different sectors and hierarchies between legal mechanisms have been omitted. Examples are given under each heading in the three main boxes; these are not exhaustive and are included to give an indication of the complexity involved.[xii]

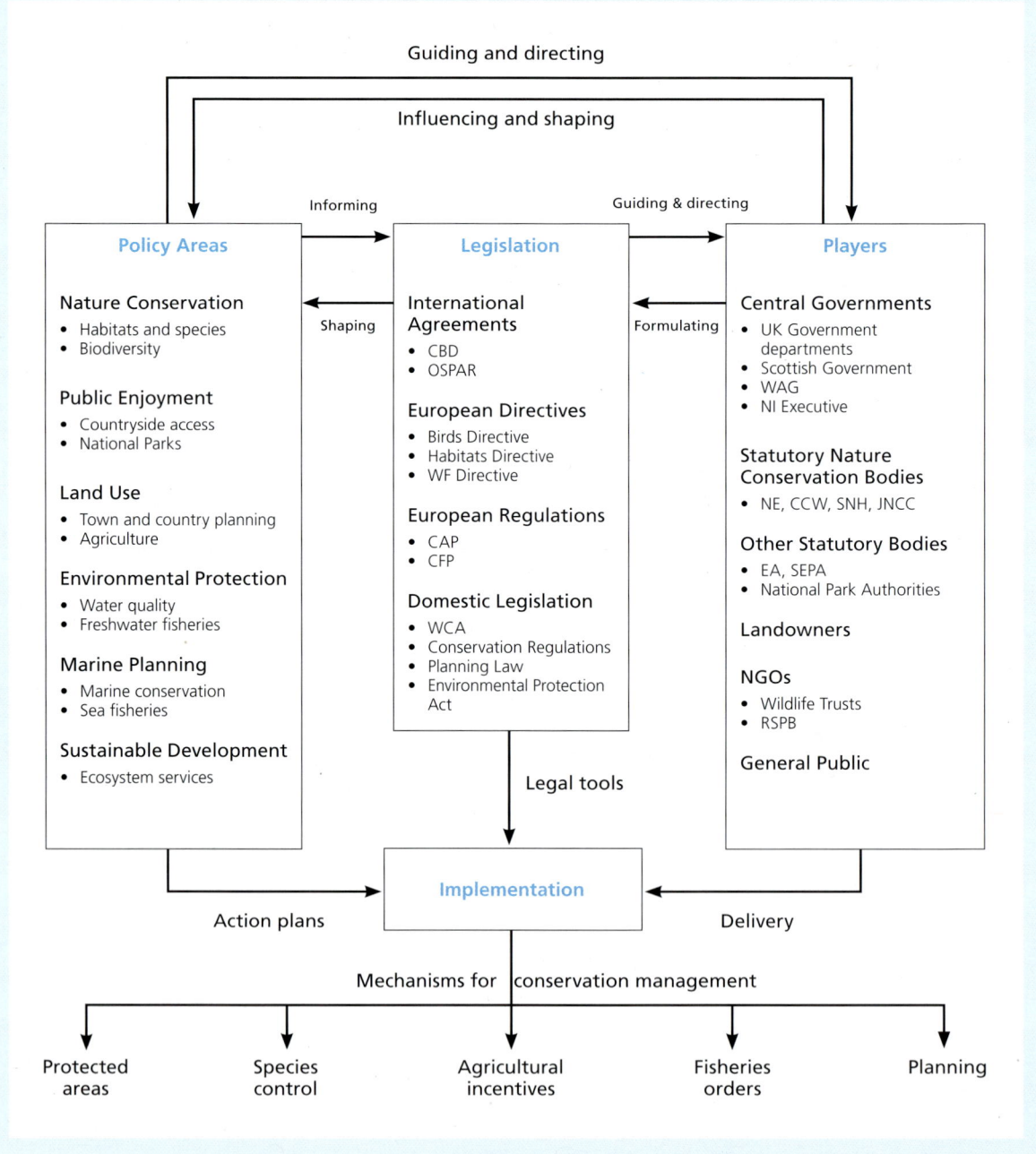

3.101 More than 250 Special Protection Areas (SPAs) covering 1,600,000 hectares have been protected under the Birds Directive and more than 600 Special Areas of Conservation (SACs) covering 2,600,000 hectares have been protected under the Habitats Directive. These UK sites contribute to the European Natura 2000 network of areas of high conservation importance. In all, nearly 10% of the UK's terrestrial and freshwater environment is protected under these international designations or as Local or National Nature Reserves and SSSIs/ASSIs. While the patchwork of designated sites was not established in the context of a changing climate, the resulting network is clearly an important framework for incorporation into adaptation strategies.

3.102 Until relatively recently, the institutional arrangements for marine conservation were different from those applying on land, and the conservation bodies had only a limited remit for marine areas. The Birds and Habitats Directives changed this so that there are now comparable legal measures for marine and terrestrial species and habitats at the European level. The area of the marine environment protected by statutory designations is currently much lower than for terrestrial sites – perhaps only in the region of 2% – but with the implementation of the new Marine and Coastal Access Act, and the Marine (Scotland) Bill currently before the Scottish Parliament, this should begin to change.

3.103 The underlying policy for nature conservation has gradually changed over the years but these changes have not been explicitly recognised in legislation. The original thinking focused on the concept of 'natural beauty' expressed in terms of scientific or aesthetic interest. Most recently the concept of ecosystem services has gained credence and nature conservation bodies have changed their agendas accordingly. However, there has been little consideration of what these different approaches actually mean for the future of biodiversity. Existing legal and institutional arrangements are being used to deliver very different objectives without any fundamental assessment of their appropriateness.

3.104 In recognition that climate change is an important challenge facing biodiversity in this country, the Secretary of State for Environment, Food and Rural Affairs recently announced a review of ecological networks in England which may go some way towards addressing the appropriateness of existing protected area mechanisms.[xiii] Furthermore, 'Securing Biodiversity' is a new framework in which Defra and its non-departmental public bodies (NDPBs) are seeking to address the conservation needs of individual species, wherever possible through habitat management – and this brings with it a range of further benefits from the ecosystem services that those habitats provide.[85] This is complemented by the landscape-scale approach to habitat restoration that is now being taken (in part) to enable biodiversity to adapt to climate change.[xiv]

3.105 As we have described in the previous chapter, climate change will result in dramatic changes to our flora and fauna, in terms of species composition, abundance and distribution. Thinking on how to deliver conservation under changing environmental conditions has focused on the need to be flexible and has tended to lead to discussions about landscape-level measures, wildlife corridors and a 'space for nature' – a protected space where organisms can find refuge in a changing world. There has been no discussion of what society might want from biodiversity in the future; for example, how much need will there be for open recreational spaces, and will protected areas

---

xiii   Declaration of Interest: The review of ecological networks is being chaired by Sir John Lawton, Chairman of the Commission.

xiv   See, for example, the work of the Wildlife Trusts described in 3.107.

be valued if they attract species that are deemed harmful? These will be important questions when determining the objectives and assessing the effectiveness of institutional arrangements for biodiversity.

3.106 These questions are for others to address but it is worth considering whether current measures of success are likely to be appropriate. Over recent years, nature conservation bodies have spent considerable time and money assessing the conservation status of their protected areas and taking action to improve and/or maintain that status. This can involve a level of micro-analysis and management that is difficult to deliver. More importantly, it implies a static understanding of what good conservation status is, which is ill-suited to a world in which climate is changing rapidly.

3.107 Conservation bodies are responding accordingly. The Wildlife Trusts' 'Living Landscapes' initiative, for instance, places the protected area network in a broader landscape context, enlarging, improving and joining protected areas together.[86] The national conservation agencies have responsibility for conservation at the landscape scale as well as for the protection of designated sites. Agri-environment funds from Pillar 2 of the Common Agricultural Policy supported by strategies for catchment sensitive farming will provide resources to integrate biodiversity into broader land use strategies that build resilience to climate change.

3.108 Natural England has recently reported on pilot studies in four of the 159 'Character Areas' in England (namely the Broads, Shropshire Hills, Cumbria High Fells and Dorset Downs/ Cranbourne Chase) in order to identify local responses required to safeguard the natural environment as the climate changes, and further studies are in hand.[87] The reports set out how the vulnerability of these systems can be assessed and the actions required to improve their resilience. There are a number of common adaptation responses, such as bringing existing habitats into a healthy status, extending existing habitats and creating new areas, and restoring the structure and function of river channels and drainage systems. Whilst providing valuable examples of how to develop adaptation strategies, these reports also illustrate some issues that need to be considered in future. For example, assessment of risks from a single policy perspective may make securing cross-functional action on adaptation more difficult.

CONCLUSION

3.109 Governance of adaptation to climate change, both for the areas of the exemplars and beyond, is clearly complex, involving many institutions and subject to a variety of institutional arrangements. Some of this complexity is inevitable, given the pervasive nature of adaptation to climate change. It will be an increasing challenge as our climate continues to change, and this challenge must be recognised and addressed. Leadership, both within specific institutions and in cross-cutting institutions such as the governments' adaptation programmes and the Adaptation Sub-Committee, will be crucial. In the next chapter, we take this analysis forward and consider how institutions should address these and other challenges.

Chapter 4

ADAPTING TO CLIMATE CHANGE: DEVELOPING INSTITUTIONAL RESPONSES

INTRODUCTION

4.1 Chapters 2 and 3 highlighted the effects that climate change will have on the exemplars we chose and some of the implications of these changes for the relevant institutions. This chapter aims to assist all institutions in building adaptive capacity[i,1] in order to cope with climate change.

4.2 We identify four overlapping challenges. These are uncertainty, complexity, path dependency, and equity and efficiency – described in detail below. In confronting these challenges, organisations will have to pay particular attention to how they frame the issue of adaptation, how they learn and how they implement policy responses. In performing these tasks of framing, learning and implementation against the background of the four challenges, we have identified a number of key elements which need to be considered. These will be discussed later in this chapter and many lead to the recommendations in Chapter 5 directed primarily at governments.

4.3 Adaptation to climate change is one example of the problems that institutions face in responding to change and risk. The effects of climate change are pervasive; they will be felt at different times and across a broad range of activities. But as with mitigation, the challenges presented by the need to adapt to climate change are also an opportunity for society to be proactive and to exploit the possibilities of achieving multiple benefits.

4.4 As discussed in Chapter 3, institutions addressing adaptation include both organisations and institutional arrangements. What follows is more immediately applicable to organisations that have the capacity to formulate and implement programmes and policies. However, other types of institution do not exist in a vacuum; for these, the discussion below will relate to the bodies responsible for their administration, or to wider society in the case of behavioural patterns.

WHAT ARE THE CHALLENGES OF CLIMATE CHANGE ADAPTATION?

4.5 The Commission has identified four challenges that institutions will face when adapting to climate change:

- planning in situations of **uncertainty**;
- coping with **complexity**;
- the problem of inbuilt **path dependency**; and
- the need to deliver both **equity and efficiency**.

These are intensely inter-related, not discrete challenges.

---

i   'Adaptive capacity' is defined here as the ability or potential of a system to respond successfully to climate variability and change.

UNCERTAINTY

4.6   Four causes of uncertainty[ii] need to be considered in the context of climate change adaptation:

- uncertainty of input data in climate models;

- uncertainty inherent in the methodologies used to produce climate models;

- uncertainty as to the impacts of climate change and the responses of natural systems; and

- uncertainty in social and technological systems (for example, the rate and direction of techno-logical change).

4.7   The first three types of uncertainty were addressed in Chapter 2. Uncertainty in the Global Circulation Models (GCMs), uncertainties about the impacts of climate change and uncertainties about the responses of natural systems mean that while we understand the direction of future change, it will often not be possible to predict accurately the magnitude and rate of the change, nor its precise expression. Institutions must therefore be able to understand and work with uncertainty and risk.

4.8   Whilst some institutions are very capable of managing uncertainty and risk, others fall back on a 'predict and provide' approach, which can offer an attractive appearance of certainty and which readily translates into organisational goals and objectives (which are frequently short term). Whilst prediction and provision are important tasks for any organisation, in that all must make plans for the future, the term 'predict and provide' can denote a narrow approach that assumes a high level of confidence in future predictions, and an assumption that the policy is simply to meet the predicted circumstances irrespective of wider considerations.

4.9   The nature of the challenge is illustrated in Figure 4-I, which provides a schematic representation of the different levels of understanding about any risk issue, based on knowledge about the likelihood of occurrence and the probable outcomes. Those who make policy or investment decisions often presume that a given problem falls into the top-left quadrant, where outcomes or impacts are well defined and there is a reasonable basis for estimating probabilities using traditional risk assessment, decision analysis and/or cost–benefit approaches. The issue is simply one of managing risks.

4.10   Climate change does not, however, fall into this category. It may fall into the 'uncertainty', 'ambiguity' or even 'ignorance' quadrants in Figure 4-I according to understanding of likelihoods and outcomes. With increasing uncertainty and lack of knowledge, different decision approaches become important – from probabilistic risk modelling and sensitivity testing under conditions of data and information uncertainty, through to scenario analysis under conditions of ambiguity and more general horizon scanning and enhanced research under conditions of ignorance. High levels of uncertainty are the main reason why a crude 'predict and provide' model of adaptation response, where predictions are in the form of precise forecasts of, say, future rainfall patterns, may not be helpful for policy making.

---

ii   We use the term 'uncertainty' in the broad sense as defined by the Oxford English Dictionary: The quality of being uncertain in respect of duration, continuance, occurrence, etc.; the quality of being indeterminate as to the magnitude or value.

4.11   Figure 4-I also introduces the need for enhanced discussion, debate and negotiation as uncertainty increases and ambiguity or ignorance becomes evident. When there is a high level of knowledge about likelihoods and outcomes (top-left quadrant, Figure 4-I) a focus on expert and agency engagement in risk assessments and cost–benefit analysis may be appropriate. However, the context of climate change adaptation is one where knowledge is uncertain, risk–benefit and risk–cost trade-offs become more complex, and issues of equity for current and future generations are important. In such circumstances a more open learning environment has to be created. Stakeholder and public engagement in the decision process become essential. Expert assumptions must be open to challenge, and other values and interests need to be heard and debated: what is widely referred to as 'deliberative engagement'. Opening decision processes to deliberative participation or engagement inherently enhances both organisational and social learning. What is important is that climate change decision-makers and agencies understand from the outset that the adaptation problem is more likely to sit in the 'ambiguity' or 'ignorance' quadrants of Figure 4-I. This understanding should help to ensure the appropriate selection of decision tools and engagement approaches.

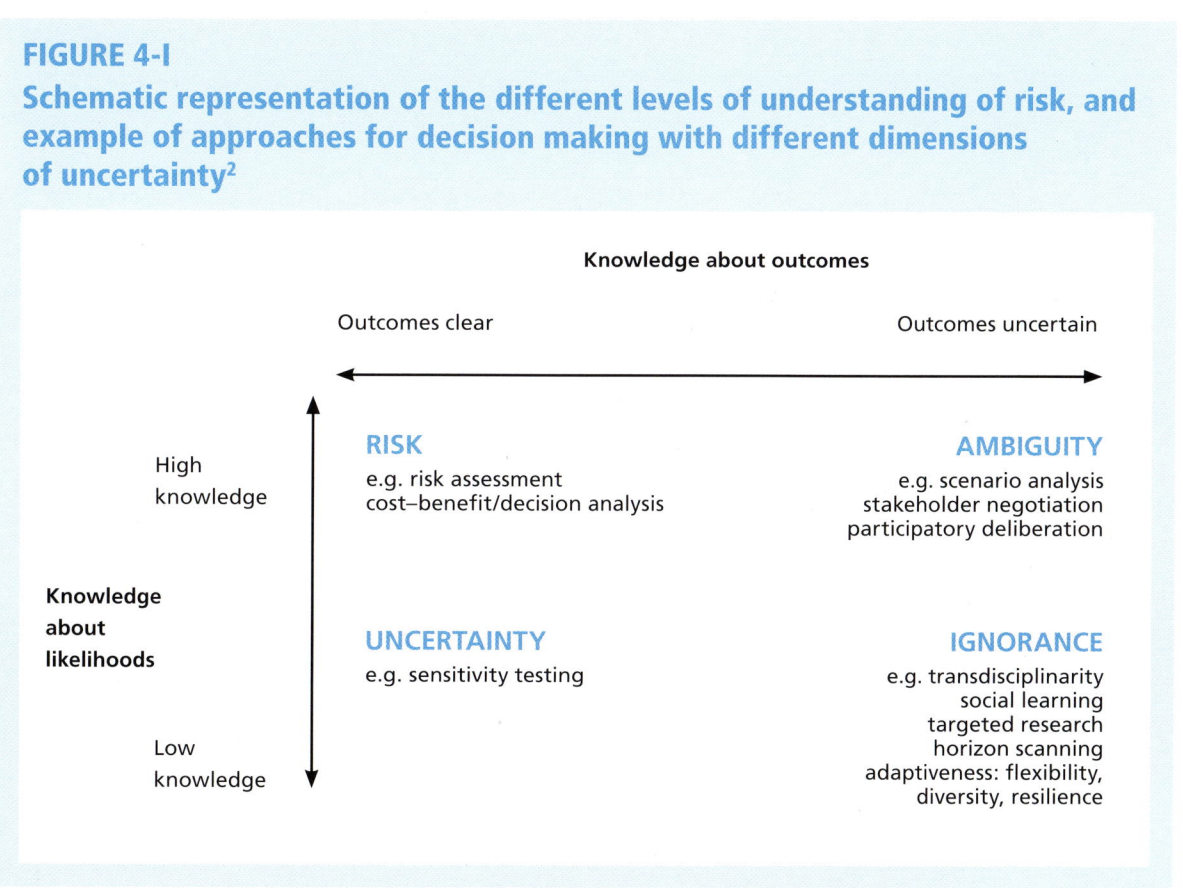

FIGURE 4-I

Schematic representation of the different levels of understanding of risk, and example of approaches for decision making with different dimensions of uncertainty[2]

4.12   Again, as seen in Chapter 2, a further source of considerable uncertainty about the future lies with the impact of other key drivers of social and technical change, such as an increasingly mobile population, future climate change mitigation efforts, or the state of the global economy. Many aspects of society will change in ways that are extremely difficult to forecast. Indeed, modelling the climate is relatively straightforward in comparison. Changes in society, both nationally and globally, and changes in technology will have an impact on the UK that is just as large, if not larger, than climate change itself. As a nation, we will have to adapt to climate change 50 or 100 years from now in a world that is utterly different from ours, and in multiple ways that we can only dimly perceive.

4.13 Importantly, flexibility has to be built into the decision-making processes as well as into the final decisions, so that future strategies can adapt if and when improved knowledge becomes available. Flexible approaches acknowledge that where low levels of knowledge about outcomes and likelihood are present, different methodological approaches are appropriate. This is demonstrated by the Thames Estuary 2100 (TE2100) project (Box 3E), which acknowledges the limitations of 'predict and provide' and instead aims to "develop an adaptable long term plan in the context of a changing estuary … changing in relation to its climate, people and property in the flood plain and an underlying essential but ageing flood defence system".[3] Attempts at prediction must acknowledge that accuracy and precision are impossible. The example provided by projects such as TE2100 shows that this uncertainty need not lead to despair; it simply requires a more flexible approach.

4.14 Even if we were able to fully understand what the climate system will do, it would not mean that we could predict how natural systems will respond. This is especially true for biodiversity (2.83-2.103). This uncertainty presents a particular challenge to those institutions focused on the conservation of species and habitats. The Commission has noted that it is still not clear how conservation practices should be adapted for the future, and how existing powers should best be used to achieve this.

COMPLEXITY

4.15 The next of the four challenges is complexity,[iii] both of the problem itself and in the way it is managed. The wider changes in society referred to in 4.12 are part of the complexity. In terms of Figure 4-I, if institutions do not recognise when issues fall into the 'uncertainty', 'ambiguity' or 'ignorance' quadrants rather than the 'risk' quadrant, they will not be able to manage the complexities of climate and other changes, their impacts and their vulnerabilities.

4.16 Complexity can be seen in the way we manage current situations, in terms of the sheer number of institutions and differing arrangements involved. For example, complexity in organisations may relate to the number of actors, the scope of their networks, their terms of engagement, the styles of governance that prevail, and so on. This is evident in the exemplars in Chapter 3, and it is particularly striking when considering the coastal zone (3.72-3.94). Complexity may be unavoidable due to the pervasive nature of the adaptation challenge, multilevel governance and the urgent need for public engagement, but efforts should be made where possible to reduce it.

4.17 As discussed in Chapters 1 and 3, actions to adapt to climate change will primarily be local – firmly rooted in, and specific to, a particular place – and a number of organisations may be involved. Some of these organisations and associated institutional arrangements will themselves be local, whilst others will be regional, national or European. Some may be specialist agencies whilst others, such as the district or county council for the area, will have a much broader remit. Some agencies will be governmental, others will be non-governmental organisations (NGOs), or bodies such as the Severn Estuary Partnership which themselves bring together a range of public and private bodies. Effective solutions can be developed only if all relevant bodies are involved and, with many players, complexity is inevitable.

---

iii   Again, 'complexity' is used here in its broad sense. We are aware that systems theory regards a system as complex when it consists of many elements which are highly interdependent or linked, and where a change in any one element of the system will produce a wide range of changes elsewhere in the system, not all of them easily predicted. Systems theory differentiates a complex system from one which is complicated: where there are many elements but where the relationships between them are less interdependent. We recognise that both complex and complicated systems are relevant to adaptation, but we did not feel it necessary to make the distinction for the purposes of this discussion.

PATH DEPENDENCY

4.18 Just like an oil tanker, it can be difficult to 'turn around' when we are locked into structures, policies, technologies and ways of doing things: this is path dependency, the third challenge. Path dependency[4] means that current and future states, actions, or decisions depend on the path of previous states, actions or decisions.[iv] Two categories of path dependency concern us here: lock-in and self-reinforcement. In both, strong structural forces dominate and therefore progress tends to be incremental rather than radical. Although path dependency can make it difficult to identify or enable new ways of working, it is not inherently problematic. In many cases it is unavoidable and the chosen path may be entirely appropriate. In some cases it could be unwise to change the established path, because greater success may be achievable by modifying the existing institutions.

4.19 However, path dependency means that institutions may acquire a political stability so strong that considerable effort is needed to shift policy onto a new trajectory.[5] The Brundtland Report recognised this when summarising the challenges of sustainability:[6]

> "... most of the institutions facing these challenges tend to be independent, fragmented, working to relatively narrow mandates with closed decision processes ... The real world of economic and ecological systems will change: the policies and institutions concerned must."

4.20 We have observed evidence of regulatory path dependency. We were told by several organisations that some European directives are inflexible. There is certainly a widespread *perception* of inflexibility. When institutions believe that they are inhibited by a law, directive, policy or something similar, they will maintain a set path with some vigour, whether or not these limits actually exist.

4.21 The EU Water Framework Directive (WFD, see Box 3C) is an example of a directive that has been developed with deliberate and generic flexibility which should in theory at least support adaptation, because it recognises that the nature of water bodies will change in the future.

4.22 However, whilst much of the WFD has the capacity for flexibility (despite widespread belief that it does not), some of the tools that are being used in the UK to monitor compliance with the WFD, such as RIVPACS, are more obviously path dependent (see Box 4A). It is important to note that monitoring tools are not specified by the WFD but require appropriate development and interpretation by regulatory bodies in the Member States. RIVPACS is an existing monitoring tool focusing on ecological status; and it has been adopted by preference and is now embedded in monitoring culture – but with insufficient attention to its relevance in a changing climate. Other European countries are also struggling to develop flexible, responsive monitoring tools. We might also note that, with its commitment to quantitative standards that are difficult to change, the approach to chemical quality in the WFD is less amenable to flexible interpretation than other parts of the Directive.

---

iv   This is the common interpretation of the term 'path dependency', which has "four related causes: increasing returns, self-reinforcement, positive feedbacks, and lock-in. Though related, these causes differ. Increasing returns means that the more a choice is made or an action is taken, the greater its benefits. Self-reinforcement means that making a choice or taking an action puts in place a set of forces or complementary institutions that encourage that choice to be sustained. With positive feedbacks, an action or choice creates positive externalities when that same choice is made by other people. Finally, lock-in means that one choice or action becomes better than any other because a sufficient number of people have already made that choice."

BOX 4A THE RIVER INVERTEBRATE PREDICTION AND CLASSIFICATION SYSTEM (RIVPACS)[7]

Although the approach to ecological quality in the EU Water Framework Directive (WFD) itself is flexible (see Box 3C), the River InVertebrate Prediction And Classification System (RIVPACS) is an example of how national interpretation could reduce that flexibility. RIVPACS is a classification system used by the UK to monitor water quality through the presence and abundance of invertebrate species, against a predicted baseline of 'undisturbed conditions'.

RIVPACS predicts the expected species composition of aquatic invertebrates for rivers in good (undisturbed) conditions based on their geographical distributions. As the geographical ranges of species change with climate change (2.67), so there might be a diminution in the ability of the model to predict which species to expect because it is based on a reference dataset which was collected primarily in the late 1970s. The Commission received conflicting evidence on whether the reference dataset is regularly updated.[8] However, time lags in species' responses to climate change are inevitable, and RIVPACS cannot predict the presence of species which are not well represented in the reference database, such as newly arriving species. The ecological classification of water bodies is therefore tied to a reference state that will inevitably change as the climate changes.

The potential impact of climate change on the efficacy of ecological classification tools, and the resulting implications for compliance with the WFD, have not yet been fully resolved. However, through not strictly defining 'undisturbed conditions', the language of the WFD allows for the species baseline to be dynamic. Furthermore, the WFD has a review process built into it that works on a six-year cycle, through which reference conditions can be revisited. This provides a mechanism by which any shifts in species distributions can be incorporated into improved management and compliance.

4.23   Another example of path dependency results from the outcome of the fragmentation of responsibility and accountability across government, its agencies, regulators and (largely private sector) operators, as illustrated in Chapter 3. This can encourage a narrow view of the world, where agencies find it difficult to consider issues beyond their own brief, and which necessitates careful co-operation and dialogue. In Scotland, for example, responsibilities for different elements of flood risk management are shared between the Scottish Environment Protection Agency (SEPA) and local authorities, whereas land management responsibility is shared by a plethora of bodies. Such fragmentation can be problematic: there can be significant inertia to structural change, not least because the costs involved can be high – although in this example the land use strategy under the Climate Change (Scotland) Act 2009 has the potential to improve matters.

4.24   Examples of path dependency can also be found in the statutory responsibilities that are placed on an institution, which clearly define the functions that should be delivered and which are often quite tightly defined. The Commission notes, for example, that although economic regulation of water services is required to have regard to or contribute to the achievement of sustainable development, it has tended to give priority to consumer interests and to the sustainability of water utilities (whilst meeting the environmental and water conservation objectives). There has been some recent evolution of regulation, but the balance of the focus is unlikely to change radically until the statutory duties are revised.

4.25   Another way of considering the problem is to ask what is required to build flexibility into policy outcomes over the longer timescales that adaptation to climate change may demand. In other words, is it possible to avoid lock-in to actions over long time frames? The Thames Estuary 2100 project (Box 3E) is one example of a decision process that has sought to prioritise flexibility to encourage short-term engagement within the context of a long-term but inherently flexible plan of action. Such an approach may not be suitable in every case, but it shows what can be done when the stakes are considered to be sufficiently high.

4.26   Given the local characteristics of adaptation to climate change, the most important policy tool is the planning system, which typically considers change and impacts over 20-30-year periods. In theory, planning policy is sufficiently flexible to build climate change adaptation into development planning. However, we heard concerns that most local authorities place transport and housing priorities higher on the agenda than climate change. The aim should be to create processes which are responsive and sustainable under changing climatic conditions, but planners cautioned against making adaptation to climate change more important than other considerations. Instead, planners we heard from thought that there was a need for adaptive capacity to become a routine consideration within, not additional to, other key non-climate policy areas.[9]

4.27   Infrastructure lock-in, which can result in stranded assets and reduce an organisation's ability to respond flexibly to changing climate, is another example of path dependency. In the Anglian region, the Commission heard from Anglian Water about how they are trying to reduce the danger of infrastructure lock-in by moving away from large pumps controlling water over larger areas to more, but smaller, local pumps controlling smaller catchments, creating a modular approach which enhances their ability to deal with unpredictable flooding and reduces the impact of localised power cuts.

Equity and efficiency

4.28   The fourth challenge is managing potential tensions between equity and efficiency. 'Equity' has many (often contending) definitions but broadly refers to perceptions of fairness between different people. Efficiency is the relationship between objectives (outputs) and the resources used to achieve them (inputs). Efficiency improves when the achievement of a given objective uses fewer resources than previously, and this is central to many organisations' objectives. Least-cost (efficient) outcomes may be inequitable because the efficiency calculation does not consider the distribution of costs and benefits of the outcome to different parties. The emphasis placed on these will vary from institution to institution, and indeed from person to person, depending on their values, objectives and priorities.

Equity

4.29   The Commission received a considerable body of evidence on the importance of involving stakeholders – in particular, local communities – in developing adaptation responses and ensuring that issues of both distributional and governance equity are taken into consideration. In the cases of the Manhood Peninsula in West Sussex[10] and the village of Happisburgh in Norfolk,[11] both of which are areas facing increasing coastal erosion driven at least in part by climate change, the distributional effects of abandoning coastal defences were not considered sufficiently, and the proposed abandonment of the defences led to major difficulties in implementing changes, and a deep feeling of unfairness in the affected communities. Fairness has many dimensions, and whilst distributional issues loom large, processes of decision making that are perceived to be fair by those affected (listening to and taking proper account of their concerns, for example) are also a crucial part of adaptation to climate change. We return to this below.

4.30   The communities in Happisburgh and the Manhood Peninsula felt they did not have sufficient opportunity to take part in framing the issues or solutions, and so equity issues remain unresolved (for example, the loss in value of properties that are no longer likely to be protected from erosion and are not eligible for compensation).[12] Whether losses should lie where they fall or be treated as broader responsibilities (and, if so, how) are difficult social choices. Whilst conservation and human interests are by no means always in conflict in this context, similar issues arise when considering the resources available to compensate for loss of habitat (as required by the Habitats and Birds Directives) when contrasted with those available to compensate vulnerable human communities.

4.31   The difficulties of ensuring equitable adaptive responses to the changing climate come about because of the uneven distribution of the impacts. The uneven distribution of the burdens of climate change is most devastating and most obvious at a global level, but it is also apparent at the national level.[13] This distributional dimension of climate change is especially acute in respect of flooding and coastal erosion, although it may arise elsewhere, for example, in increased water scarcity or reduced access to blue or green space.

4.32   Uneven distribution can be *spatial*, *social* and *temporal*. *Spatially*, some communities are naturally more vulnerable to coastal erosion and flooding but, more significantly in respect of institutional arrangements, some of these communities will be protected by public defence works whilst others will not. The planning system has an important role to play in addressing these vulnerabilities.

4.33   *Socially*, whilst the evidence is complicated, a report for the Environment Agency concluded that "more deprived populations are more likely than less deprived populations to be living within zones at risk from flooding".[14] Many coastal towns experience high levels of social deprivation.[15] Equally, vulnerability to the effects once flooding has occurred is unevenly distributed between social groups. We have also received evidence suggesting that "socially marginalised communities, institutions and sectors of lesser economic importance" lack the capacity to make proper use of the UK Climate Projections and hence may have lower levels of preparedness.[16]

4.34   Climate change is likely to increase inland and coastal flooding, and coastal erosion. There will be locations where it is not sustainable to build or maintain defence structures.[17] Difficult decisions will have to be taken, potentially causing dismay and disruption, which will have to be dealt with. The deliberate abandonment of land to the sea can have beneficial effects for nature and conservation (Figure 2-V). But unplanned coastal erosion and flooding can have enormous impacts on property (2.64). This has received a great deal of political attention,[v] but property is only part of the conundrum and those who own no land and have little personal property may also bear costs. Intangible losses include the loss of 'community', business and employment, and the disruption of health, educational and social services. As well as being potentially unevenly distributed, these less tangible losses may be unevenly experienced, for example by the elderly or in low-income households.

4.35   *Temporally*, the impacts of climate change and of our responses are likely to extend far into the future. Decisions taken for the current generation, for example to protect a coastline, may create costs for future generations, especially if, as is likely, such protection encourages development on vulnerable coastlines or flood plains.[18] The temporal distribution of the effects of climate change raises difficult questions about intergenerational equity.

---

v   See for example, Lord Smith, Chair of the Environment Agency, in *The Times*, 7 November 2009.

Efficiency

4.36 Efficiency is about achieving the best relationship between inputs and outputs. Operationally, this often means using cost–benefit analysis (CBA), where the benefits and costs can each be quantified, to decide whether the benefits of a policy or programme are sufficient to justify its costs; alternatively, a cost-effectiveness analysis can be used, where the objective is given and the task is to minimise the cost of achieving it. Efficiency in adaptation practice can be difficult to measure: while costs are usually relatively straightforward to determine, benefits can be harder to quantify because of uncertainties about the nature and extent of future climate change.

4.37 As observed earlier, efficiency and equity objectives may be in tension, because the policies which minimise resource use may lead to unfairness, for example by concentrating the costs of policies on those least able to bear them. Advice to UK public authorities in assessing efficiency is that they should follow the Treasury's Green Book,[19] involving an approach derived from orthodox economics and requiring, where feasible, the use of formal cost–benefit analysis, and this is now recommended by the Department for Environment, Food and Rural Affairs (Defra) for appraisal decisions throughout Government.

4.38 Cost–benefit analysis is most useful where problems lie in the 'risk' quadrant in Figure 4-I above. However, the problems surrounding adaptation to climate change lie firmly in the other quadrants, making application of CBA problematic. While costs of action are often well defined, benefits in the case of adaptation are often difficult to define with any precision and may lie in a distant future. It is still necessary to decide how best to use scarce resources, but it will sometimes be necessary to use CBA where an objective is defined, and then the cheapest alternative way of fulfilling it will be preferred.

4.39 Even where benefits can be clearly defined, cost–benefit analysis has limitations. First, benefits are measured by observing or inferring people's willingness to pay. There are two issues here: consumers and citizens do not have the necessary knowledge to make rational decisions about the benefits of, say, biodiversity in 50 years' time; and, secondly, people's willingness to pay is constrained by their ability to pay, i.e. by income inequalities. Government advice sometimes recommends that compensation for these inequalities should be brought into CBA by a weighting scheme that gives higher relative values to the views of, and impacts on, the poor. While this is attractive, it also undermines one of the important theoretical claims of 'pure' CBA, which is that it provides a guide to an *efficient* decision under the given distribution of income, i.e. that the project with the highest value represents the *socially* most efficient (resource-minimising or benefit-maximising) outcome. Where income or other weightings are used to achieve social goals, CBA can no longer claim theoretical pre-eminence over other more pluralistic methods of appraisal, often encompassing multiple objectives and involving direct input from stakeholders and the public.

4.40 In addition, CBA suppresses the visibility of the multiple objectives that policy often pursues by putting single monetary values on appraisal outcomes. For adaptation (as in other areas of policy, such as radioactive waste management),[20] equity objectives as well as economic objectives are significant and it is important to explore analytical techniques that explicitly incorporate multiple objectives.

4.41 The second limitation of cost–benefit analysis concerns valuation over time, when, as in the case of adaptation, long-term outcomes are important. Conventionally, CBA uses a positive discount rate – in other words, costs and benefits are given progressively lower valuations the further into the future they are expected to occur. The Treasury has in recent years given detailed guidance on discounting over the long term, especially beyond 50 years, but nevertheless still argues for a positive discount rate into the indefinite future. This renders very long-term benefits apparently trivial as seen from today's perspective. For example, under Treasury advice that discount rates should decline from 3.5% per year to around 1% per year over long future periods, an event expected to occur 300 years from now has a perceived value today that amounts to only 0.1% of the value that would apply if it were expected tomorrow. There are, of course, important ethical issues of intergenerational equity involved in decisions with implications that extend into the far future, and no-one imagines that the discount rate can alone bear the weight of major intergenerational decisions.

4.42 The considerations outlined in these last four paragraphs mean that great care needs to be exercised in applying cost–benefit analysis in adaptation policy making, and that other methods, including multi-criteria methods and those involving public and stakeholder engagement, are needed as replacements or supplements.

ADDRESSING THE CHALLENGES

4.43 The previous section has explored the four challenges facing institutions adapting to climate change: **uncertainty, complexity, path dependency**, and **equity and efficiency**. As noted, these challenges are not unique to adaptation; rather, it is their specific manifestations and pervasive nature that make adaptation such a difficult issue. What are organisations to do about these challenges and what actions might they take? A great deal of evidence indicated that organisations 'need to build their adaptive capacity',[21] but what does this involve? We believe that there are three essential and integrated components in building adaptive capacity. These are:

- **framing** – recognising and understanding the problem and challenges of adaptation (4.50-4.70);

- **implementation** – taking actions both to adapt to climate change and to build the capacity to adapt (4.71-4.99); and

- **learning** – gathering information and learning about adaptation (4.100-4.118).

4.44 When framing, implementing and learning, institutions will inevitably and repeatedly face the four challenges outlined in the first half of this chapter. Framing, implementing and learning are explored in more detail below. For each stage, we have identified key elements but have not attempted to be comprehensive.

4.45 Framing adaptation in particular lies at the heart of an effective decision-making process. We deliberately focus on framing issues as a support to learning and implementation because, as in all aspects of good risk management, it is essential to include as wide a range of views and values as possible before coming to a decision.

4.46 There are some parallels between successful approaches to climate change adaptation and established approaches to business management, although the context in which these approaches take shape is very different in these two settings. Effective businesses recognise that concepts such as Customer Service Orientation[22] and Total Quality Management,[23] together with innovation and flexibility, must underpin sustained success in delivering products or services. We saw evidence that these approaches have been successfully used in a water utility.[24] Key relevant principles include leadership from top management, continual improvement (learning) and employee participation. We recognise, however, that different approaches to business management will be appropriate for different organisations; for example, a command and control approach may suit the needs of some organisations but not others.[25] We return to the issue of 'learning organisations' at 4.113.

4.47 While the analogy with business methods is not exact, adaptation will require practical actions which have similarities with business behaviour. How corporations manage information, uncertainties and complexities, and how they create lasting expertise and adaptable attitudes can provide valuable lessons for those seeking to manage adaptation. Similarly, the need for a pervasive institutional focus on adaptation to climate change could be seen as equivalent to the priority accorded by business to the customer.

4.48 Successful businesses also identify and nurture the core competencies they need for sustained achievement of their objectives. The Commission believes that for organisations to adapt it will be necessary to recognise, define and promote core competencies in climate change adaptation, including the challenges and opportunities which adaptation presents. This implies a desire to act in a way which reduces the risks of a changing climate to current and future stakeholders to acceptable levels, and means focusing efforts on discovering what the range of possible changes will be, and then responding effectively, efficiently and fairly. We return to this issue in Chapter 5.

4.49 The components shown in Figure 4-II are neither new nor exclusive to the adaptation debate. They draw on the contemporary language and definitions of risk management, not least in that the latter prioritises the appropriate framing and scoping of risks prior to their assessment and evaluation, the implementation of actions to mitigate unacceptable risks and the monitoring of effectiveness of actions.

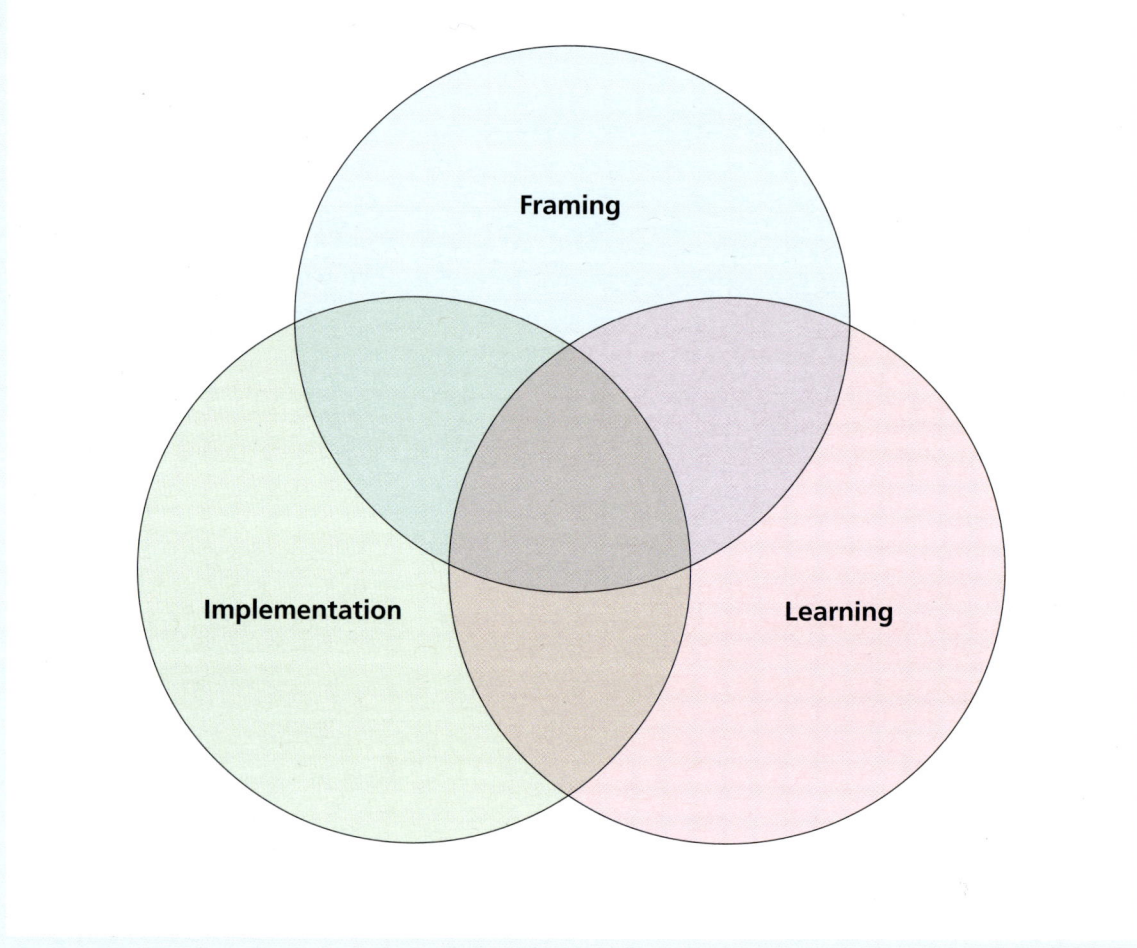

FIGURE 4-II
Schematic illustrating framing, implementing and learning

Framing, implementing and learning are components of a flexible, iterative, non-linear framework. Organisations will typically start by framing the problem. The components will often overlap, for example organisations will learn throughout their framing and implementing. Public engagement should support all three components.

FRAMING

4.50   Framing a problem involves recognising its existence, and understanding its nature and its direct and indirect implications for the particular institution. This is perhaps the most challenging aspect of building adaptive capacity.

4.51   Because adaptation is hard to frame, it is difficult to determine the actions to be taken and the capacities which should be built. It is easy to frame wrongly (for example by using the wrong timescales), incompletely (for example by thinking solely in terms of flood defence instead of flood risk management) or not at all. Because adaptation is hard to frame, it is also difficult to define 'successful' adaptation or metrics for measuring progress or outcome.

4.52   The Commission identified a set of issues to do with framing, relating to how institutions recognise the challenges of adaptation, the factors involved, and how institutions recognise what they must do to build their adaptive capacity.

4.53 The key elements of framing the adaptation problem are:

- the role of climate in relation to the **key missions** of an institution (4.54-4.55);

- the role of other relevant actors in **partnerships** (4.56-4.58);

- **competition** with other goals (4.59-4.63);

- the tendency to '**short-termism**' in decision making (4.64-4.65); and

- the existence of **different values and interests** (4.66-4.70).

BOX 4B FRAMING THE PROBLEM: UKCIP's IMPACTS AND VULNERABILITIES APPROACH

The UK Climate Impacts Programme's (UKCIP's) approach to framing is an example of an effective one. Adaptation is viewed in terms of vulnerability and impacts. Vulnerability is the degree to which a system is susceptible to, and unable to cope with, adverse effects of a changing climate, including variability and extremes, and is a function of exposure, sensitivity and adaptive capacity. Impacts are the effects of a changing climate, including variability and extremes, and are a function of exposure and sensitivity. Impacts feed into climate and socio-economic scenarios alongside information on current climate and socio-economic conditions. This comprehensive approach to reducing risks and vulnerabilities is illustrated below.[26]

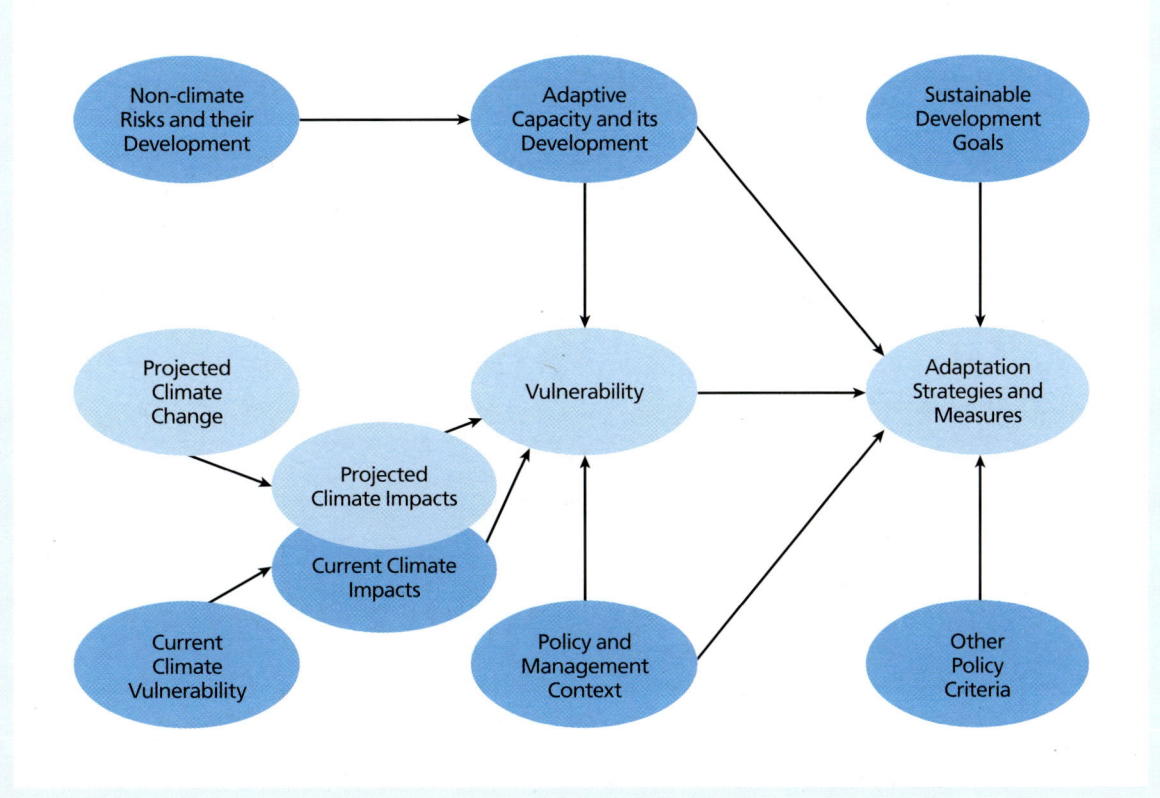

The role of climate in relation to the key missions of an institution

4.54 An institution's approach to framing adaptation is to a large degree determined by its key missions. Institutions may be placed within a mission 'spectrum' in which climate change has varying priority. Adaptation will be framed differently in each of the following types of institution:

- institutions with a primary mission of dealing with the consequences of climate change, such as the Climate Change Act 2008 and the UK Climate Impacts Programme (UKCIP);

- institutions where this mission is significant but sits alongside other responsibilities, for example the Environment Agency and local authorities such as Hampshire County Council (Box 4C);

- institutions where the need for adaptation is not currently recognised (but could be); and

- institutions where there is no business case for the inclusion of climate change adaptation in its mission.

BOX 4C HAMPSHIRE COUNTY COUNCIL

Climate change is a difficult issue which is hard to communicate. Although it is vital to acknowledge the dangers, apocalyptic scenarios can be alienating and counterproductive. It can be helpful to develop a 'story' or narrative that is meaningful to people to illustrate the issues.

Hampshire County Council (HCC) achieved this by identifying a city with a present climate similar to the future projected climate for Hampshire, namely Bordeaux in south-west France. The Council recognised that the climate is changing, that the effects will be felt in all sectors of society and the economy, and that the impacts will be fundamental to wellbeing and security. The ability to make direct comparisons with a tangible real-world example helped the politicians to understand the risks and opportunities, and to be prepared to take action.

HCC has been engaged with climate change issues since the late 1990s, and it sees its role as that of community leader (not least in the new era of more limited strategic engagement for county councils with the new regional spatial planning structures and Local Development Plans). The Council signed the Nottingham Declaration, took part in pilot projects such as Councils for Climate Protection, was a founder member of the South East Climate Change Partnership and has signed up to the Aalborg commitments for sustainable cities. The Council was also a partner on the BRANCH project and has been part of the Advisory Group to the European Commission on Adaptation to Climate Change. HCC led the ESPACE project (Box 3B).

The ESPACE Project elaborated an existing Organisational Change Tool developed from the business management literature which has identified different typologies of organisational environmental engagement.[27] The tool was designed to help organisations develop higher levels of performance in addressing climate change. There are six levels from '1 – Core Business Focused' through to '6 – The Champion Organisation', although as in the business literature these are not presented as stand-alone or discrete levels.

HCC has also created the 'performance acceleration capacity-building tool' (PACT) to help identify its progress against national indicator NI188 (3.25). The Council is looking at different approaches to measuring its performance against NI188 because it believes that the cumulative effect of adaptation may be more important than making the transition from one level to the next. The Council observed that, when it comes to adaptation, "the more you know, the more you realise you don't know". This led HCC to score itself more moderately against NI188 than some other local authorities, who have possibly not explored adaptation to the same depth.

4.55 We have also observed that where climate change is not a defined part of the mission of an institution, the capacity to respond can be hampered. For example, neither the EU Birds Directive nor the Habitats Directive considers the possibility of climate change (Box 4D), which has left many actors uncertain as to how well these instruments will be able to respond to biodiversity changes resulting from climate change, as discussed in the section on path dependency (4.18-4.27). There are also cases where an institution's legal and policy framework, whilst not ignoring environmental and social issues (including climate change adaptation), places them in a secondary role. The economic regulation of water services is a good example. Ofwat has a number of statutory duties, including duties to protect the interests of consumers and to secure a reasonable return for water companies, as well as a duty, which is 'subject to' those former duties, to exercise its powers in the way best calculated to contribute to the achievement of sustainable development. The fact that 'consumers' are defined to include future consumers gives considerable scope to Ofwat in respect of adaptation to climate change; and, indeed, Ofwat has taken steps to respond to the challenge.[28] However, pragmatically, given the legal and policy framework, its focus is on ensuring that water services are affordable for consumers. There are signs, from statements by water companies in England and Wales about the recent determinations of prices for 2010-15,[vi] that there are tensions around the provision of finance for investment now and longer-term objectives. This was addressed in part by Ofwat in the final determinations[29] but recognised as a matter needing some further reform before the review of prices for 2015-20.

BOX 4D THE EU BIRDS AND HABITATS DIRECTIVES

The EU Birds Directive (79/409/EEC) was one of the earliest environmental instruments adopted by the European Union, and views conservation in terms of overall wellbeing rather than as a specific sectoral interest. The Directive requires Member States to act to restore or maintain populations of all species of birds occurring naturally in the wild in Europe at levels corresponding to ecological, scientific and cultural requirements. The requisite measures include those needed to preserve, maintain or re-establish a sufficient diversity and area of habitats. The provisions should form the fundamental basis for conservation in Member States. The Directive also requires Member States to establish Special Protection Areas (SPAs) for listed rare, vulnerable or endangered species.

The Royal Society for the Protection of Birds (RSPB) sought legal advice on whether the Birds Directive (as amended by the Habitats Directive) is sufficiently flexible to meet the challenges which may arise from climate change. This advice concluded that, overall, the Birds Directive will continue to provide protection for birds even where climate change has led to changes in bird distributions and broad habitat ranges. It also established that deterioration in 'bird quality' in the UK as a result of climate change will not allow the authorities to abandon or lessen their attempts to protect birds. It does not, however, address the question of whether (and, if so, how) a network of protected areas identified and designated under one set of climatic conditions will be effective when conditions change.

vi   Water companies are required to prepare a 25-year strategy, and prices are determined for five-year periods within this.

The EU Habitats Directive (92/43/EEC) aims to 'promote the maintenance of biodiversity' and thereby make a contribution to sustainable development. Measures at an EU level are regarded as necessary because of the deterioration of habitats and threats to species that are often of a transboundary nature. The Directive requires Member States to identify possible sites of Community Importance for species and habitats listed in Annexes of the Directive, from which the Commission selects a suite of Special Areas of Conservation (SACs) known as Natura 2000. In addition, Member States are obliged "where they consider it necessary to endeavour to improve the ecological coherence of Natura 2000 by maintaining, and where appropriate developing, features of the landscape which are of major importance for wild fauna and flora". The Directive can be interpreted as a defensive, reactive response to what is regarded as an unfavourable natural status for some habitats and species.

Article 3 of the Habitats Directive provides for the establishment of the Natura 2000 ecological network whereby each Member State contributes to its creation in proportion to the representation within its territory of habitats and species of Community interest. The definition of 'Community interest' is quite rigid and this, along with the focus on establishing the Natura 2000 network of fixed sites, has led to questions about its flexibility in the face of climate change. Article 9 nevertheless allows for the possibility that an SAC may need to be declassified "where this is warranted by natural developments noted as a result of surveillance" as provided for in Article 11. This is, however, an area that needs further attention and work.

The role of other relevant actors in partnerships

4.56   In framing the problem of adaptation, organisations need to consider the roles of other relevant actors. For example, we were told in Wales that heavy rainstorms can lead to run-off being contaminated with sheep and cattle faeces from farmland, which ultimately finds its way to the sea via streams and rivers and pollutes beaches, causing them to lose favourable status for bathing and impacting on tourism. Events like this will occur more often in the future, and the problem requires a co-ordinated response, in this case between the Welsh Assembly Government, the Environment Agency, local farmers and the tourism industry, to understand the problem and work together to find ways of reducing it. Similarly, effective responses to the risk of flash flooding in central London require co-operation between the Environment Agency, Westminster Council, local public, private and third sector organisations, and residents. Working in partnership in these cases is essential as a way of managing the transfer of risk from one place or group to another.

4.57   Acting alone, any single body is unlikely to be able to understand the full nature of the issue or identify a solution that meets the requirements of all the actors, and so each organisation has to look outside its own remit to fully frame the problem. As adaptation is relevant to so many institutions, a co-ordinated approach can help overcome the fragmentation of powers and responsibilities which might otherwise hinder an effective response. And because of the number of institutions with an involvement in adapting to climate change, it is inevitable that there will be some overlap in jurisdictions and sectors. The coastal zone (Chapter 3) is a good example.

4.58   Overlap in jurisdictions and the need to consider other actors is particularly obvious in the multi-layered governance arrangements in the UK – at the highest level from Europe, through national and devolved governments, to regional and local administrations. One advantage is that such arrangements allow for different approaches to be tried in different places, for example in each of the Devolved Administrations. For many issues, there are scales at which it is most appropriate for adaptation to take place; and whilst this will typically be local, it must usually happen within an overarching strategic framework set by (for instance) planning laws or European directives. Flood risk management, for example, needs to have an overall strategy, often at the catchment level, but is best delivered by considering what is required at a very local level. While it is easy to stress the need for local and national responses to be complementary, this is not to downplay the frequent and significant tensions between requirements and responses at these different scales. We revisit some of these issues when we consider co-ordination later (4.86-4.89).

Competition with other goals

4.59   One of the key elements in framing adaptation is recognising the competition with other goals, for example, economic recovery in a time of recession or the provision of housing in areas at risk of flooding. Finding a balance can be challenging. For example, many water companies face changes in the future availability of water and there may eventually be a conflict between the duty to provide water and the need to preserve it. Again, the TE2100 project is an example of where reducing the risk from storm surges has been balanced with development, housing provision, managing habitats and local aspirations through a major programme of stakeholder engagement and consultation, leading to a proposal that should enable the Thames estuary region to develop and adapt to climate change for the next 90 years (Box 3E).

4.60   The nature of adaptation can also vary according to differing attitudes to risk, as organisations weigh up competing goals, as well as to disposition (for example, a willingness to contemplate change versus a desire for stability) and attitudes (optimistic versus pessimistic).[30] An interesting small study revealed that even amongst a set of construction companies in one English region, radically different adaptation strategies were adopted by different firms in the face of the same apparent risk (increased flooding), ranging from withdrawal from the area to investment in engineering solutions.[31]

4.61   Competition with other goals can sometimes hamper adaptation. The Commission received evidence of projects such as the proposal to create flood plain woodland in the Laver catchment to help manage flood risk in Ripon. Although this was agreed in principle by all parties, the project did not proceed because, in the end, the financial incentives proved insufficient given the greater financial returns to individual landowners from alternative forms of land use that did not involve planting trees.[32]

4.62   An enormous range of social and economic objectives are pursued through the land use planning system, and adaptation may compete for attention with these other objectives (3.29-3.44). We argue in Chapter 5 that adaptation should not necessarily be seen as being in competition with, for example, housing provision or economic development: we should think not about housing or adaptation, but about housing that will best cope with a changing climate (5.58). In the long term, and in the collective interest, this compatibility is reasonably straightforward. But in the short term, poorly adapted flood-prone housing, for example, may seem to be necessary to satisfy an immediate demand for more homes.

4.63   From the evidence it was clear that adaptation often takes place as part of addressing another priority; as such it may be difficult to attribute the allocation of resource as being for adaptation, with the result that it is hard to tell whether or not adaptation is a priority for an institution.[33] Whilst it could be argued that this does not matter so long as the desired outcome is being achieved, organisations need to understand just how much of their resources are actually being focused on adaptation, to avoid false or misleading discussions about expenditure on adaptation versus expenditure in pursuit of other goals.

The tendency to 'short-termism' in decision making

4.64   Politicians, with an understandable eye on election cycles, are often focused on short-term decisions and outcomes, and in the financial world investors prefer business decisions that yield quick returns. Such 'short-termism' may not be in the best interests of adapting to climate change. The above example (4.61) of a failed attempt at flood risk management by planting trees is a good example of a short-term decision preventing an adaptive response, with potentially serious long-term consequences.

4.65   The time frame for decisions relating to adaptation depends on the nature of the action that is required. Long time frames involve infrastructures with a lifetime of decades (or even centuries in the case of housing), whereas in other cases a short-term approach is suitable, for instance when farmers decide what crops to plant next year, or if an institution launches an exercise focusing on learning and developing capacity. The challenge is recognising the appropriate time frame for the response. The water companies, for example, are encouraged to consider the longer term by preparing a 25-year strategy to support their spending plans for each (shorter-term) five-year price review, and they provide a model of how to deal flexibly with conflicting time frames and the possibility of changing priorities.

The existence of different values and interests

4.66   Nature conservation illustrates very clearly how different values and interests may have profound consequences for the way in which responses to climate change are framed. We have seen that maintaining the *status quo* in species composition, distribution, and abundance of UK wildlife in the face of climate change will be impossible (2.103). Virtually all the evidence we received from the statutory and voluntary conservation bodies accepts that change is inevitable. The problem is, who will decide what future protected areas will be like? How should society decide? Indeed, should society decide, or should nature be left to get on with it? Should species currently regarded as undesirable aliens be vigorously exterminated? And so on.

4.67   Not everybody in our society would accept that nature conservation 'is a good thing', and some would regard people, jobs and economic growth (for instance) as much more important than wildlife conservation. These individuals might frame their responses to climate change in a very different way from a member of the Royal Society for the Protection of Birds (RSPB). But even within the conservation movement itself, framing the debate is far from straightforward and again involves different values and interests.

4.68   Many reasons for conserving biodiversity are not based on science, just as the reasons for conserving mediaeval cathedrals, Mozart concertos and Monet paintings have nothing to do with science. Many individuals within society value such things because they enrich our lives, or because they feel an ethical and moral responsibility to care for the world around them, or because they take spiritual comfort from wild places. Others, of course, beg to differ. Science can inform and underpin conservation strategies but it cannot tell society what or why to conserve particular species, habitats or ecosystems.

4.69   There are also profoundly important practical and economic reasons for nature conservation in the form of the 'services' which ecosystems provide for society: species that can be harvested for food or fibre, pollinators, healthy soils, wetlands that clean water and help control flooding in urban areas, nature tourism, and so on. The science underpinning the evaluation of ecosystem services is growing rapidly.[34] The Commission has been encouraged that Defra is pioneering methodologies that enable ecosystems services to be valued.

4.70   There was a dilemma running through much of the evidence we received from conservation bodies about the impacts of climate change, which on the one hand generally welcomed the arrival in the UK of new species that are 'nice' (little egrets being a good example), whilst lamenting the potential loss of native species (2.84-2.90; and Arctic–alpine plants, for instance), and the invasion of aliens that are deemed 'nasty' (2.92). There are some very difficult issues here that involve people's cherished world views, and an understandable human desire to maintain the *status quo* (even though we know it will ultimately be futile) that goes to the very heart of what conservation is trying (or hoping) to achieve.

IMPLEMENTATION

4.71   Implementation is the second component in addressing the challenges of adaptation. Implementation has two aspects: institutions need to make the decision to take action ('decide to do things') and to take action ('do things'). 'Deciding to do things' involves such activities as valuation (see 4.36-4.42 on economic efficiency), consultation and ongoing public engagement.

4.72   Issues when considering implementation are discussed further below and comprise:

- **up-scaling** local and small-scale initiatives (4.73-4.74);

- **enabling mechanisms** for adaptation goals (4.75-4.78);

- **engaging** public support (4.79-4.85);

- **co-ordination** between actors, both horizontally and vertically (4.86-4.89);

- **resources** – people, skills and finance (4.90-4.91); and

- **distribution** of costs (4.92-4.99).

Up-scaling local and small-scale initiatives

4.73   There are many examples of adaptation actions being taken at a relatively small, local scale. There are, however, questions about how institutions take the experience of small-scale exercises and scale these up to larger projects, whether this is appropriate, and how it can best be achieved. The Exmoor Mire Restoration project (Box 4E) is a good example where the partners are keen to expand the initiative from Exmoor (relatively small scale) to Dartmoor (a much bigger scale).

4.74   Enabling successful small-scale demonstration projects to continue in the longer term is a related issue. The catchment sensitive farming (CSF) scheme from the River Glaven (Box 3D) is an example of a small-scale initiative that the conservation agencies have applied elsewhere, and which many are keen to continue past the current round of funding. This type of project allows members of different organisations to work together, exchange practice and learn from one another in ways that large-scale formalised partnerships may not permit.

BOX 4E THE EXMOOR MIRE RESTORATION PROJECT[35]

Exmoor was draining heavily following the digging of drainage ditches (known as grips) in the 20th century. Draining changed the moorland habitat, damaging biodiversity, and allowed water to flow off the moors faster than before, leading to rapid rises in river levels in times of heavy rain. The solution was to block these drainage channels, which has reduced the flooding problems, improved biodiversity management and had the additional benefit for the relevant water company (South West Water) that Exmoor is now acting as a water store that regulates flow throughout the year. Another benefit for the water company of reduced flooding is that there is less need to purify water that is carrying agricultural run-off or sediment. Here, as elsewhere, it will be important to monitor progress to be sure that such ongoing benefits do indeed flow from the project.

Enabling mechanisms for adaptation goals

4.75　One of the main constraints on adaptation is the absence of enabling mechanisms. A simple example given to the Commission involved another tree-planting scheme, this time in Wharfedale, which could manage flood risk if 5% of the catchment was planted with trees but only if trees were planted in very specific areas of the catchment. There is at present no mechanism by which such a scheme could be made to happen other than by obtaining agreement from all relevant landowners. Nature conservation provides a more subtle example, because mechanisms to designate sites for species that are likely to arrive as the climate changes (i.e. providing nature reserves for species that are not there yet, or a 'space for nature') do not currently exist. Compulsory purchase powers, which could theoretically play a role in both these cases, are normally used for the purpose of building developments rather than for soft engineering or green infrastructure.

4.76　Schedule 1 of the Flood and Water Management Bill will allow for the designation of structures or other features which may affect flooding or coastal erosion risk and will prohibit their alteration without the consent of the responsible authority. Similarly, the approach to 'risk management' in this Bill would allow for increased probability of flooding in one place to reduce the probability of flooding in another (Clause 3(2)).

4.77　The planning system provides, as discussed in Chapter 3 (3.29-3.44), a potentially powerful institutional structure for adaptation to climate change. But whilst the planning system has the final say as to whether a proposed development goes ahead, and can even seek to encourage particular forms of development through development planning, it cannot compel positive action (as in the example of Wharfedale above). In this sense, the planning system is in the main 'enabling' and 'permissive', and has limited scope to promote new schemes or to enable adaptation of the existing built environment. Although development planning, with its emphasis on sustainable development, is a material consideration in development control decisions, the demand for positive action must largely come from elsewhere.

4.78　Central Government enjoys considerable power in the planning system (through control of policy and nationally significant infrastructure, the calling-in of controversial decisions, decisions on appeal, etc.), but the planning system is characterised by significant discretion, and final decisions are in many cases taken by locally-elected politicians. Given the local nature of climate change impacts, and the capacity of the planning system to engage local publics, this is appropriate. However, all local authorities, regardless of local political imperatives, need to address climate change. A range of mechanisms (policy, statutory powers and duties, monitoring and reporting) are in place to try to ensure that this happens. It is possible to move to more robust requirements when specific measures are necessary. So, for example, whilst the use of sustainable drainage systems was encouraged in the 2007 Planning Policy Statement on planning and climate change,[36] under the Flood and Water Management Bill (Schedule 3) construction with drainage implications will only be possible following approval of the drainage system. The effectiveness of these provisions will depend on the rigour of the standards set for sustainable drainage, but they indicate how regulation can be strengthened.

Engaging public support

4.79   Many studies confirm that most members of the public are now very aware of climate change and express significant concern about the issues. However, survey results also confirm that people do not understand climate change as an imminent or high-priority personal risk, and that climate projections are weak tools for promoting action.[37] So how should individuals, the public and organisations respond to projected major changes in the climate?

4.80   Studies in both the US and the UK have shown that people tend to see climate change as a problem for others rather than themselves.[38] Researchers have examined potential responses to different scenarios of rapid climate change and identified a complex set of beliefs amongst the public.[39] These range from concern, to scepticism, to calls for action, to apprehension. 'Concern' was the dominant response, supported by a belief in the role of both individuals and government in addressing climate change. There was a significant lack of clarity about what this meant in reality. We have found no evidence in more recent studies of any general increase in levels of societal concern or understanding, and, importantly, no surveys that report any increase in public awareness of the need for adaptation.[40]

4.81   Despite a considerable body of work to test the power of visual images of the consequences of climate change, and the dissemination of scenarios and probabilities, the literature concludes that these of themselves are relatively weak tools of persuasion. Indeed, psychological and sociological research over at least three decades suggests that if people are to be motivated to adapt then they must feel both imminently threatened and able to take action.

4.82   Of course, as individuals we can readily engage with probabilities when faced with an immediate or imminent personal decision – in healthcare, for example, probabilities are commonly discussed with patients in relation to treatment choices. But in this context a number of characteristics of engagement are apparent. First, there is direct one-to-one engagement between a trusted expert (doctor) and the individual (patient). Second, the decision relates to the direct potential for short-term or even immediate personal benefit. Such crucial characteristics are missing from the climate change debate, where experts do not or only rarely interact directly with the public. Most engagement on climate change happens through intermediaries (local planning officers, Environment Agency officers, the media, etc.) rather than through climate scientists themselves.

4.83   Basically, many people are aware that climate change exists and could be a problem, but they are not likely to take action in the near future to do anything about it. Clearly this needs to change. In order to engage public support, institutions responsible for adaptation need to ensure that a wide range of views are fed into the process in a transparent and inclusive manner. We therefore welcome the emphasis in Defra's *Consultation on Coastal Change Policy* on local participation and engagement in issues around coastal change, and we look forward to seeing this being brought into effect.[41]

4.84   However, aside from coastal erosion and flood protection, we have seen little evidence of public debate about the changes we may see as a result of adaptation decisions. It is important, particularly with the publication of the 2009 UK Climate Projections (UKCP09), that efforts are made by government, community leaders, business, the voluntary sector and conservation organisations to identify the issues, dilemmas and choices, so that as adaptation takes place there is a reduced likelihood of reactionary responses from individuals and organisations. The scale at which engagement takes place is important and in many cases will need to be local, but often in a regional context – again, the TE2100 project (Box 3E) is a good example. The Commission also notes that, of the engagement that is taking place, much of it is related to flood and coastal erosion risk management issues. Although biodiversity in the UK is likely to undergo significant changes that may require different or additional areas of land for habitat protection, this does not yet seem to be a subject for extensive discussion.

4.85   Public engagement is important for a range of reasons. We are familiar with the idea, for example, that only an engaged and informed public will encourage or tolerate some of the difficult choices required for the mitigation of climate change. But the same applies to adaptation, for example with respect to communities facing coastal erosion (a longstanding problem which is likely to be exacerbated by climate change). A decision-making process which those affected perceive to be open and fair can go a long way to enhancing tolerance and even acceptance of outcomes.[42]

Co-ordination between actors

4.86   Co-ordination between actors is crucial for building adaptive capacity. But as discussed earlier, the sheer number of actors and the complexity of potential relationships between them means that co-ordination is a challenge. Co-ordination can take different forms depending on the 'mode' of governance. This can be: a hierarchical mode, in which co-ordination of different actors is ensured through formal regulations, command and control; a market mode, where the price mechanism of the market ensures co-ordination; or a network mode of governance, where co-ordination is a result of debating and bargaining.[43] Different mixes of governance modes will impact on the way that institutions communicate and co-ordinate with one another.

4.87   During our visit to the Netherlands, it was apparent that Dutch management of flood risk is based on a system with different levels of governance, from the state through to local and municipal areas. A range of actors share responsibility for ensuring that the flood defences work as a complete system. The 'hot-spot' approach described in Box 4F is an example from the Netherlands of a way of including multiple stakeholders in the decision-making process.

BOX 4F THE HOT-SPOT APPROACH: AN EXAMPLE FROM THE NETHERLANDS

Water management in the Netherlands is paid for through taxes at the state and water-board levels. The Rijk (national Government) is responsible for strategic flood defence, including sea defences. There are then 12 *Provincies* (regional governments), who are asked to deliver regional plans on behalf of Government, and 26 *Waterschaps* (water-boards) who are responsible for water quality and quantity. Because the risk of flooding is recognised at all levels of government and society, there is a national level of awareness and often intense debate about the issues.

One method taken by the Dutch to deal with the many stakeholders involved in making adaptation decisions about flood risk is to take a 'hot-spot' approach. This is time consuming and involves extensive and intensive discussions, but it recognises that different places have different levels of risk and require different solutions. For instance, the actions that need to be taken to protect Schiphol airport are very different to those required to prevent Rotterdam from flooding. Hot-spots are those parts of the country most at risk from flooding, and where the problems are likely to get worse because of climate change and rising sea levels. In each hot-spot the local authorities lead the process (another aspect of framing the issue) to decide what the most effective local actions should be, within a nationally coherent framework.

Some of the proposed courses of action to protect hot-spots are imaginative. In Provincie Zuid Holland, sea defences are expected to become too weak within 10 years, but the proposed works will ensure they meet the required safety standards for a further 50 years. This will be done on the basis of integrated development of the coastline, which means that at the same time as improving the defences they will create space for nature and recreation as well as business and habitation (so making innovative use of the opportunity). One engineering solution is to dredge vast quantities of sand and either transfer it to the land (to counteract subsidence) or place it offshore to create a 'sand engine' whereby natural processes will continue to feed the shore and provide coastal defence.

The national debate in the Netherlands about these issues continues. In late 2008, the Delta Commission published a report into the state of the nation's flood defences, and identified many areas where they believe considerably more work needs to be done to improve flood defences in the face of climate change (an example of learning about the issue), arguing that in some places defences need to be adequate even for a once-in-10,000-year event. The Netherlands is currently debating how to respond to this report and what the most appropriate implementation path will be.

4.88   At our Edinburgh seminar in September 2008,[44] which was attended by representatives of the Northern Ireland Executive and Scottish Government, delegates identified a mismatch in national and local scales of action; impacts will be felt locally but national plans inevitably have poor detail at the local level. It was also suggested that national planning for climate change does not always properly take account of regional variation, especially in the Devolved Administrations. In Northern Ireland, water is recognised as being a cross-border issue, requiring horizontal co-ordination and shared responsibility with the Republic of Ireland.

4.89   Agriculture was also raised as an example of the dangers of 'silo' (or stand-alone) thinking, encouraging insufficient horizontal co-ordination. Adapting agriculture to climate change will require the environment and agriculture departments of devolved governments to work together. The agricultural industry itself can and will adapt very quickly, especially if the subsidy system is used to incentivise change. Such changes could have significant environmental impacts, and environmental actors need to understand what these changes might be and how their impact on biodiversity, soil systems and water might be minimised or used beneficially. Environment and agriculture departments must also ensure that attempts to improve co-ordination are no more complicated than absolutely necessary.

Resources – people, skills and finance

4.90   Adaptation requires the right number of people, with the right skills and training, and sufficient financial resources. Evidence received by the Commission highlighted the need for more engineers, and greater capacity in the planning system, to deal with the challenges of climate change.[45] These are specific disciplines, but there is a wider need for training for a variety of professions to be set into the context of a changing climate so as to enable institutions to take a broad and multidisciplinary view.[46]

4.91 During the course of our 26th study on the urban environment,[47] we heard that there was a shortage of planning officers and we recommended that local authority planning departments be adequately resourced and organised to maximise environmental benefits. The resourcing of planning departments was again highlighted during the current study. Evidence from our workshop on the role of the planning system in adaptation suggested that "the planning service was not perceived to be a priority area within the management team of a local authority, and it therefore lacks the resources to deliver to its full potential", and that planning budgets are often reduced in the face of pressures from other statutory and 'front-line' services such as education and housing, despite the crucial role of the planning system in climate change adaptation (see also Chapter 3).[48]

Distribution of costs

4.92 The burdens of climate change will, as discussed above (4.33-4.34), be unevenly distributed. This applies generally but is most acutely the case in respect of flooding and coastal protection. Questions of cost distribution include both how public resources for risk management are allocated and the response when risk management interventions, such as hard flood defences, fail or are withdrawn. These two parts of the dilemma seem currently to be considered separately. For example, we have had evidence that suggests that 'protect or abandon' have been straightforward alternatives in the coastal zone.[49]

4.93 The provision of flood and coastal defences is a discretionary power, rather than a duty, and the process for exercising this discretion, and allocating resources, is dominated by cost–benefit analysis (4.36-4.42). Valuation is not limited to a narrow calculation of infrastructure value, since Treasury rules allow for consideration of social wellbeing as well as distributional impacts. We note that the Defra consultation document on coastal change policy says that the Environment Agency is introducing a new policy statement on the subject, encouraging "the assessment of a greater range of benefits and options" from the provision of flood and coastal defences.[50]

4.94 The scale for decision making on these powers is obviously controversial. Implementation is likely to be local, and the frustration of local people who feel excluded from the process emphasises the need for a clear local voice in decision making.[51] But some broader national process is necessary, both to provide adequate funds and to distribute those funds in a sensible way. Under the Flood and Water Management Bill, the Environment Agency and the Welsh Ministers are to have a central strategic role, developing a flood and coastal erosion strategy for England and Wales respectively.

4.95 Although some European nations (for example, the Netherlands) compensate property owners in respect of those rare cases of the catastrophic failure of dykes, Government policy in this country is not to provide direct compensation for coastal erosion or flooding.[52] The Commission notes that losses from coastal erosion and flooding do not necessarily lie where they fall. Beyond emergency relief provided during flooding,[53] and the ordinary security (for example, re-housing) provided by the welfare state, the main existing mechanisms for redistributing costs are private or public law liabilities and insurance; both focus on property losses rather than broader impacts. Further discussion of the legal aspects of flooding and coastal erosion is provided in Box 4G.

BOX 4G LEGAL ASPECTS OF COASTAL PROTECTION

The Royal Commission on Environmental Pollution commissioned a review of the 'Legal Liabilities for Coastal Erosion and Flooding in the United Kingdom due to Climate Change' and published a report of the same name in 2009.[54] The report provides a detailed overview of the subject, and here we simply extract some key issues.

The common law does not provide a coherent or easily predictable response to flooding or coastal erosion, although in some cases it does redistribute costs. Common law powers and duties to provide protection from water have developed over centuries and are intimately affected by piecemeal (and also more comprehensive) statutory interventions. As a result, legal liabilities are complicated and context-dependent.[55]

Some of the issues can be seen in a Court of Appeal decision in respect of the loss of a Yorkshire cliff-top hotel as a result of coastal erosion.[56] The land that 'slipped' was owned by Scarborough Borough Council. The Court of Appeal held that the Council (or any other owner or occupier of such land) does indeed owe a 'measured duty of care' to prevent danger to a neighbour's land from lack of support due to natural causes. This duty applies when the owner or occupier knows (or could be presumed to know) of the condition on his land giving rise to the danger, and where it was reasonably foreseeable that the defect or condition would cause damage to the neighbour's land. The Court emphasised questions of cost and reasonableness in determining the nature of the duty owed. In this case the Council was not responsible, but there is considerable scope for debate on the facts in future cases.

The common law situation might be more straightforward if, for example, engineering work upstream or along the coast had caused the flooding or erosion; liability for something done is easier to establish than liability for a failure to act, and a straightforward 'reasonable person' test is likely to be applied.

The Human Rights Act 1998 may also be invoked in a way which could rearrange costs and liabilities. The rights most likely to be invoked are the right to respect for private and family life and home, and the right to peaceful enjoyment of possessions.

Neither right is absolute. The right to respect for private and family life and home may be interfered with "as is in accordance with the law and is necessary in a democratic society in the interests of national security, public safety or the economic well-being of the country, for the prevention of disorder or crime, for the protection of health or morals, or for the protection of the rights and freedoms of others." And the right to peaceful enjoyment of possessions can be interfered with "in the public interest and subject to the conditions provided for by law and by the general principles of international law"; nor does the right prevent "such laws as [the State] deems necessary to control the use of property in accordance with the general interest …".[57]

As with the common law, the position under the Human Rights Act is difficult and unclear. A House of Lords' decision on recurrent flooding of domestic property with sewage illustrates some of the issues. The parties in this case agreed that such flooding is a *prima facie* violation of the rights both to property and private and family life. Although the case established the need for a fair balance to be struck between the interests of the individual and the community as a whole, the claimants failed in their claim for compensation because the statutory scheme for assessing the priority for sewage works was compatible with the European Convention on Human Rights.[58]

Both common law and human rights law are developing areas. We have not yet seen litigation over planned land abandonment, and presumably the complete loss of property or home will at least bring with it a greater burden of justification in human rights law. Loss of life would also potentially raise different issues.

A number of specific statutory liabilities apply to damage resulting from flood defence work,[59] although they are unlikely to apply to a decision not to carry out flood defence work, which will fall to the common law (for example, s 177 and Schedule 21 of the Water Resources Act 1991).

4.96 Legal liabilities aside, insurance is another social mechanism for spreading risks and sharing costs, and it can mitigate the disruption of flooding. It is when loss becomes uninsurable (as is already happening in some parts of the UK both for flooding and coastal erosion) that claims for the sharing of burdens are most energetically made of the state.

4.97 The agreement between Government and the insurance industry in respect of the availability of insurance for residential property on flood plains is an important institutional intervention in the distribution of burdens, albeit contingent on public funding of flood defence work within a specific period.[60] The amount of loss that is uninsurable through ordinary market processes may increase with climate change.

4.98 Current policies to enhance awareness and uptake of insurance by members of groups likely to be underinsured or uninsured is another, albeit partial, response to the uneven distribution of climate impacts. The Government's *Financial Inclusion: An action plan for 2008-11*[61] was backed by a £130 million Financial Inclusion Fund. It welcomed the new focus on uptake of insurance and recommended that Government and the insurance industry work together to deliver a public education programme setting out the benefits of insurance in the context of flooding.

4.99 More generally, we welcome Government recognition of the need to "support communities in [the] process of adapting to both the physical effects of coastal change and the social and economic impacts",[62] and the beginnings of the development of a policy on this issue, including through the coastal change pathfinders programme (3.94).[63] It remains to be seen whether the scale of the challenge is really being recognised across the board.

LEARNING

4.100 Learning is the third of the essential components required to build adaptive capacity. The four big challenges of uncertainty, complexity, path dependency, and equity and efficiency mean that without continual and effective learning, institutions will quickly find the challenges unmanageable. Without uncertainty, for example, there would be little need for learning because institutions would simply be able to draw up a set of guidelines to be followed, with few revisions. We discuss the concept of a 'learning organisation' further at 4.113.

4.101 There are two relevant types of learning here that derive from long-developed theories of transformational and social learning:[64,65]

- *instrumental learning* or cognitive enhancement through the acquisition of new skills or information and knowledge; and

- *communicative learning* in terms of how a person (or, for our purposes, institution) approaches a situation or point of view and learns how to co-operate with others in solving collective problems, including developing a sense of group solidarity. Importantly, communicative learning often involves values, intentions and feelings, which can be defined only in their specific and often local contexts.

4.102 Importantly, both these components of learning are known to be essential in responding to complex environmental problems and in promoting environmental citizenship.[66] Instrumental learning (e.g. simply learning about the potential effects of climate change) is insufficient to support institutional or individual behavioural change and response.

4.103 The key elements of an integrated approach to instrumental and communicative learning include:

- the **generation and sharing** of information, particularly in a discussion-based environment (4.106-4.112);

- use of **information and knowledge** (numbers, projections, assessments, models, targets, valuations, etc.) (4.113-4.114);

- **strategic memory** and **social learning** (4.115-4.116); and

- **innovative** (non-standard) approaches (4.117-4.118).

4.104 Although framing, implementation and learning have been discussed separately, we repeat that they are not discrete activities. This is particularly important when considering learning: it should occur throughout framing and implementation.

4.105 It can be hard to measure the progress of learning because, as we have seen, there are currently no widely agreed indicators for adaptation. There is also potentially a problem with the translation of science research into social policy, which can lead to delays in learning and application of the best knowledge, for example the time delays between International Panel on Climate Change (IPCC) reports, or the interval between the production of UKCIP scenarios. Skills and capacity are important, and some of the evidence we have seen has suggested that there is a shortage of both engineers and planners which could impact on the UK's adaptive capacity.[67] But decision-makers also need to learn how to interpret and use information, particularly the UKCP09 projections, which will require appropriate training.

The generation and sharing of information

4.106 Effective learning depends on where institutions source their information and how that information is shared. There was a high level of commonality in where institutions sourced their information from in the evidence we received: many cited the UKCIP02 projections and were waiting in anticipation for UKCP09 (published during the course of this study, Box 2B). Others mentioned the IPCC reports as valuable sources of information. One of the concerns that the Commission has already mentioned is that there can be an over-reliance on the information that UKCP09 provides; it needs to be used appropriately, recognising the inherent uncertainties that exist in its projections.

4.107 There is already extensive sharing of information on climate change through network organisations, for example the sharing of good practice between local authorities through the local government associations. National indicator NI188 in England (3.25) attempts to measure adaptation to climate change, and around one-third of local authorities have signed up to it. Some local authorities who assess their performance against this indicator have looked deeply at the challenge of adaptation, such as Hampshire County Council (Box 4C). In doing so, they have tended to score their performance as lower than that of others who have not engaged in as much detail with the issue. Clearly, the challenge is to raise awareness and knowledge in all local authorities. The opportunity to share this kind of information is a valuable part of the learning process. The local government associations have recognised the need for a more integrated approach and have disseminated guidance and initiated pilot projects linking local authorities and national agencies in order to develop regional approaches to climate change adaptation.

4.108 An online survey of public sector organisations carried out on behalf of the Trades Union Congress (TUC) during 2008 pointed out that the introduction of NI188 in England had stimulated a wide range of adaptation activities in local government.[68] The Government's Adapting to Climate Change Programme recognises the need to provide support and guidance to local authorities and to stimulate networking to encourage 'bottom-up' learning. Since 2008, the Programme has worked with several partners (including UKCIP, the Environment Agency, the Government Office network and the Local and Regional Adaptation Partnership (LRAP) Board) to disseminate information through regional workshops. The TUC study concluded that local authorities which had engaged with UKCIP previously were much more likely to have carried out vulnerability studies or climate change risk assessments, and were more likely to have embarked on a communications programme.[69]

4.109 The Audit Commission, through its Comprehensive Area Assessment, has a strong interest in the performances of local authorities, and is keen to encourage the sharing of best practice. The Audit Commission's submission to the Commission recognised the challenges in providing assurances on the responses of local authorities to NI188, particularly as the indicator is currently process based not outcome based.[70] The Audit Commission has proposed a specific study on adaptation to climate change as part of its future national study programme.

4.110 The role of the planning system in monitoring adaptation progress has been recognised in England in the climate change supplement to Planning Policy Statement (PPS) 1.[71] Indicators should be selected by planning bodies to allow for monitoring and reporting in annual monitoring reports.

4.111 The Scotland and Northern Ireland Forum for Environmental Research (SNIFFER) works to conduct research and horizon scanning, and to share knowledge across two of the countries of the UK.[72] SNIFFER also acts as the Secretariat for the Northern Ireland Climate Change Impacts Partnership (NICCIP) and the Scottish Climate Change Impacts Partnership (SCCIP). There are also regional climate partnerships throughout England; these provide a valuable platform for a range of organisations to come together to discuss their experiences, challenges and aims with regards to climate change; importantly, the membership of these partnerships spans the public, private and third sectors. Similar functions are performed in Wales by the Welsh Climate Change Commission.

4.112 The cross-government Adapting to Climate Change (ACC) Programme for England is a major initiative focusing on adaptation. One of the key roles of this Programme is to generate information where it is currently lacking, and to share information. Also important is the Adaptation Programme Board (a cross-Whitehall body which champions and promotes adaptation) because adaptation is not limited to a single department. The Commission believes that the approach being taken should help to drive effective adaptation, provided that the ACC Programme remains alert to new developments and does not become too committed to any single path of action.

Use of information and knowledge

4.113   Once sourced, institutions need to ensure that information and knowledge (in the form of progress against targets and use of projections, for example) are fed into the learning process. A 'learning organisation' (defined by the European Consortium for the Learning Organisation)[vii] uses the management tools and techniques referred to in 4.46-4.48 to do this. It accepts the importance of having flexible management practices which have clear processes for managing data, information and knowledge through organisational and personal wisdom. It learns from successes and failures, and it combines written information with operating experiences.

4.114   But we have also seen examples where there are difficulties, for instance in the translation of information and knowledge in planning. Whilst the policy and legislative frameworks in the planning field are well established and capable of delivering effective approaches to adaptation, the importance of adaptation seems not always to be recognised in development control decisions on the ground (for example, in specifying drainage system design in large commercial projects). In part this is about the ability of hard-pressed local authority planning departments to recognise the scope of adaptation, and its urgency.

Strategic memory and social learning

4.115   The way in which organisations manage strategic or corporate memory is important for adaptation. Once again, we refer to the TE2100 project (Box 3E), which realised that a great deal of knowledge was tied up in individuals who were nearing retirement, threatening the loss of this hugely valuable institutional memory. Hence one of the aims of the project was to formally record and make available (for example, on its intranet site) options for managing flood risk in the future.

4.116   The Environment Agency and other organisations in the UK with a responsibility for managing flood risk are usually statutory consultees on all developments in flood risk areas, providing a mechanism by which the strategic memory of flood risk is institutionalised. A flood-prone area is still vulnerable to flooding even though this may not have happened for some years, and people easily forget. Trade bodies and organisations such as Water UK and the Water Research Centre, which have a common membership, also have a role in sharing practice and facilitating social learning.

Innovative (non-standard) approaches

4.117   The Commission has received evidence that encouraging experimentation in adaptation can lead to increased adaptive capacity and helps to ensure that path dependency is not limiting the opportunities to adapt. As we have already noted, the Exmoor Mire Restoration project is an example of how statutory bodies (the Environment Agency, Natural England and English Heritage), a water company (South West Water), and local recreation and conservation organisations have tried a new approach to improve water and biodiversity management in the uplands of Exmoor (Box 4E).

vii   See European Consortium for the Learning Organisation website at: http://www.eclo.org/. Accessed 10 December 2009.

4.118 We have also already pointed out that adaptation will require practical actions which have similarities with the outputs from successful businesses. How corporations manage information, uncertainties and complexities, and particularly how they innovate to create lasting expertise and adaptable attitudes, can provide valuable lessons for all organisations grappling with climate change. Almost by definition, 'business as usual' will become increasingly difficult and ultimately irrelevant. To survive and remain effective in the face of climate change, organisations will have to be innovative.

THE CIRCLES OF ADAPTIVE CAPACITY

4.119 In summary, institutions addressing adaptation face four challenges: uncertainty, complexity, path dependency, and equity and efficiency. In order to build their adaptive capacity, institutions will also need to consider how to frame the issue of adaptation, how to learn, and how to implement. This will be the vital first step in ensuring effective responses. In this chapter we have explored how each of these components is multi-faceted and each is inter-linked (Figure 4-III). In the next chapter we make a number of more specific recommendations designed to help institutions address them in practice.

FIGURE 4-III
The circles of adaptive capacity

This diagram illustrates a flexible, iterative, non-linear framework for building adaptive capacity, together with the main components, actions and institutional activities that contribute to each part of the process.

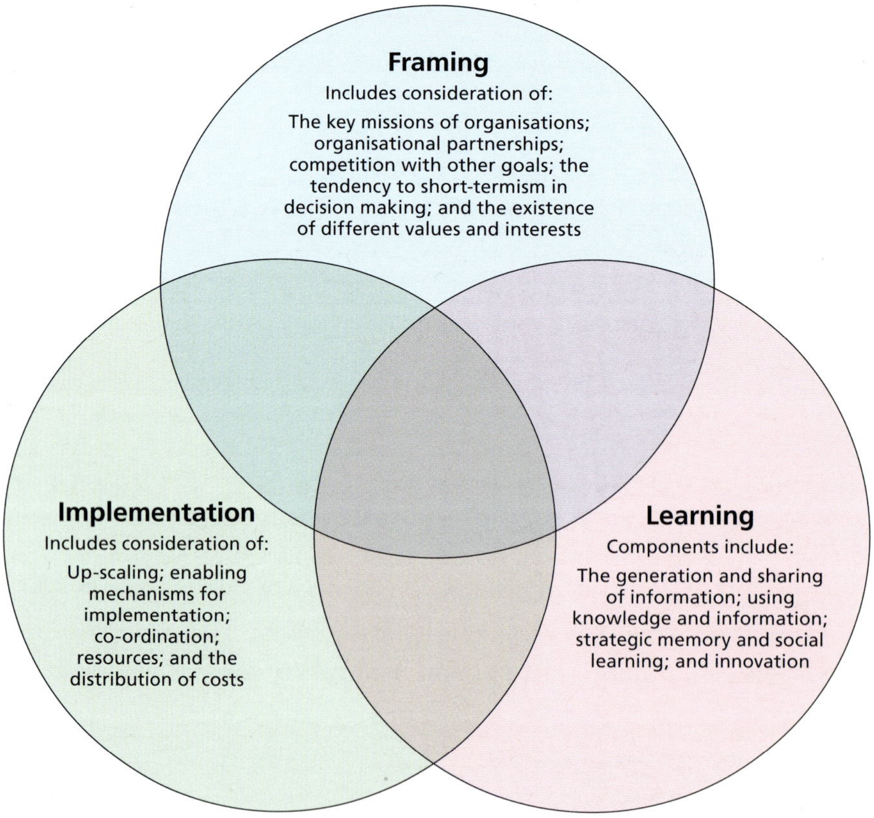

Framing
Includes consideration of:

The key missions of organisations; organisational partnerships; competition with other goals; the tendency to short-termism in decision making; and the existence of different values and interests

Implementation
Includes consideration of:

Up-scaling; enabling mechanisms for implementation; co-ordination; resources; and the distribution of costs

Learning
Components include:

The generation and sharing of information; using knowledge and information; strategic memory and social learning; and innovation

94

Chapter 5

DEVELOPING ADAPTIVE CAPACITY

INTRODUCTION

5.1 Societies have always had to adapt pragmatically to their current climate, with varying degrees of success (1.4). In the UK we can deal with most weather conditions reasonably well, but extreme weather can cause severe disruption – as the heatwaves of 2003, floods in 2007 and late 2009, and the cold weather at the end of 2009 and the start of 2010 demonstrated. Often these events lead to reviews, and lessons are learnt which increase our capacity to cope with similar events in future. But that learning can often be slow, and it is usually in reaction to events rather than anticipatory.

5.2 Climate change presents adaptation challenges of a different order: extreme events will occur more often, and will potentially be more extreme and more widespread. It will never be possible (or affordable) to plan to cope with all the circumstances which the country or local areas may face. But the Commission firmly believes that as a country we need to recognise that our vulnerability will increase, and that institutions should address this proactively and systematically on the basis of the principles set out in the previous chapter.

5.3 We saw in Chapter 4 how institutions face four challenges when dealing with adaptation: uncertainty, complexity, path dependency, and equity and efficiency. In addressing these challenges, institutions will need to consider how to frame, incorporate learning and implement their approaches to adaptation. It is only by following these principles that institutions can build adaptive capacity soundly.

5.4 Framing, implementation and learning are not linear processes but, rather, are flexible and iterative approaches for understanding and characterising the issues that emerge from the four high-level challenges. Of the many difficulties we have outlined in this report, it is common for organisations when faced with a problem to focus on what actions they need to take immediately, whereas often it would also be appropriate to concentrate on how to build capacity to frame, learn about, and implement appropriately. Then adaptation actions will not only be effective in the short term but can remain sufficiently flexible in the face of an uncertain climate in the longer term.

5.5 The key message is that building adaptive capacity needs to be embedded as part of the routine business of institutions. The circles of adaptive capacity (Figure 4-III) provide a framework to understand how the different components of adaptive capacity can be developed so that the challenges can be addressed.

5.6 But how do organisations embed adaptation within their business? How can government ensure that the policy framework for delivering services and programmes is made more relevant to a world with a changing climate? Leadership and capacity building are the key prerequisites. We believe strongly that addressing these themes is essential if organisations are to frame, implement and learn successfully.

5.7 In contrast to mitigation, where the challenge is to reduce greenhouse gas emissions, there is no predefined blueprint, end-point or programme for adaptation. This report is not about the myriad of practical actions which will be required. Instead, our recommendations aim to assist in building institutional capacity to address vulnerability to a climate which is both changing and becoming more variable. The point is not to identify short-term fixes which might seem appropriate now, but to seek to ensure that all institutions are equipped to respond to the changing and uncertain demands of adaptation. The nature of the task of building adaptive capacity will vary according to context. In this sense, adaptation is intensely local.

5.8 We have chosen to focus our investigations on three exemplars, but the lessons we have learned extend much more broadly, and many of the recommendations apply across government departments and agencies, rather than simply to those concerned with freshwater, coasts and biodiversity. Furthermore, while our recommendations are directed primarily at governments and public sector agencies, many are also relevant to private sector organisations. In all cases, it is our view that urgent and purposeful action is required to ensure that adaptation is embedded in all aspects of institutional design and operation.

5.9 Given the potentially large number of actions that may need to be taken to adapt, it will not always be easy to decide what to do first and what can be left until later. It may sometimes be appropriate to prioritise policies which, though designed to deal with a particular aspect of the adaptation challenge, also contribute to the attainment of other goals. Terms such as 'no regret' or 'win–win' (generally involving multiple benefits) are often used to describe such actions. For example, creating migration pathways to allow animals to move as the climate changes as an adaptation response can also create recreational opportunities for activities such as walking or cycling, and creating new wetland can both help buffer water supply and provide new habitats for species – both of which contribute to adaptation. In some cases it is possible to take actions which will contribute to both mitigation and adaptation. But building adaptive capacity and, especially, taking specific adaptation actions will in virtually all cases have a net cost, even if the actions can be described as 'no regret' or 'win–win' – though in many cases the benefits may be multiple and substantial.

5.10 We set out in the following paragraphs recommendations intended to help organisations to address adaptation. In summary, organisations will need to ensure that their policies and programmes address, and reduce, vulnerability to climate change, and exploit opportunities to increase resilience. We present first a series of cross-cutting recommendations, aimed at ensuring that policies and programmes address adaptation. We believe this can be achieved by introducing an 'adaptation test', backed up by new duties on public bodies to address adaptation and by arrangements for monitoring progress. Second, we make more specific recommendations flowing from our examination of current institutional arrangements. Third, we consider measures to ensure that we have the information, tools, skills and resources required. Fourth, we consider the important issue of equity. Finally, we address issues of public engagement. Adaptation may appear a technical issue, but the choices we face are far from merely technical – the discussion of equity in Chapter 4 (4.29-4.35) is one example.

5.11 A number of our recommendations are addressed to the Adaptation Sub-Committee, established by the Climate Change Act 2008. These are summarised at the end of the chapter (5.81). We recognise that the Sub-Committee – and the equivalent body in Scotland if one is established – will need to determine the extent to which it is equipped to perform effectively the tasks which we identify; if they fall outside the remit of the Sub-Committee it will be for the Department for Environment, Food and Rural Affairs (Defra) and the Devolved Administrations to decide who should take responsibility for addressing the Commission's recommendations.

THE POLICY FRAMEWORK

5.12 Our first series of recommendations is aimed at ensuring that adaptation is embedded in policy making and investment appraisal, that all public bodies have a duty to advance adaptation, and that monitoring arrangements are in place to ensure accountability.

POLICY APPRAISAL

5.13 Organisations need to examine both their current and future policies and programmes, to assess whether they will be suitable and appropriate for a future in which the climate will be more extreme and variable. Organisations will also need to consider whether their policies and programmes will make it more or less difficult for adaptation to take place, or will increase our vulnerability to climate change. We propose that institutions should adopt an 'adaptation test'. This should apply not only to the legislative, policy, regulatory or administrative decisions made by public bodies, but also in the private sector where important infrastructure or services are at stake, and could apply more widely as part of good practice for any business. **The Commission recommends that an 'adaptation test' appropriate to the circumstances be integrated into public and private decision making. The objective of this test should be to reduce exposure to the risk of damage through climate change; to develop the capacity to cope with unavoidable damages; and to encourage organisations to take advantage of new opportunities.**[i]

5.14 For public bodies, the adaptation test should be integrated into existing frameworks for policy development and impact assessment, required by both the European and national procedures. A test should also apply to individual projects as well as policies and plans. It should include consideration of alternatives from a climate resilience perspective.

INVESTMENT APPRAISAL

5.15 Decisions on what policy or programme to pursue will often require an investment appraisal if financial investment is involved, usually in the form of a cost–benefit analysis. Organisations need to be aware of the limitations of orthodox cost–benefit analysis in appraising investment (outlined in 4.36-4.42). In particular, cost–benefit analysis cannot deal with multiple objectives and does not explicitly take account of ethical problems which arise when valuing over long timescales and when discounting methodologies are applied. In these circumstances, the use of multi-criteria analytical approaches has advantages, particularly when open to public and stakeholder input. These approaches can help capture the complexity of projects, including those involving novel technologies or approaches, and can assist in managing some of the intergenerational equity issues associated with discounting the impacts of current behaviour on future generations.

---

i   The three objectives suggested for an adaptation test reflect a typology set out in the Third Assessment Report of the Intergovernmental Panel on Climate Change. Available at: http://www.ipcc.ch.

5.16   The Department for Communities and Local Government (CLG) has published extensive guidance on multi-criteria methods that should be used in evaluating investment options.[1] In addition, Defra has also published guidance on valuing ecosystem services.[2] While this is a welcome development, there remain significant difficulties in applying such valuation methods. The revision to the Treasury Green Book on investment appraisal[3] also advocates the use of option values, a major modification to standard cost–benefit analysis, which the Commission believes is particularly useful for any project for which climate variability is a consideration, because the technique increases flexibility in the investment appraisal process.

5.17   The Commission commends the Government for advocating and in some cases pioneering these new approaches to valuation and appraisal. **The Commission recommends that the new flexibilities in the supplementary guidance to the Treasury Green Book are fully used by public sector bodies in making investment appraisals, particularly for infrastructure investment.**

5.18   **The Commission also recommends the use of a range of alternative discount rates (including zero) in appraising investments with very long-term impacts, given the ethical problems involved in discounting the impacts of current behaviour on future generations.**

AN ADAPTATION DUTY

5.19   An adaptation test will be an important means of ensuring that adaptation is embedded in decision making. But it is also important that public bodies have a clear responsibility for addressing the issue.

5.20   The Climate Change (Scotland) Act 2009 imposes a duty on public bodies, requiring them to exercise their functions in the way best calculated to contribute to the delivery of the Scottish Government's climate change adaptation programme. Similarly, in 2007 a duty was placed on the Mayor of London and the London Assembly to "address climate change" and to "take action with a view to mitigation of, or adaptation to, climate change" (3.7).[4]

5.21   The Climate Change Act 2008 stops short of imposing a more general obligation of this kind. **The Commission recommends that the Climate Change Act 2008 should be amended to impose an adaptation duty on public bodies of the kind included in the Climate Change (Scotland) Act 2009 or the Greater London Authority Act 2007.**

REPORTING AND MONITORING

5.22   Introducing a duty of this kind raises the issue of how compliance with it is to be monitored. The Climate Change (Scotland) Act 2009 provides the possibility of establishing a monitoring body to fulfil this function. In the event that a duty of this kind were to be introduced in other parts of the United Kingdom, it would be important to consider which body or bodies could play this role. **The Commission recommends that the Adaptation Sub-Committee should be responsible for ensuring that appropriate and transparent systems of accountability are in place for monitoring compliance with a general adaptation duty imposed on public bodies.** One possible system of accountability could be based on the concept of peer review, for example by one local authority reviewing the work of another.

5.23   The Climate Change Act 2008 empowers the Government and Welsh Ministers to direct public bodies to prepare and report on risk assessments and action plans. Defra has recently issued a strategy about which bodies should be regarded as priority reporting authorities (Box 3A and 3.20-3.22). There are bodies which satisfy Defra's criteria as priority reporting authorities but which do not meet the definition of a reporting authority for the purpose of the Climate Change Act (for example, petroleum and electronic communications companies, and the food sector). Defra is proposing to ask these bodies to report on a voluntary basis. **The Commission recommends that Government regularly review, and if necessary update, the definition of a reporting authority in the Climate Change Act 2008, in order to ensure that reporting obligations can be imposed on all bodies identified as meeting the Defra criteria for selection as priority reporting authorities.**

5.24   There are also bodies which meet Defra's criteria for priority reporting and are reporting authorities within the definition in the Climate Change Act, but which will nonetheless not (initially at least) be required to report. For example, local authorities are excluded from Defra's initial list, because they report in accordance with national indicator NI188 (3.25-3.27). Defra recognises the importance of keeping alternative arrangements such as these under review, and we welcome this. In addition, **the Commission recommends that the Adaptation Sub-Committee should evaluate and ensure the adequacy of the arrangements which apply to bodies which meet Defra's criteria for priority reporting bodies but are excluded from Defra's initial list of those required to report.**

INDICATORS OF ADAPTIVE CAPACITY

5.25   It will be important for organisations to monitor and evaluate their performance in building capacity. This is, however, difficult: measuring adaptation, or adaptive capacity, is not straight-forward (4.51) because there is no end-point or quantifiable target for adaptation which can be set, and the circumstances of each organisation are different.

5.26   There is considerable debate as to how baselines can be set when the climate is changing, or what form meaningful indicators can take when the goal is to build the capacity to adapt now and in the future. Simple outcome indicators can be too narrow to account for the complexity of adaptation, and sometimes misleading where adaptive success involves the absence of an effect, for example flooding. It will be important to avoid a system of targets which can unintentionally create perverse incentives.

5.27   The definition of the targets must follow from a correct framing of the problem, and reflect the uncertainties and the complexities which we have identified. The Defra guidance for departmental adaptation plans requires Departments to define indicators to help them define what successful adaptation looks like;[5] the Scottish Government is developing its own indicators.

5.28   It is also clear to us that in view of the complexity of the adaptation challenge there is no simple indicator that can be applied to all institutions and all sectors. It is likely that at first organisations will use primarily process-based indicators. Over time, as they become more experienced in building adaptive capacity, they may be able to move towards greater use of outcome-based indicators. Both are important, and we would encourage the development and use of both process- and outcome-based indicators as soon as possible.

Specific institutional arrangements

5.29　Our second series of recommendations is addressed at specific institutional arrangements. We identified in Chapter 3 some of the complex institutional arrangements involved in delivering climate change adaptation. Some of our recommendations flow from our analysis of particular exemplars, but many will have much wider application.

5.30　As we have noted, adaptation is often local (see, for example, 1.13, 3.3 and 4.58) but the organisations which deliver local services or make investment decisions about projects operate within a multi-level governance framework. Actors at all levels play a role in adaptation – as is clear from the descriptions we have given in Chapter 3. Different places will experience climate change in different ways, requiring locally-tailored responses and public engagement about the form that these responses should take; however, in some circumstances there are good reasons for actors operating at higher levels to be involved. Action at a local level may spill over and affect people in other areas, so co-ordinated responses may be required. Equally, the capacity of local actors to take steps to increase resilience to the effects of climate change will be determined to an important degree by policy and fiscal frameworks put in place elsewhere.

5.31　In England, Defra has set up the Adapting to Climate Change Programme (3.9 and Figure 3-I), which co-ordinates action across Government. As one element, Defra has engaged with the Environment Agency, the UK Climate Impacts Programme (UKCIP) and a number of regional and local bodies to establish the Local and Regional Adaptation Partnership (LRAP) Board. The aim of LRAP is to facilitate "at the regional and local level, a robust approach to identifying and managing the risks and opportunities of unavoidable climate change in a co-ordinated and consultative way",[6] and to do so by 2011. **The Commission recommends that Defra extend the Local and Regional Adaptation Partnership Board beyond the current term of 2011 to continue to take advantage of collaborative working across national and regional organisations.** Adaptation is a process with no definable end-point, and there will be a continuing need for a forum to facilitate the exchange of information at a regional and local level. This is particularly important given that the first UK-wide climate change risk assessment is not due until the end of LRAP's currently anticipated life.

5.32　In many places, authorities will need to work together to build adaptive capacity. For example, neighbouring local authorities may need to co-operate where co-ordinated action is needed over a larger geographical scale than the area of one authority. Partnerships and multi-area agreements provide mechanisms to facilitate joint working, though these are voluntary arrangements. We encourage the Government to require joint reporting, where appropriate, in accordance with the terms of the Climate Change Acts.

The land use planning system

5.33　The Commission is convinced that the land use planning system will be extremely important in delivering adaptation. We are concerned at the pressures being placed on the system, given that we know that many planning departments are under-resourced.[7] For the planning system to deliver adaptive capacity fully and effectively, there needs to be the opportunity for planners to learn about adaptation, and also the organisational culture and operational mechanisms to allow them to incorporate adaptation into development planning and planning control decisions. **The Commission recommends that local authorities ensure that planning departments are adequately resourced and organised to enable their responsibilities in relation to adaptation to be met.**

5.34   Two of our earlier recommendations are of clear relevance to the planning system. An 'adaptation test' (5.13) should be integrated into all relevant stages of the planning process. Similarly, the introduction of an adaptation duty on all public bodies (5.21) would greatly strengthen the place of adaptation within planning policy.

5.35   The commitment of local politicians to adaptation to climate change (Box 4C), and their recognition of the importance of the task, is mixed. Given that the process of development control is very often subject to competing pressures and objectives, awareness of the significance of adaptation is crucial if it is to be adequately taken into account and adequately prioritised.

5.36   There is also the possibility that bodies such as Local Strategic Partnerships (3.24-3.25) can help set the high-level policy and raise awareness of the need to include adaptation in development planning.

5.37   The planning system is subject to a large number of legislative and policy obligations in respect of adaptation to climate change, as discussed in Chapter 3. Although the Committee on Climate Change is a statutory consultee on National Policy Statements under the Planning Act 2008, there are no other explicit links between the Committee and the planning system. Such links would facilitate learning and capacity building. **The Commission recommends that the Adaptation Sub-Committee should scrutinise planning policy guidance to assess and advise on the recognition within spatial planning of the importance of adapting to climate change. The Sub-Committee should also scrutinise the activities of the Infrastructure Planning Commission in the context of adaptation to climate change.**

LESSONS FROM THE EXEMPLARS

5.38   The Commission identified a number of shortcomings in existing policy frameworks as a result of its analysis of the three exemplar areas. Some illustrate broader challenges which must be addressed if policy frameworks are to facilitate and not hinder adaptation. We highlight below a number of steps to confront these challenges.

5.39   ***Review and where necessary revise the 'missions' of organisations***: It is essential that adaptation is firmly embedded in the key missions or duties of organisations, and that it is accorded a sufficiently high priority alongside other important goals. To this end it is crucial that organisations review their own key missions from an adaptation perspective and where necessary revise them.

5.40   For example, in Chapter 4 (4.55) we noted that whilst economic regulation of water services is required to contribute to or to have regard to sustainable development, it gives priority to consumer interests and to the sustainability of water utilities. **The Commission recommends that organisations, including those subject to statutory duties, review and where necessary revise their mission and objectives from an adaptation perspective. For priority reporting authorities, the Adaptation Sub-Committee should scrutinise these reviews, and where necessary recommend revisions to their mission and objectives.**

5.41   ***Scrutinise new and existing legislative frameworks and implementing measures to ensure flexibility***: Flexible policy frameworks enhance the ability of organisations to respond to the challenge of climate change adaptation. We saw this in relation to the EU Water Framework

Directive (Box 3C), in which flexibility derives not only from the broadly expressed nature of the policy goals and from the presence of context-specific exceptions, but also from the institutional arrangements which have been put in place at both EU and national level to examine regularly the operation and implementation of the Directive and the appropriateness of its underlying concepts and goals. The inbuilt flexibility of the Water Framework Directive is a useful model for how policies can be framed to allow for environmental change.

5.42 Adopting a similar approach with respect to the EU Birds and Habitats Directives would enhance their value as tools for integrating adaptation into conservation policy. A rigid application of these Directives can result in protected areas being viewed as static entities designed to preserve the *status quo* rather than as a tool for providing space for nature that can accommodate change. The main aim of the Habitats Directive (Box 4D), namely to promote the maintenance of biodiversity, cannot be met unless the primary tool for achieving this aim – the Natura 2000 network – is applied in the light of a changing environment. **The Commission recommends that in implementing EU directives, including those on conservation, governments utilise the flexibility inherent in the directives in order to facilitate adaptation.**

5.43 Ensuring appropriate flexibility may require hard questions to be asked about long-established and taken-for-granted concepts. For example, water quality models for inland waters have been based on historical time series of river flows. Changes in rainfall will affect river flow profiles (2.35). Water quality models will have to be recalibrated to reflect these changes, which may well be manifested in additional requirements for treatment, particularly of sewage. **The Commission recommends that environmental regulators ensure that the assumptions underpinning water management models are updated so that they remain appropriate for the maintenance of water resources and quality in a changing climate.**

5.44 ***Ensure a cross-sectoral approach to policy making and implementation***: The Commission has concluded that governments have made significant progress in providing a policy framework for a cross-sectoral approach to adaptation. However, delivery of these policies in relation to future management of natural resources and conservation of biodiversity will require much greater collaboration between government agencies. The Commission considers that a cross-sectoral approach to the delivery of ecosystem services is also an essential element in building resilience into land management. The launch of a UK-wide National Ecosystem Assessment[ii] is an important step towards developing a national framework.

5.45 The Natural England studies which we highlight in Chapter 3 (3.108) emphasise that vulnerability assessments need to be cross-sectoral if all aspects of environmental change are to be assessed. In addition, action plans designed to build resilience will require the commitment of resources across several government agencies. Delivery agencies need to work in partnership to ensure that projects aimed at assessing vulnerability and improving resilience at the local level will be fully integrated.

ii   See http://uknea.unep-wcmc.org/ for more information about the National Ecosystem Assessment.

5.46 **The Commission recommends that the Government's Adapting to Climate Change Programme ensures there is a framework for collaboration on a cross-sectoral approach to the development of the National Risk Assessment**[iii] **and subsequent Action Plans for adaptation to climate change.**

RESOURCES TO BUILD CAPACITY

5.47 Our third series of recommendations is aimed at developing leadership, raising awareness, developing the knowledge and skills which organisations will need to build adaptive capacity, and ensuring the resources will be available.

THE IMPORTANCE OF LEADERSHIP AND CULTURAL CHANGE

5.48 Building adaptive capacity will require knowledgeable individuals who can think strategically about what climate change means for their organisation and who can embed resilience to climate change into their organisation's business. The Commission welcomes Defra's guidance on formulating Departmental Adaptation Plans (3.13), which requires Government departments to act now to plan for adaptation.

5.49 Leadership is particularly important in addressing climate change, because of the endemic uncertainty and complexity. In addition, leadership may be necessary to ensure the right level of support, resources and acceptance for current policy changes or investment now to deal with future problems. The need to consider adaptation must be embedded throughout organisations, and this can only be achieved through appropriate leadership. The Commission has observed that adaptive capacity has been built in organisations where there are climate change champions and, where relevant, supportive politicians.

5.50 The culture of building adaptive capacity should pervade a whole organisation. Leadership is necessary if organisations are to understand the need for adaptation, to frame the issue effectively, and to be vigilant in exposing and tackling damaging path dependencies. A list of ten initial questions to help decision-makers address adaptation is given at Box 5A later in this chapter. Defra guidance for Departmental Adaptation Plans[8] recommends that responsibility for departmental adaptation should be owned at Management Board or at least Director level. This principle should be adopted by all organisations affected by climate change. This will also require active steps to develop the competencies necessary to create the learning organisation which will deliver effective climate change adaptation (4.48). **The Commission recommends that organisations (both public and private) should ensure that responsibility for building adaptive capacity and putting in place arrangements to develop and utilise the competencies necessary for climate change adaptation is assigned at Management Board or Director level.**

5.51 The Government has taken important steps to increase awareness of the challenge of adaptation, in particular through the Adapting to Climate Change Programme, and by way of its support for the UK Climate Impacts Programme. In England and Wales, the Local Government Association (LGA) has also done much to raise awareness amongst local authorities, not least through the LGA's annual climate change conference. But it is not yet clear how far this awareness is reaching into public and private sector organisations. Work needs to continue if organisations, and the

iii   The Climate Change Act 2008 commits the UK Government to carrying out an assessment of the risks to the UK of climate change every five years. The first cycle is required to report to Parliament by the end of January 2012. See http://www.defra.gov.uk/environment/climate/adaptation/assess-risk.htm.

103

leaders within them, are to be properly supported in embedding adaptation. There are both vulnerabilities and opportunities associated with climate change. Adaptation is about 'doing the day job differently and better' rather than simply being an additional burden.

5.52   There is considerable scope for leaders to learn from others who are pioneering mitigation and adaptation in the UK, Europe and other parts of the world. The Commission has noted that networks, such as the C40 Cities Climate Leadership Group[iv] at the international level or the Nottingham Declaration Partnership[v] at the national level, can and should be used as a means of sharing information and good practice. To be effective these networks need to be supported and resourced appropriately.

INCREASING KNOWLEDGE AND SKILLS

5.53   The learning organisation we refer to at 5.50 (and 4.113) must invest in training and professional learning about climate change adaptation. The learning must be factored into everyday work and must be done now if we are to have the capacity to adapt to current and future climate. It is crucial that this investment takes place at all levels of an organisation. In addition, adaptation must be integrated into school and university curricula to ensure that there is a steady stream of skilled people available in future years.

5.54   The 2009 Climate Projections (UKCP09) are the major information resource for adaptation in the UK. The Commission believes that they are a valuable resource, if used appropriately. Organisations such as the UK Climate Impacts Programme (UKCIP) and the regional and devolved climate change partnerships can also be invaluable in helping organisations to improve their understanding of adaptation and to develop adaptation strategies. The Commission is concerned that the resources provided to support these institutions are not commensurate with the scale of the adaptation challenge. **The Commission recommends that Government should ensure that the UK capability to produce and interpret climate change projections is maintained and enhanced.**

5.55   Governments should ensure that professional training on awareness of climate change is included in programmes for the development of the Senior Civil Service as they are the professional managers of the public sector. It is also important to raise awareness for business professionals. **The Commission recommends that the governments and UKCIP work with professional institutions (for example, those bodies representing planners and engineers) to create continuing professional development that increases understanding of the need for adaptation.** Where appropriate, they should also work with professional institutions to support the inclusion of climate change adaptation within relevant higher education syllabi, including those developed by business schools.

5.56   Many organisations will rely on external contracted expertise to help understand what UKCP09 means for them and how it should be applied to their business. The Commission has already observed that the information provided by the climate projections needs to be properly

---

iv   The C40 Cities Climate Leadership Group is a group of the world's largest cities committed to tackling climate change. It was established in October 2005 when representatives of 18 leading world cities met in London to discuss joining forces to tackle global warming and climate change (see: http://www.c40cities.org/; accessed November 2009).

v   The Nottingham Declaration was launched in October 2000 in Nottingham. By signing the Declaration, councils and their partners pledge to systematically address the causes of climate change and to prepare their community for its impacts. The Declaration has now been signed by more than 300 English councils (see: http://www.energysavingtrust.org.uk/nottingham; accessed November 2009).

understood in order that it can be used appropriately. The Commission is aware of the importance of maintaining quality control for those offering consultancy services in relation to adaptation. It suggests that quality control could be achieved through the development of a scheme of 'accredited practitioners' of UKCP09. **The Commission recommends that governments and relevant bodies build climate change adaptation into existing personal and corporate accreditation schemes to help ensure that climate projection information is being interpreted and used appropriately.**

5.57   In the longer term the multidisciplinary Living With Environmental Change (LWEC) programme described in Chapter 2 will be an important source of new insights that could contribute to our adaptive capacity and be used to inform adaptation action. To ensure that institutions generally can benefit from this information, there needs to be effective knowledge transfer mechanisms in place for all research activity of relevance to adaptation and, as LWEC is such a large programme, it should be a leader in this. **The Commission recommends that the Living With Environmental Change partners develop an extensive and proactive knowledge transfer programme to ensure that new information on climate change adaptation is shared widely and effectively.**

ENSURING RESOURCES ARE AVAILABLE

5.58   Finally, adaptation should not be set in competition with other goals but should be viewed as a core element of an organisation's primary activities. This does not mean that building adaptive capacity will not cost money. Inevitably competition for resources will lead to tensions between competing objectives, as we have seen in spatial planning (Chapter 3). The Commission was disappointed to learn that the Treasury's approach to the provision of additional funds for adaptation does not appear be in keeping with the scale and urgency of the problem, or indeed with Government's own ambitious targets for adaptation.[9]

5.59   The Treasury acknowledges that there is uncertainty over the total economic impact of climate change and is awaiting the publication of the UK Climate Change Risk Assessment and Economic Analysis (due in January 2012) "... in order to inform further consideration of climate change risks and policy development."[10] We are concerned that sufficient resources will not be available to meet the scale of the challenge of adaptation, and that the scale of the challenge is not yet adequately reflected in the frameworks for setting and prioritising departmental objectives. **We recommend that Government departments ensure that at the next (and at future) comprehensive spending reviews sufficient resources are committed to building adaptive capacity, and that appropriate recognition of the need for adaptation is included in the frameworks for setting and prioritising departmental objectives.**

EQUITY

5.60   Aspects of the uneven distribution of costs of climate change are outlined in Chapter 3 (3.72-3.94). This is not unique to the issue of climate change: there are many examples where the costs and benefits of action, or inaction, fall differentially. It is clear that governments need to continue to develop an adequate process which does not unreasonably favour some individuals or interests (for example property interests or conservation interests) in the allocation of resources for protection from flood and coastal erosion. Decisions on protection (or not) should be taken alongside decisions on the treatment of those most disadvantaged by climate change.

105

5.61 A basic question is whether the costs of flooding and coastal erosion, which are likely to increase with a changing climate, should lie where they fall and, if not, how they should be redistributed (it is already the case that nationally-funded flood and coastal erosion defences involve a redistribution of resources through government taxation and expenditure).

5.62 Public and political attention at the moment is focused on demands for financial compensation of those facing immediate property losses due to coastal erosion. This could take a variety of forms, including a simple payment of market value for the property, government initiated or sponsored insurance schemes, or, where loss of property is not imminent and rental of the property is an attractive option, a 'purchase and lease-back' scheme. Local authority pathfinders are exploring some of these options (3.94 and 4.99). Compensation, particularly for residential property from which historical protection by the state has been withdrawn, might seem an intuitively attractive response to the burdens of coastal change; but this solution is far from straightforward.

5.63 Questions of moral hazard (for instance, encouraging development in vulnerable areas) comprise one of the problems. This difficulty is probably manageable, although attempts at management, for example, by making compensation available only for property purchased before a particular date, could have their own blighting effect. The potentially open-ended redistribution of resources contemplated by financial compensation proposals is a more significant difficulty. The scale of land abandonment or uninsurable flood damage in the longer term is uncertain, and it reminds us that compensation by the state may have implications in other areas – money used for compensation is not then available for investment elsewhere.

5.64 Equally significantly, as discussed in Chapter 3, property does not capture the full scale of the community disruption of flood and coastal erosion, and addressing only property will leave some of the most vulnerable without assistance. **The Commission recommends that the Adaptation Sub-Committee should explore the range of options available to address issues such as the loss of community, business and employment, and the disruption to health, educational and social services, which may be a direct or indirect consequence of climate change.**

5.65 Government might focus on assisting in the rebuilding (literally or metaphorically) or relocation of affected communities, including community and social services, just as it carries out compensation 'in kind' for conservation losses. Whilst there is no clear 'right' to publicly provided defence from water or to associated rights to compensation, simply ignoring questions of property ownership would be controversial. That does not necessarily imply that full financial compensation for lost property is the right response, simply that it should be considered alongside other options such as partial compensation or compensation in kind, and together with approaches that can apply equally to property owners and those who do not own property.

5.66 Deciding between the full range of the options available cannot be resolved by a technical analysis or an abstract discussion of existing legal rights and duties. Selecting any single option (for example, full compensation for lost property) requires a particular approach to distributive justice (or simply fairness) when in fact as a society we take very different approaches depending on the circumstances. For example, some forms of legal liability require full compensation of all loss (even beyond property loss); compulsory purchase provides for full compensation of property losses in limited circumstances; many misfortunes which fall outside the reach of legal liabilities lead to recourse to the welfare state; and even welfare state provision varies depending on the type of assistance being sought. As a nation, our approach to distributive justice is inconsistent, and often a result of historical accident; it is something society should consider afresh in the light of the new circumstances created by climate change.

5.67 There is no obvious or easy answer to the question of how and whether the state should redistribute the costs of climate change. The far-reaching political nature of this question, which implies a range of questions about the social and physical world in which we wish to live, should be recognised. In the absence so far of public and political debate on the subject, it would be premature to make a recommendation on the institutional solution to the uneven distribution of climate change impacts. However, there is a pressing need for such a debate.

5.68 As the Government has noted (3.67 concerning the Flood and Water Management Bill), there is also a need for debate about the circumstances in which local funding to maintain or improve defences is a fair and appropriate response. This may be a solution in some cases, serving at the least to 'buy time' for consideration of other options. It assumes, however, that the defences are being withdrawn for economic reasons only, and that locally-funded defences would not simply send the water or the wave energy elsewhere – in which case wealthy communities could adversely affect poorer ones.

5.69 Governments have a responsibility to address the distributional aspect of climate change, including less tangible losses, in an explicit, open and collaborative way. **The Commission recommends that governments should initiate and sustain an informed political and public debate on the distribution of the costs of the impacts of climate change and of adaptation. This should cover the consequences of flooding and coastal erosion, the impact on communities and questions of compensation, and the costs of maintaining or improving defences. Governments should make policy decisions on the basis of this informed political and public debate.**

5.70 Equity is not just about the distribution of costs, but also about the ways in which decisions are made about those issues. A key element of good decision making is public engagement, to which we turn next.

PUBLIC ENGAGEMENT

5.71 We have stressed that the effects of climate change are felt locally. Even in a country as relatively small as the UK, for some the manifestations of climate change are already real while for others they are still a remote risk. Significant changes to localities will directly affect and shape the ways in which individuals will be able to interact with, and benefit from, their natural and social environments in the future. As one expert has said: "the implications of a changing physical environment touch the core of how individuals and cultures may define themselves and their interactions with the world around them."[11] How can society ensure that the fundamental impacts of climate change are fully debated and appropriate opportunity provided for individuals and communities to consider the implications, the decision dilemmas that arise and the need to weigh up potentially differing outcomes?

5.72 We believe that there is a need for better public access to, and debate about, issues raised by climate change projections, particularly those produced by UKCP09. If these scenarios are to inform institutional and policy responses, it is essential that all stakeholders – including members of the public – can understand them. As we discussed in Chapter 3, public responses will be dependent on people understanding what climate change means for them and their families, in their own context. This is an essential component of both the framing and learning processes.

5.73 The implications of climate change needs to be made 'real' for people. This will require considerable effort to provide multiple opportunities (both passive and active) for individuals to engage with the data and to ensure that as the scenarios develop over time there continues to be effective communication and discussion. We have seen in the example of Hampshire County Council (Box 4C) how local politicians needed to envision their local landscape in the context of a future climate similar to that currently experienced in Bordeaux in order to frame the issue of climate change and adaptation. **The Commission recommends that Defra, environmental regulators and local authorities, and the equivalent for the Devolved Administrations, pay urgent attention to the presentation of national and regional narratives or stories which describe what climate change will mean for institutions, communities and individuals, and the relevant adaptation priorities.**

5.74 Climate change adaptation must be embedded as a routine part of both public discussion and decision making on all subjects, and not as something special undertaken only by agencies or institutions focusing on climate change. People adapt to climate change in the way in which they use and engage with resources, infrastructure and the environment. So decisions about nature conservation, water resource management, coastal protection, new housing provision or sustainable transport, for example, will be where adaptation is actually implemented. We have already made a recommendation about an adaptation test to be applied to policies, programmes and plans, but there also needs to be engagement with the public in devising them. There are already requirements for public consultation on draft plans, etc., in many of these areas. However, **the Commission recommends that public authorities make greater use of discussion-based public engagement much earlier in their decision processes, to help frame the issues relevant to adaptation and to gather public concerns and views to inform decision making, as opposed to limited passive consultation on draft actions.**

5.75 This is not just about informing people. People will have important and often personal information about their local environment and their experience of engaging with it that they can bring to any discussion of appropriate adaptation strategies. So engagement with the scenarios and predictions in the local context should be a two-way process of the sharing of knowledge and information. This represents the communicative approach to learning discussed in Chapter 4 (4.101 and 4.103).

5.76 But even if more direct engagement between climate predictions and members of the public can be facilitated, there is still the problem of making adaptation a personally and socially relevant issue which gains community and individual support. Interpretations of danger are specific to particular contexts and are strongly impacted by embedded cultural and societal norms and values, world views, habitual behaviour, experience and social status. This complex interplay of impacts operates at individual decision-making levels and potentially constrains collective action.

5.77 The goals of adaptation vary according to differing attitudes to risk, to disposition (e.g. progressive versus conservative ethos) and to the adaptive capacity of future generations (optimistic versus pessimistic).[12] An interesting small study revealed that, even amongst a set of construction companies in one English region, radically different adaptation strategies were adopted by different firms in the face of the same apparent risk (increased flooding), ranging from withdrawal from the area to investment in engineering solutions.[13]

5.78 In our 27th report *Novel Materials in the Environment*[14] we introduced the concept of continual social intelligence gathering and recommended this as a desirable move beyond one-off public engagement projects in the governance of innovation. We conclude here that the challenge of building adaptive capacity around climate change has common characteristics to those that underpin the need for the governance of innovation as opposed to the simple governance of risk. Not only is adaptation to climate change an issue of significant uncertainty and complexity but there is a need to deliver both equity and efficiency (4.28-4.42).

5.79 So, our final observation is that institutions need to recognise that climate change is a social, political and normative challenge as much as a purely technical or environmental challenge. Institutions need to be sensitive to the values that may be embedded in assumptions about, for example, acceptable levels of risk and the appropriate distribution of the costs and benefits of climate change and of adaptation strategies. We have discussed this particularly in the context of issues of equity in relation to coastal zone management (3.72-3.94).

THE ADAPTATION SUB-COMMITTEE

5.80 It will be apparent that the Commission is placing much emphasis upon the possible role of the Adaptation Sub-Committee. The Sub-Committee's precise remit, roles and responsibilities are not yet fully defined. Therefore we recognise the need for the Sub-Committee to determine the extent to which it is equipped to perform effectively the tasks which we identify. In the event that the Sub-Committee does not consider itself the appropriate body to perform these tasks, the Commission recommends that another body with adequate resources and expertise be charged with fulfilling these functions.

5.81 To summarise, the Commission has addressed the following recommendations to the Adaptation Sub-Committee, which should be read in the light of the paragraph above:

- the Sub-Committee should be responsible for ensuring that appropriate and transparent systems of accountability are in place for monitoring compliance with a general adaptation duty imposed on public bodies (5.22);

- the Sub-Committee should evaluate and ensure the adequacy of the arrangements which apply to bodies which meet Defra's criteria for priority reporting bodies but are excluded from Defra's initial list of those required to report (5.24);

- the Sub-Committee should scrutinise planning policy guidance to assess and advise on the recognition within spatial planning of the importance of adapting to climate change. The Sub-Committee should also scrutinise the activities of the Infrastructure Planning Commission in the context of adaptation to climate change (5.37);

- in the context of the recommendation that organisations, including those subject to statutory duties, should review and where necessary revise their mission and objectives from an adaptation perspective, the Adaptation Sub-Committee should scrutinise the reviews of priority reporting authorities, and where necessary recommend revisions to their mission and objectives (5.40); and

- the Sub-Committee should explore the range of options available to address issues such as the loss of community, business and employment, and the disruption to health, educational and social services, which may be a direct or indirect consequence of climate change (5.64).

CONCLUSION

5.82　We welcome the fact that governments and other agencies have begun the process of addressing adaptation seriously over the last two years: since we began our study legislation has been put in place and adaptation strategies and programmes have been established. This is a good start. But much more needs be done if adaptation is to be embedded throughout all institutions, and our recommendations will help that process.

5.83　Not all adaptation efforts will deliver the expected outcome in full – institutions will get it wrong sometimes. But this does not mean those efforts be without value. A key aspect of building adaptive capacity is learning what does and does not work, and feeding this back into the process of framing and implementing the next steps in what will be a continuous journey without a defined end-point.

5.84　We fully accept that our message is a difficult one. Adaptation is complicated, and it is likely to be messy: much of what will happen cannot be predicted, or at least not with great certainty.[15] This report does not offer specific solutions to the problems that each institution will face, as these will be unique to the circumstance of each. By setting out the issues that institutions could usefully address in order to understand what climate adaptation means for them and how to build their capacity accordingly, we hope that it will be possible to build institutional capacity across the board to be better equipped to deal with the changing climate.

5.85　Finally, we offer, in Box 5A, a list of ten questions which organisations – in both the public and private sectors – might use to start their consideration of the need for adaptation. We hope that these questions will stimulate those who have not yet begun to face that challenge of adapting to climate change to do so.

BOX 5A AN INDICATIVE LIST OF TEN QUESTIONS ON ADAPTATION

1. Have you identified the possible range of impacts of climate change on the activities and responsibilities of your institution or business, and their timescales?

2. Do you understand the nature of, and limitations in, the climate projections in UKCP09?

3. Do you understand that adaptation to climate change is an open-ended process, not a single action that will solve your problems or reduce your risks?

4. Have you framed the questions and issues to be addressed adequately, so as to avoid tackling the wrong problem, or making matters worse? Do you understand how the risks posed by climate change interact with, and might change, the other risks your organisation has to respond to?

5. Have you identified options for adaptation, and devised flexible plans and strategies that can deal with uncertainty?

6. Are you embedding consideration of adaptation into your core business? Is there the right accountability for actions at the most senior levels of your organisation?

7. Are the objectives and aims of your institution fit for purpose in a changing world? Are you aware of the powers and duties affecting your institution?

8. Who are the significant other stakeholders (including members of the public) with whom you need to interact to deliver adaptation? Are there barriers (perceived or real) that might make collaboration difficult? How do you plan to negotiate these barriers?

9. Do you have mechanisms in place to listen and respond to alternative views on the ways of dealing with climate change, new ways of thinking, and ways of evaluating the success of past actions in relation to climate change?

10. Do your organisation's planning and investment cycles allow for new insights and information about climate change to be taken into account?

ALL OF WHICH WE HUMBLY SUBMIT FOR YOUR MAJESTY'S GRACIOUS CONSIDERATION

John Lawton *Chairman*

Nicholas Cumpsty

Michael Depledge

Ian Graham-Bryce

Jeffrey Jowell

Maria Lee

Peter Liss

Peter Matthews

Judith Petts

Steve Rayner

Michael Roberts

Joanne Scott

Lynda Warren

Gordon MacKerron
Economic Advisor to the Commission

John Roberts   *Secretary*

Jon Freeman

Joanna Foreman

Noel Nelson   *Secretariat*

Laura Pleasants

Rachael Yokoo-Laurence

References

CHAPTER 1

1   Royal Commission on Environmental Pollution (RCEP) (2000). *22nd report: Energy – The Changing Climate*. Available at: http://www.rcep.org.uk.

2   The [UK] Climate Change Act 2008.

3   *Key Messages from the Congress*. International Scientific Congress on Climate Change: Global Risks, Challenges and Decisions. 10-12 March 2009, Copenhagen. Available at: http://climatecongress. ku.dk/newsroom/congress_key_messages/. Accessed 13 November 2009.

4   Intergovernmental Panel on Climate Change (IPCC) (2007). *Climate Change 2007: Impacts, Adaptation and Vulnerability*. Contribution of Working Group II to the Fourth Assessment Report of the Intergovernmental Panel on Climate Change. Cambridge University Press. Pages 869-883. Available at: http://www.ipcc.ch/publications_and_data/publications_and_data_reports.htm.

5   IPCC (2001). *Climate Change 2001*. Third Assessment Report of the Intergovernmental Panel on Climate Change. Cambridge University Press. Available at: http://www.ipcc.chpublications_and_ data/publications_and_data_reports.htm

6   Richardson, K. (2009). The science is clear. *Public Service Review: Science and Technology*, Issue 4, 9.

7   The Copenhagen Accord, December 2009. Available at: http://unfccc.int/resource/docs/2009/ cop15/eng/l07.pdf. Accessed 15 January 2010.

8   Richardson (2009).

9   Dessai, S., Adger, N.W., Hulme, M., Turnpenny, J., Kohler, J. and Warren, R. (2004). Defining and experiencing dangerous climate change. *Climatic Change*, **64**, 11-25.

10 Schellnhuber, H.J., Cramer, W., Nakicenovic, N., Wigley, T. and Yohe, G. (Eds.) (2006). *Avoiding Dangerous Climate Change*. Cambridge University Press.

11 *The Pitt Review: Learning lessons from the 2007 floods*. Cabinet Office. June 2008. Available at: http:// archive.cabinetoffice.gov.uk/pittreview/thepittreview.html. Accessed 13 November 2009.

CHAPTER 2

1   Brohan, P., Kennedy, J.J., Harris, I., Tett, S.F.B. and Jones, P.D. (2005). Uncertainty estimates in regional and global observed temperature changes: A new dataset from 1850. *J. Geophys. Res.*, **111**, D12106.

2   Intergovernmental Panel on Climate Change (IPCC) (2007a). *Climate Change 2007: The Physical Science Basis*. Contribution of Working Group I to the Fourth Assessment Report of the Intergovernmental Panel on Climate Change. Cambridge University Press. Pages 235-336. Available at: http: www.ipcc.ch/publications–and–data/publications–and–data–reports.htm.

3   IPCC (2007a).

4   Jones, P.D., New, M., Parker, D.E., Martin, S. and Rigor, I.G. (1999). Surface air temperature and its variations over the last 150 years. *Reviews of Geophysics*, **37**, 173-199.

5   Jenkins, G., Murphy, J., Sexton, D., Lowe, J., Jones, P. and Kilsby, C. (2009). *UKCP09 Briefing Report*. UK Climate Projections. June 2009. See Section 2. Available at: http://ukclimateprojections. defra.gov.uk/content/view/826/519/. Accessed 4 December 2009.

6   See the Met Office website at: http://www.metoffice.gov.uk/climatechange/policymakers/policy/slowdown.html. Accessed 17 December 2009.

7   IPCC (2001). *Climate Change 2001: The Scientific Basis.* Contribution of Working Group I to the Third Assessment Report of the Intergovernmental Panel on Climate Change. Cambridge University Press. Available at: http://www.ipcc.ch/publications_and_data/publications_and_data_reports.htm.

8   IPCC (2007b). *Climate Change 2007: Synthesis Report.* Contribution of Working Groups I, II and III to the Fourth Assessment Report of the Intergovernmental Panel on Climate Change. Available at: http://www.ipcc.ch/publications_and_data/publications_and_data_reports.htm.

9   IPCC (2007a).

10   *Ibid.*

11   *Ibid.*

12   See the Met Office Heat-Health Watch website at: http://www.metoffice.gov.uk/weather/uk/heathealth/. Accessed 20 January 2010.

13   IPCC (2007a).

14   See UK Climate Projections website, Key finding: Observed trends at: http://ukclimateprojections.defra.gov.uk/content/view/512/9/. Accessed 14 January 2010.

15   Stott, P.A., Stone, D.A. and Allen, M.R. (2004). Human contribution to the European heatwave of 2003. *Nature,* **432,** 610-614.

16   See http://www.metoffice.gov.uk/climatechange/. Accessed 20 January 2010.

17   See http://www.tyndall.ac.uk/. Accessed 20 January 2010.

18   See http://ukcip.org.uk/. Accessed 20 January 2010.

19   See http://ukclimateprojections.defra.gov.uk/content/view/824/517/. Accessed 20 January 2010.

20   Dessai, S., Hulme, M., Lempert, R. and Pielke Jr., R. (2009). Climate prediction: A limit to adaptation? In: Adger, W.N., Lorenzoni, I. and O'Brien, K.L. (Eds.) (2009). *Adapting to Climate Change: Thresholds, Values and Governance.* Cambridge University Press. Pages 64-78; Heffernan, O. (2009). Asking the impossible. *Nature Reports. Climate Change.* Published online 1 July 2009. doi:10.1038/climate.2009.64.

21   IPCC (2000). *Special Report on Emission Scenarios.* See http://www.grida.no/publications/other/ipcc_sr/?src=/climate/ipcc/emission/. Accessed 19 January 2010.

22   Murphy, J.M., Booth, B.B.B., Collins, M., Harris, G.R., Sexton, D.M.H. and Webb, M.J. (2007). A methodology for probabilistic predictions of regional climate change from perturbed physics ensembles. *Phil. Trans. R. Soc. A,* **365,** 1993-2028.

23   See http://ukclimateprojections.defra.gov.uk/images/stories/Other_images/UKCP09_Review.pdf; see also http://ukclimateprojections.defra.gov.uk/content/view/824/517/; and http://ukclimateprojections.defra.gov.uk/content/view/1140/664/. Accessed 15 January 2010.

24   *Ibid.*

25   Murphy *et al.* (2007).

26   More generally, see: Berry, D.A. (1996). *Statistics: A Bayesian Perspective.* Duxbury, London.

27   Data from the UK Climate Projections. Available at: http://ukclimateprojections.defra.gov.uk/ content/view/2067/517/. Accessed 19 January 2010.

28   *Ibid.*

29   Data from the UK Climate Projections. Available at: http://ukclimateprojections.defra.gov.uk/ content/view/2068/517/. Accessed 19 January 2010.

30   IPCC (2007a).

31   *4 Degrees and Beyond. International Climate Conference.* 28-30 September 2009, Environmental Change Institute, University of Oxford. Available at: http://www.eci.ox.ac.uk/4degrees/. Accessed 5 December 2009.

32   Climate change: Prepare for global temperature rise of 4°C, warns top scientist. *Guardian,* 7 August 2008. Available at: http://www.guardian.co.uk/environment/2008/aug/06/climatechange. scienceofclimatechange. Accessed September 2009.

33   Adger, W.N., Lorenzoni, I. and O'Brien, K.L. (Eds.) (2009). *Adapting to Climate Change: Thresholds, Values and Governance.* Cambridge University Press.

34   Stott *et al.* (2004).

35   Environment Agency (2009). *Water for People and the Environment. Water Resources Strategy for England and Wales.* March 2009. Available at: http://www.environment-agency.gov.uk/research/library/ publications/40731.aspx. Accessed 5 December 2009.

36   *Ibid.*

37   See the Met Office website at: http://www.metoffice.gov.uk/climate/uk/ne/print.html. Accessed 1 February 2010.

38   Royal Commission on Environmental Pollution (RCEP) (2006). *26th report: The Urban Environment.* Paragraphs 4.76-4.86. Available at: http://www.rcep.org.uk.

39   See the Environment Agency website on bathing water quality at: http://www.environment-agency.gov.uk/research/library/data/34381.aspx#improve . Accessed 21 January 2010.

40   See the Met Office website at: http://www.metoffice.gov.uk/corporate/pressoffice/2009/ ht20091123.html?zoneid=79048. Accessed 21 December 2009.

41   *The Pitt Review: Learning lessons from the 2007 floods.* Cabinet Office. June 2008. Available at: http:// archive.cabinetoffice.gov.uk/pittreview/thepittreview.html. Accessed 13 November 2009.

42   House of Commons Environment Committee (1992). *Coastal Zone Protection and Planning.* Volume 1, Session 1991-92. HMSO, London.

43   Box 2D has been adapted from *The Earth in Our Hands No. 7. Coastal Erosion* published by the Geological Society of London (2001).

44   Evidence from Commission visit to the Gower Peninsula, Wales, December 2008, organised by the National Trust.

45   Evidence from Commission visit to Happisburgh, Norfolk, February 2009.

46   See the Met Office website at: http://www.metoffice.gov.uk/corporate/pressoffice/anniversary/ floods1953.html. Accessed 1 February 2010.

47   Clayton, K.M. (1989). Sediment inputs from the north Norfolk cliffs, Eastern England – A century of coast protection and its effect. *Journal of Coastal Research,* **5**, 433-442.

48   Klein, R.J.T., Nicholls, R.J., Ragoonaden, S., Capobianco, M., Aston, J. and Buckley, E.N. (2001). Technological options for adaptation to climate change in coastal zones. *Journal of Coastal Research*, **17**(3), 531-543.

49   Reproduced from *RSPB Reserves 2009*, 34: Restoring the Ribble Saltmarshes. Available at: http://www.rspb.org.uk/Images/reserves1_tcm9-229499.pdf. Accessed 21 January 2010.

50   Stern, N. (2007). *The Economics of Climate Change. The Stern Review*. Cambridge University Press. Page 93.

51   Lawton, J.H. (2000). Community Ecology in a Changing World. *Excellence in Ecology 11*. Ecology Institute, Oldendorf/Luhe, Germany.

52   Gaston, K.J. (Ed.) (2009). Geographic range limits of species. *Proceedings of the Royal Society B*, **276**, 1391-2911.

53   Huntley, B., Green, R.E., Collingham, Y.C. and Willis, S.G. (2007). *A Climatic Atlas of European Breeding Birds*. Published as a partnership between Durham University, the Royal Society for the Protection of Birds and Lynx Edicions in association with the University of Cambridge, BirdLife International and the European Bird Census Council. Lynx Edicions, Barcelona.

54   Walmsley, C.A., Smithers, R.J., Berry, P.M., Harley, M., Stevenson, M.J. and Catchpole, R. (Eds.) (2007). *MONARCH – Modelling Natural Resource Responses to Climate Change – A synthesis for biodiversity conservation*. UK Climate Impacts Programme, Oxford.

55   Huntley *et al.* (2007).

56   Walmsley *et al.* (2007).

57   Huntley *et al.* (2007).

58   Evidence received from the Centre for Ecology and Hydrology (CEH), January 2009. Available at: www.rcep.org.uk.

59   *Ibid.*

60   Berthold, P. (1996). *Control of Bird Migration*. Chapman and Hall, London.

61   Bearhop, S., Fiedler, W., Furness, R.W., Votier, S.C., Wladron, S., Newton, J., Bowen, G.J., Berthold, P. and Farnsworth, K. (2005). Assortative mating as a mechanism for rapid evolution of a migratory divide. *Science,* **310**, 502-504.

62   Hopkins, J.J., Allison, H.M., Walmsley, C.A., Gaywood, M. and Thurgate, G. (2007). *Conserving Biodiversity in a Changing Climate: Guidance on building capacity to adapt*. Department for Environment, Food and Rural Affairs (Defra) on behalf of the UK Biodiversity Partnership, London; evidence received from the British Ecological Society (BES), January 2009; CEH, January 2009; Natural England, November 2008; and the Wildlife Trusts, January 2009. Available at: http://www.rcep.org.uk.

63   Parmesan, C. and Yohe, G. (2003). A globally coherent fingerprint of climate change impacts across natural systems. *Nature,* **421**, 37-42.

64   Hopkins *et al.* (2007).

65   See for example: Thomas, C.D. and Jones, P.M. (1993). Partial recovery of a skipper butterfly (*Hesperis comma*) from population refuges: Lessons for conservation in fragmented landscapes. *Journal of Animal Ecology*, **62**, 472-481.

66 Willis, S.G., Hill, J.K., Thomas, C.D., Roy, D.B., Fox, R., Blakeley, D.S. and Huntley, B. (2009). Assisted colonization in a changing climate: A test-study using two UK butterflies. *Conservation Letters*, **2**(1), 45-52.

67 Eaton, M.A., Brown, A.F., Noble, D.G., Musgrove, A.J., Hearn, R.D., Aebisher, N.J., Gibbons, D.W., Evans, A. and Gregory, R.D. (2009). Birds of conservation concern. 3: The population status of birds in the United Kingdom, Channel Islands and Isle of Man. *British Birds*, **102**, 296-341.

68 Thomas, C.D., Cameron, A., Green, R.E., Bakkenes, M., Beaumont, L.J., Collingham, Y.C., Erasmus, B.F.N., Ferreira de Siqueira, M., Grainger, A., Hannah, L., Hughes, L., Huntley, B., van Jaarsveld, A.S., Midgely, G.F., Miles, L., Ortega-Huerta, M.A., Peterson, A.T., Phillips, O.L. and Williams, S.E. (2004). Extinction risk from climate change. *Nature*, **427**, 145-148.

69 Maclean, I.M.D., Austin, G.E., Rehfisch, M.M., Blew, J., Crowe, O., Delany, S., Devos, K., Deceuninck, B., Günther, K., Laursen, K., van Roomen, M. and Wahl, J. (2008). Climate change causes rapid changes in the distribution and site abundance of birds in winter. *Global Change Biology*, **14**, 2489-2500.

70 Evidence received from Defra, December 2008. Available at: http://www.rcep.org.uk.

71 *Ibid.*

72 *Ibid.*

73 Evidence received from CEH, January 2009. Available at: http://www.rcep.org.uk.

74 Marris, E. (2009). Planting the forest of the future. *Nature*, **459**, 905-908; evidence received from CEH, January 2009; the Forestry Commission, January 2009; the Royal Society for the Protection of Birds (RSPB), January 2009; and the Woodland Trust, November 2008. Available at: http://www.rcep.org.uk.

75 Hopkins *et al.* (2007); evidence received from CEH, January 2009; and Natural England, November 2008. Available at: http://www.rcep.org.uk.

76 Both, C., Bouwhuis, S., Lessells, C.M. and Visser, M.E. (2006). Climate change and population declines in a long-distance migratory bird. *Nature*, **441**, 81-83.

77 Møller, A.P., Rubolini, D. and Lehikoinen, E. (2008). Populations of migratory bird species that did not show phonological response to climate change are declining. *PNAS*, **105**, 16195-16200.

78 Lawton (2000).

79 Hopkins *et al.* (2007).

80 Mitchell, R.J., Morecroft, M.D., Acreman, M., Crick, H.Q.P., Frost, M., Harley, M., Maclean, I.M.D., Mountford, O., Piper, J., Pontier, H., Rehfisch, M.M., Ross, L.C., Smithers, R.J., Stott, A., Walmsley, C.A., Watts, O. and Wilson, E. (2007). *England Biodiversity Strategy – Towards adaptation to climate change*. Final Report to Defra for research contract CRO327.

81 Hopkins *et al.* (2007).

82 Smithers, R.J., Cowan, C., Harley, M., Hopkins, J.J., Pontier, H. and Watts, O. (2008). *England Biodiversity Strategy: Climate Change Adaptation Principles*. Published by Defra.

83 Hopkins *et al.* (2007).

84 Evidence from Commission visit to the Thames Barrier, 29 January 2009.

85 Lee, M. (2001). Coastal defence and the Habitats Directive: Predictions of habitat change in England and Wales. *The Geographical Journal*, **167**(1), 39-56.

86   Millennium Ecosystem Assessment (2005). *Ecosystems and Human Well-being*. Island Press, Washington DC.

87   European Commission (2009). *Adapting to Climate Change: Towards a European framework for action.* White Paper. COM(2009)147 Final. Commission of the European Communities, Brussels.

88   Eigenbrod, F., Anderson, B.J., Armsworth, P.R., Heinemeyer, A., Jackson, S.F., Parnell, M., Thomas, C.D. and Gaston, K.J. (2009). Ecosystem service benefits of contrasting conservation strategies in a human-dominated landscape. *Proceedings of the Royal Society B*, **276**, 2903-2911.

89   Peterson, G. (2009). Ecological limits of adaptation to climate change. In: Adger *et al.* (2009), pages 25-41.

90   Eigenbrod *et al.* (2009).

91   For example, evidence received from BES, January 2009; CEH, January 2009; Defra, December 2008; the Joint Nature Conservation Committee, January 2009; Natural England, November 2008; RSPB, January 2009; and the Woodland Trust, November 2008. Available at: http://www.rcep.org.uk.

CHAPTER 3

1   European Commission (2009a). *Adapting to Climate Change: Towards a European framework for action.* White Paper. COM(2009)147 Final. Commission of the European Communities, Brussels.

2   See http://europa.eu/rapid/pressReleasesAction.do?reference=SPEECH/09/401&format=HTML&aged=0&language=EN&guiLanguage=en, and http://ec.europa.eu/commission_designate_2009-2014/mission_letters/pdf/hedegaard_climate_en.pdf. Accessed 18 January 2010.

3   Committee on Climate Change (2009). *Preparing for Climate Change: Adaptation Sub-Committee Work Programme*. December 2009. Available at: http://hmccc.s3.amazonaws.com/ASC/ASC%20Booklet%20-%20SCREEN.pdf. Accessed 18 January 2010.

4   See Part 4 of the Climate Change Act 2008 and Part 5, Chapter 1 of the Climate Change (Scotland) Act 2009.

5   For further details of the Adaptation Sub-Committee (ASC) see: http://www.theccc.org.uk/asc-home. Accessed 6 January 2010.

6   See generally Part 4 of the Climate Change (Scotland) Act 2009 for further details.

7   Department for Environment, Food and Rural Affairs (Defra) (2009a). *Adapting to Climate Change: Ensuring Progress in Key Sectors*. Available at: http://www.defra.gov.uk/environment/climate/documents/ensuring-progress.pdf. Accessed 6 January 2010.

8   Figure 3 in National Audit Office (NAO) (2009). *Adapting to Climate Change. A Review for the Environmental Audit Committee*. July 2009.

9   NAO (2009), Figure 4, and based on information from the Adapting to Climate Change Programme.

10   NAO (2009), Figure 8, and based on information from Government departments.

11   NAO (2009).

12   Scottish Government (2009a). *Scotland's Climate Change Adaptation Framework*. Available at: http://www.scotland.gov.uk/Topics/Environment/climatechange/scotlands-action/adaptation/AdaptaitonFramework/TheFramework. Accessed 17 January 2010.

13   *Ibid*, page 12.

14   For further details of the Living With Environmental Change initiative see: http://www.nerc.ac.uk/research/programmes/lwec/. Accessed 15 December 2005.

15   Cabinet Office (2008). *The National Risk Register.* Available at: http://www.cabinetoffice.gov.uk/media/cabinetoffice/corp/assets/publications/reports/national_risk_register/national_risk_register.pdf. Accessed 19 January 2010.

16   Department of Health (2009). *Heatwave Plan for England 2009.* May 2009. Available at: http://www.dh.gov.uk/en/Publicationsandstatistics/Publications/PublicationsPolicyAndGuidance/DH_099015. Accessed 5 December 2009.

17   Welsh Assembly Government (2009a). *Heatwave Plan for Wales 2009: A framework for preparedness and response.* Available at: http://new.wales.gov.uk/topics/health/ocmo/publications/cmo/cmo09/heatwave/. Accessed 21 December 2009.

18   Defra (2008a). *The Government's Response to Sir Michael Pitt's Review of the Summer 2007 Floods.* December 2008. Available at: http://www.defra.gov.uk/environment/flooding/documents/risk/govtresp-topitt.pdf. Accessed 5 December 2009.

19   See http://www.defra.gov.uk/environment/climate/adaptation/assess-risk.htm. Accessed 19 January 2010.

20   Defra (2009a).

21   *Ibid.*

22   Department for Communities and Local Government (CLG) (2006a). *Strong and Prosperous Communities – The Local Government White Paper.* October 2006. Available at: http://www.communities.gov.uk/publications/localgovernment/strongprosperous. Accessed 5 December 2009.

23   Town and Country Planning Association (TCPA) (2009). *Helping to Deliver Climate Change Adaptation through the UK Planning System.* Available at: http://www.rcep.org.uk/reports/28-adaptation/documents/TCPA%20reportforRCEP.pdf. Accessed 14 January 2010.

24   The Planning Act 2008, Section 181.

25   The Local Democracy, Economic Development and Construction Act 2009, Section 70(4).

26   The Planning Act 2008, Section 182.

27   The Climate Change (Scotland) Act 2009, Sections 44(1)(b) and 53.

28   CLG (2007). *Planning Policy Statement: Planning and Climate Change – Supplement to Planning Policy Statement 1.* December 2007. Available at: http://www.communities.gov.uk/planningandbuilding/planning/planningpolicyguidance/planningpolicystatements/planningpolicystatements/ppsclimatechange/. Accessed 5 December 2009.

29   Welsh Assembly Government (2004). *Technical Advice Note (TAN) 15: Development and Flood Risk.* Available at: http://wales.gov.uk/topics/planning/policy/tans/tan15?lang=en. Accessed 21 December 2009.

30   Welsh Assembly Government (2009b). *Technical Advice Note (TAN) 12: Design.* Available at: http://wales.gov.uk/topics/planning/policy/tans/tan12/?lang=en. Accessed 21 December 2009.

31   Scottish Government (2009b). *National Planning Framework for Scotland 2.* Available at: http://www.scotland.gov.uk/Publications/2009/07/02105627/0. Accessed 11 January 2010.

32   Welsh Assembly Government (2009c). *Revised Technical Advice Note (TAN) 5: Nature Conservation and Planning.* September 2009. Available at: http://wales.gov.uk/topics/planning/policy/tans/tan5/;jsessionid=FZQsLh6MBlWLGzz42JCchy0kQsf3Frfrzr2VBsHMVT1Ychcdpd0k!1963699030?lang=en. Accessed 5 December 2009.

33   Scottish Government (2009a).

34   Defra (2005). *Making Space for Water. Taking forward a new Government strategy for flood and coastal erosion risk management in England.* First Government response to the autumn 2004 *Making space for water* consultation exercise. March 2005. Available at: http://www.defra.gov.uk/environment/flooding/documents/policy/strategy/strategy-response1.pdf. Accessed 5 December 2009.

35   CLG (2006b). *Planning Policy Statement 25: Development and Flood Risk.* December 2006. Available at: http://www.communities.gov.uk/planningandbuilding/planning/planningpolicyguidance/planningpolicystatements/planningpolicystatements/pps25/. Accessed 5 December 2009.

36   Environment Agency (2009a). *Flooding in England: A National Assessment of Flood Risk.* Available at: http://publications.environment-agency.gov.uk/pdf/GEHO0609BQDS-E-E.pdf. Accessed 18 January 2010.

37   Welsh Assembly Government (2004).

38   CLG (2009a). *World Class Places – The Government's strategy for improving the quality of place.* Available at: http://www.communities.gov.uk/documents/planningandbuilding/pdf/1229344.pdf. Accessed 14 December 2009.

39   TCPA (2009), page 94.

40   The Local Democracy, Economic Development and Construction Act 2009, Section 77(2); The Planning Act 2008, Section 6(6).

41   CLG (2009a).

42   For further details of the ESPACE Project see: http://www.espace-project.org/. Accessed 15 December 2009.

43   The Planning Act 2008, Section 10.

44   *Ibid*, Section 5(5).

45   *Ibid*, Section 104(7).

46   For further details of the Department of Energy and Climate Change's consultation on the draft National Policy Statements for energy infrastructure see: https://www.energynpsconsultation.decc.gov.uk/. Accessed 17 January 2010.

47   Defra (2008b). *Future Water. The Government's water strategy for England.* Cm 7319. February 2008. Available at: http://www.defra.gov.uk/Environment/quality/water/strategy/pdf/future-water.pdf. Accessed 5 December 2009.

48   Environment Agency (2009b). *Water for People and the Environment. Water Resources Strategy for England and Wales.* March 2009. Available at: http://www.environment-agency.gov.uk/research/library/publications/40731.aspx. Accessed 6 December 2009.

49   European Commission (2009a).

50   European Commission (2009b). *Common Implementation Strategy for the Water Framework Directive (2000/60/EC). Guidance Document No. 24: River Basin Management in a Changing Climate.* Technical Report 2009-040. November 2009.

51   Ofwat (2009). *Final Determination of Price Limits*. Available at: http://www.ofwat.gov.uk/pricereview/pr09phase3/prs_web_pr09fd. Accessed 11 January 2010.

52   Defra (2008b).

53   Welsh Assembly Government (2009d). *Strategic Policy Position on Water*. Available at: http://wales.gov.uk/topics/environmentcountryside/epq/waterflooding/policystatement/?lang=en. Accessed 11 January 2010.

54   Personal communication from Professor Peter Matthews, Member of the Royal Commission on Environmental Pollution.

55   Defra (2005).

56   *The Pitt Review: Learning lessons from the 2007 floods*. Cabinet Office. June 2008. Available at: http://archive.cabinetoffice.gov.uk/pittreview/thepittreview.html. Accessed 13 November 2009.

57   The Flood Risk Regulations SI 3042/2009.

58   The Flood Risk Management (Scotland) Act 2009. Available at: http://www.opsi.gov.uk/legislation/scotland/acts2009/pdf/asp_20090006_en.pdf. Accessed 5 December 2009.

59   Directive 2007/60/EC of the European Parliament and of the Council on the assessment and management of flood risks. *Official Journal of the European Union*, **288**, 6 November 2007, page 27. Available at: http://eur-lex.europa.eu/LexUriServ/LexUriServ.do?uri=OJ:L:2007:288:0027:0034:EN:PDF. Accessed 5 December 2009.

60   The Flood and Water Management Bill 2009, Clause 3 (as introduced in the House of Commons).

61   Photograph: Sir John Lawton, 2009.

62   For further details of TE2100 see: http://www.environment-agency.gov.uk/homeandleisure/floods/104695.aspx. Accessed 21 January 2010.

63   Nicholson-Cole, S. and O'Riordan, T. (2009). Adaptive governance for a changing coastline: Science, policy and the public in search of a sustainable future. In: Adger, W.N., Lorenzoni, I. and O'Brien, K.L. (Eds.) (2009). *Adapting to Climate Change: Thresholds, Values and Governance*. Cambridge University Press. Pages 368-383.

64   Department of Environment Northern Ireland (2006). *An Integrated Coastal Zone Strategy for Northern Ireland*. Available at: http://www.doeni.gov.uk/index/protect_the_environment/natural_environment/marine_and_coast/integrated_coastal2.htm. Accessed 11 January 2010.

65   CoastNet (2007). *Scoping Study Regarding Current Coastal Activity and the National ICZM Programme, and Implications for East of England*. Prepared by CoastNet for the Sustainable Development Round Table – East. Available at: http://library.coastweb.info/967/. Accessed 5 December 2009.

66   Foresight (2004). *Future Flooding*. Available at: www.foresight.gov.uk/OurWork/Completed-Projects/Flood/index.asp. Accessed 5 December 2009.

67   Defra (2005).

68   For further details see: http://www.defra.gov.uk/environment/flooding/manage/index.htm. Accessed 11 January 2010.

69   For further details see: http://www.defra.gov.uk/environment/flooding/manage/propertylevel.htm. Accessed 11 January 2010.

70   CLG (2006b).

71   Defra (2001). *Guidance on Shoreline Management Plans. Volumes 1 and 2*. Available at: http://www.defra.gov.uk/environment/flooding/policy/guidance/smp.htm. Accessed 6 December 2009.

72   For further details of the UK Futurecoast Project (2002) see: http://www.coastalwiki.org/coastalwiki/FUTURECOAST_project,_UK. Accessed 6 December 2009.

73   Foresight (2004).

74   CLG (2009b). *Consultation Paper on a New Planning Policy on Development and Coastal Change.* July 2009. Available at: http://www.communities.gov.uk/archived/publications/planningandbuilding/consultationcoastal. Accessed 6 December 2009.

75   Adger *et al.* (2009).

76   Milligan, J., O'Riordan, T., Watkinson, A., Amundsen, H. and Parkinson, S. (2006). *Implications of the draft Shoreline Management Plan 3b on North Norfolk Coastal Communities.* Final report to North Norfolk District Council. Tyndall Centre for Climate Change Research, Norwich. Cited in: O'Riordan, T., Nicholson-Cole, S.A. and Milligan, J. (2008). Designing sustainable coastal futures. *21st Century Society*, **3**(2), 145-157.

77   Photograph taken by Secretariat during the Commission visit to Happisburgh, Norfolk, February 2009.

78   O'Riordan *et al.* (2008).

79   Nicholson-Cole and O'Riordan (2009).

80   Defra (2009b). *Consultation on Coastal Change Policy.* June 2009. Available at: http://www.defra.gov.uk/corporate/consult/coastal-change/index.htm. Accessed 6 December 2009.

81   *Ibid.*

82   CLG (2009b).

83   For further details see: http://www.defra.gov.uk/environment/flooding/manage/pathfinder/index.htm. Accessed 18 January 2010.

84   Personal communication from Professor Lynda Warren, Member of the Royal Commission on Environmental Pollution.

85   Defra/Natural England (2008). *Securing Biodiversity. A new framework for delivering priority habitats and species in England.* Natural England. Available at: http://www.naturalengland.org.uk/ourwork/conservation/biodiversity/protectandmanage/framework.aspx. Accessed 6 December 2009.

86   For example, see the latest summary report on the Living Landscapes initiative: The Wildlife Trusts (2009). *A Living Landscape. A call to restore the UK's battered ecosystems, for wildlife and people.* Available at: http://www.wildlifetrusts.org/?section=environment:livinglandscapes. Accessed 6 December 2009.

87   Natural England (2009). *Responding to the Impacts of Climate Change on the Natural Environment.* Natural England Reports NE114, NE115, NE116 and NE117.

CHAPTER 4

1   Brooks, N. and Adger, W.N. (2005). Assessing and enhancing adaptive capacity. In: Lim, B. and Spanger-Siegfried, E. (Eds.) (2005). *Adaptation Policy Frameworks for Climate Change: Developing Strategies, Policies and Measures*. Pages 165-181. UNDP-GEF. Cambridge University Press.

2   The information in Figure 4-I is adapted from Stirling, A. (2008). Science, precaution and the politics of technological risk: Converging implications in evolutionary and social and scientific perspectives. *Annals of the New York Academy of Sciences*, **1128**, 95-110.

3   Environment Agency (2009). *Thames Estuary 2100*. Available at: http://www.environment-agency. gov.uk/homeandleisure/floods/. Accessed 6 December 2009.

4   Page, S.E. (2006). Path dependence. *Quarterly Journal of Political Science*, **1**, 87-115. ISSN 1554-0626; DOI 10.1561/100.00000006.

5   O'Riordan, T. and Jordan, A. (1999). Institutions, climate change and cultural theory: Towards a common analytical framework. *Global Environmental Change*, **9**, 81-94.

6   UN World Commission on Environment and Development (1987). *Our Common Future ('The Brundtland Report')*. Oxford University Press. Page 9.

7   For further details see: http://www.ceh.ac.uk/products/software/RIVPACS.html. Accessed 9 December 2009.

8   Personal communication from the Department for Environment, Food and Rural Affairs (Defra), 2009, and Professor R. Clarke, 2010.

9   Evidence received at a joint Town and Country Planning Association – Royal Commission on Environmental Pollution (TCPA–RCEP) workshop on *Helping to Deliver Climate Change Adaptation through the UK Planning System*, 28 July 2009. Report available at: http://www.rcep.org.uk/ reports/28adaptation/documents/TCPA%20workshopreport.pdf. Accessed 10 December 2009.

10 Evidence received from the Manhood Peninsula Steering Group, October 2008. Available at: http://www.rcep.org.uk.

11 Evidence from Commission visit to Happisburgh, Norfolk, February 2009.

12 Evidence received from the Coastal Concern Action Group and the Manhood Peninsula Steering Group, October 2008. Available at: http://www.rcep.org.uk.

13 Adger, W.N., Lorenzoni, I. and O'Brien, K. (2009). *Adapting to Climate Change: Thresholds, Values, Governance*. Cambridge University Press.

14 Walker, G., Burningham, K., Fielding, J., Smith, G., Thrush, D. and Fay, H. (2006). *Addressing Environmental Inequalities: Flood Risk*. Science Report: SC020061/SR1. Environment Agency, Bristol.

15 House of Commons Communities and Local Government Committee (2006-07 Session). *Second report: Coastal Towns*. Available at: http://www.parliament.the-stationery-office.co.uk/pa/ cm200607/cmselect/cmcomloc/351/35102.htm. Accessed 9 December 2009.

16 West, C.C. and Gawith, M.J. (Eds.) (2005). *Measuring progress. Preparing for climate change through the UK Climate Impacts Programme. UKCIP Technical Report*. UKCIP, Oxford. Cited in evidence received from Dr Emma Tompkins of the University of Leeds, September 2008. Available at: http://www. rcep.org.uk.

17 Defra (2009a). *Consultation on Coastal Change Policy*. Available at: http://www.defra.gov.uk/corporate/ consult/coastal-change/consultation-doc.pdf. Accessed 10 December 2009.

123

18   Cooper, J.A.G. and McKenna, J. (2008). Social justice in coastal erosion management: the temporal and spatial dimensions. *Geoforum, 39*(1), 294-306.

19   HM Treasury (2003). *The Green Book: Appraisal and Evaluation in Central Government.* TSO, London. Available at: http://www.hm-treasury.gov.uk/d/green_book_complete.pdf. Accessed 10 December 2009.

20   See Committee on Radioactive Waste Management website: http://www.corwm.org.uk. Accessed 10 December 2009.

21   Berkhout, F., Hertin, J. and Gann, D. (2006). Learning to adapt: Organisational adaptation to climate change impacts. *Climate Change, 78*, 135-156.

22   See for example, see the British Council's pages on Customer Service Orientation at: http://www.britishcouncil.org/professionals-work-customer-service-orientation-1.htm. Accessed 10 December 2009.

23   See, for example, the European Foundation for Quality Management (EFQM), and the British Quality Foundation websites at: http://ww1.efqm.org/en/ and http://www.quality-foundation.co.uk/ respectively. Accessed 10 December 2009.

24   Ciminero, S.M. (1997). Anglian Water: Customer Service Transformation. *The Harvard Business School,* April 9, Report N9-897-093.

25   Adger *et al.* (2009).

26   Written communication from Roger Street (2008).

27   For example: Welford, R. (1995). *Environmental Strategy and Sustainable Development: The Corporate Challenge for the 21st Century.* Routledge, London.

28   See Ofwat website on climate change at: http://www.ofwat.gov.uk/sustainability/climatechange. Accessed 5 January 2010.

29   Ofwat (2009). *Final Determination of Price Limits.* Available at: http://www.ofwat.gov.uk/pricereview/pr09phase3/prs_web_pr09fd. Accessed 11 January 2010.

30   Adger *et al.* (2009).

31   Berkhout *et al.* (2006).

32   Evidence received from the Forestry Commission, October 2008.

33   Tompkins, E.L., Boyd, E., Nicholson-Cole, S.A., Weatherhead, K., Arnell, N.W. and Adger, W.N. (2005). *Linking Adaptation Research and Practice.* A report submitted to Defra as part of the Climate Change Impacts and Adaptation Cross-Regional Research Programme. Tyndall Centre for Climate Change Research, University of East Anglia.

34   See, for example, the Millennium Ecosystem Assessment project at: http://www.millenniumassessment.org/en/index.aspx. Accessed 13 January 2010.

35   See the Exmoor Mire Restoration project at: http://www.exmoor-nationalpark.gov.uk/mire. Accessed 15 January 2010.

36   Department for Communities and Local Government (CLG) (2007). *Planning Policy Statement: Planning and Climate Change – Supplement to Planning Policy Statement 1.* December 2007. Available at: http://www.communities.gov.uk/documents/planningandbuilding/pdf/ppsclimatechange.pdf. Accessed 11 December 2009.

37   There is an extensive literature on this subject. See, for example: Bulkeley, H. (2000). Common knowledge? Public understanding of climate change in Newcastle, Australia. *Public Understanding of Science*, **9**, 313-333; and Lorenzoni, I., Nicholson-Cole, S. and Whitmarsh, L. (2007). Barriers perceived to engaging with climate change among the UK public and their policy implications. *Global Environmental Change*, **17**(3-4), 445-459.

38   Lorenzoni, I. and Pidgeon, N. (2006). Public views on climate change: European and US perspectives. *Climatic Change*, **77**(10-2), 73-95.

39   Niemeyer, S., Petts, J. and Hobson, K. (2005). Rapid climate change and society: Assessing responses and thresholds. *Risk Analysis*, **25**(6), 1443-1456.

40   For example: Slovic, P. (1987). Perception of risk. *Science*, **236**, 280-285; Slovic, P. (2000). *The Perception of Risk*. Earthscan, London; and Grothmann, T. and Reusswig, F. (2006). People at risk from flooding: Why some residents take precautionary action while others do not. *Natural Hazards*, **38**, 101-120.

41   Defra (2009a).

42   See for example: Pateman, C. (1990). *Participation and Democratic Theory*. Cambridge University Press; Renn, O., Webler, T. and Wiedemann, P. (Eds.) (1995). *Fairness and Competence in Citizen Participation: Evaluating Methods for Environmental Discourse*. Kluwer Academic, Dordrecht; Renn, O., Webler, T. and Kastenholz, H. (1998). Procedural and substantive fairness in landfill siting: A Swiss case study. In: R. Lofstedt and L. Frewer (Eds.) (1998). *Risk and Modern Society*. Earthscan, London; Petts, J. (2001). Evaluating the effectiveness of deliberative processes: Waste management case studies. *Journal of Environmental Planning and Management*, **44**(2), 207-226; and Bloomfield, J.A., Collins, K., Fry, C. and Munton, R. (2001). Deliberation and inclusion: Vehicles for increasing trust in UK public governance? *Environment and Planning C*, **19**, 501-513.

43   Adger *et al.* (2009).

44   Report of the RCEP seminar in Edinburgh (2008) on *Institutional Capacity for Adaptation to Climate Change – Synergies, Gaps, Conflicts and Incentives in Scotland and Northern Ireland*. Available at: http://www.rcep.org.uk/reports/28-adaptation/documents/2008-11-27%20Scotland%20Seminar%20-%20Final%20Report.pdf. Accessed 10 December 2009.

45   TCPA–RCEP workshop report (2009).

46   Personal communication from Dr. Tim O'Riordan, 2009.

47   RCEP (2007). *26th report: The Urban Environment*. Paragraphs 6.85-6.88. Available online at: http://www.rcep.org.uk/reports/26-urban/documents/urban-environment.pdf. Accessed 10 December 2009.

48   TCPA–RCEP workshop report (2009).

49   Evidence from Commission visit to Happisburgh, Norfolk, February 2009.

50   Defra (2009a).

51   Evidence received from the Coastal Concern Action Group, October 2008.

52   Defra (2009b). *Policy Statement: Appraisal of Flood and Coastal Erosion Risk Management*. Available at: http://www.defra.gov.uk/environment/flooding/documents/policy/guidance/erosion-manage.pdf. Accessed 10 December 2009.

53   *The Pitt Review: Learning lessons from the 2007 floods. Cabinet Office, June 2008*. Available at: http://archive.cabinetoffice.gov.uk/pittreview/thepittreview.html. Accessed 13 November 2009.

54   Gibson, J. (2009). *Legal Liabilities for Coastal Erosion and Flooding in the United Kingdom due to Climate Change*. Report for the Royal Commission on Environmental Pollution. Available at: http://www.rcep.org.uk.

55   UK Environmental Law Association (UKELA) (2009). Flooding and private rights. *e-Law Bulletin*, **49** (January 2009).

56   *Holbeck Hall Hotel Ltd. and Another v Scarborough Borough Council* (2000). Q.B. 836.

57   The Human Rights Act (1998). Schedule 1. Office of Public Sector Information (OPSI). Available at: http://www.opsi.gov.uk/ACTS/acts1998/ukpga_19980042_en_1. Accessed 18 January 2010.

58   *Marcic v Thames Water Utilities* (2003). 3 WLR 1603.

59   Defra (2009b).

60   ABI/Government Statement (2008). *Flooding and Insurance for England*. Available at: http://www.abi.org.uk/Information/40469.pdf. Accessed 10 December 2009.

61   HM Treasury (2007). *Financial Inclusion Action Plan*. Available at: http://www.hm-treasury.gov.uk/d/financialinclusion_actionplan061207.pdf. Accessed 10 December 2009.

62   Defra (2009a).

63   See Defra Coastal Change Pathfinders website at: http://www.defra.gov.uk/environment/flooding/manage/pathfinder/index.htm. Accessed 18 January 2010.

64   Bandura, A. (1977). *Social Learning Theory*. Prentice Hall, London.

65   Mezirow, J. (1994). Understanding transformation theory. *Adult Education Quarterly*, **44**(4), 222-232.

66   Bull, R., Petts, J. and Evans, J. (2008). Social learning from public engagement: Dreaming the impossible? *Journal of Environmental Planning and Management*, **51**(5), 701-716.

67   TCPA–RCEP workshop report (2009).

68   Trades Union Congress (TUC) (2009). *Changing work in a changing climate. Adaptation to climate change in the UK – New research on implications for employment*. Produced by AEA for TUC. Available at: http://www.tuc.org.uk/extras/adaptation.pdf. Accessed 10 December 2009.

69   *Ibid.*

70   Evidence received from the Audit Commission, October 2008. Available at: http://www.rcep.org.uk.

71   CLG (2007).

72   See SNIFFER website at: http://www.sniffer.org.uk/. Accessed 10 December 2009.

CHAPTER 5

1   Department for Communities and Local Government (CLG) (2009). *Multi-criteria analysis: A manual*. January 2009. Available at: http://www.communities.gov.uk/publications/corporate/multicriteriaanalysismanual. Accessed 18 January 2010.

2   Department for Environment, Food and Rural Affairs (Defra) (2007). *An Introductory Guide to Valuing Ecosystems Services*. Available at: http://www.defra.gov.uk/wildlife-pets/policy/natural-environ/documents/eco-valuing.pdf. Accessed 22 December 2009.

3   HM Treasury (2003). *The Green Book: Appraisal and Evaluation in Central Government*. TSO, London. Available at: http://www.hm-treasury.gov.uk/d/green_book_complete.pdf. Accessed 10 December 2009.

4   Greater London Authority Act 2007, amending various sections of the Greater London Authority Act 1999. Available at: http://www.opsi.gov.uk/Acts/acts2007/pdf/ukpga_20070024_en.pdf. Accessed 5 January 2010.

5   Defra (2009). *Departmental Adaptation Plans: Guidance for Government Departments.*

6   Government Office for London (2008). More information available at http://www.gos.gov.uk/gol/Environment_rural/Environmental_issues/climate_change/813469/813471/. Accessed 22 December 2009.

7   Royal Commission on Environmental Pollution (RCEP) (2007). *26th report: The Urban Environment.* Available at: http://www.rcep.org.uk; and oral evidence from CLG, June 2009.

8   Defra (2009).

9   National Audit Office (2009). *Adapting to Climate Change. A review for the Environmental Audit Committee.* July 2009. Available at: http://www.nao.org.uk/publications/0809/adapting_to_climate_change.aspx#. Accessed 22 December 2009.

10   *Ibid.*

11   Adger, W.N., Lorenzoni, I. and O'Brien, K.L. (Eds.) (2009). *Adapting to Climate Change: Thresholds, Values, Governance.* Cambridge University Press. Page 349.

12   *Ibid.*

13   Berkhout, F., Hertin, J. and Gann, D.M. (2006). Learning to adapt: Organisational adaptation to climate change impacts. *Climatic Change,* **78**(1), 135-156.

14   RCEP (2008). *27th report: Novel Materials in the Environment: The case of nanotechnology.* Available at: http://www.rcep.org.uk.

15   Ney, S. (2009). *Resolving Messy Policy Problems: Handling Conflict in Environmental, Transport, Health and Ageing Policy.* Earthscan, London.

Appendix A

ANNOUNCEMENT OF THE STUDY AND INVITATION TO SUBMIT EVIDENCE

A1 ANNOUNCEMENT OF THE STUDY

The Royal Commission study on adapting institutions to climate change was announced in a news release on 19 October 2007 in the following terms. Nearly 200 organisations were invited to respond to issues described below, and around 80 responses were received.

ROYAL COMMISSION STUDY ON ADAPTING INSTITUTIONS TO CLIMATE CHANGE

The next study by the Royal Commission on Environmental Pollution will address the question of how UK institutions can adapt to climate change.

Following a very positive response to the shortlist the Royal Commission published in July this year, the decision was made to undertake a study on *Adapting the UK to Climate Change*. The comments received on the shortlist were substantial and the Royal Commission is grateful to all those organisations and individuals that took the time to share their views. Having carefully considered all of the responses, the Royal Commission noted that there was significant support for climate adaptation and has decided that this is the most appropriate topic for the next major study. Most of the other topics on the shortlist will be kept on the list for consideration for possible future study.

BACKGROUND TO THE STUDY

Climate change is unavoidable. To date, the principal focus on climate change has been on reducing greenhouse gas emissions, with considerable political effort focused on what the targets and mechanisms for reductions should be.

Identifying what adaptive measures to take is not immediately obvious. Adaptation should be conducted in concert with mitigation strategies and should, insofar as it is possible, be done in a way that minimises any unintended consequences. It is unlikely that there is a single set of answers, but there needs to be analysis of what the options are to prepare for the future.

The Stern review set a very clear benchmark for the costs of climate change and more importantly the costs of adapting to future events. The need for adaptation is becoming recognised, and features in the draft Climate Change Bill that Defra is driving forward, which proposes that there should be regular reporting by Government to Parliament on adaptation policies.

The Defra England Biodiversity Strategy is focused on adaptation to climate change, and provides a useful look at how biodiversity could be affected and approaches that can be taken to best adapt to these changes. Events such as habitat loss, species migration and changes of land use are all likely to occur, and actions to address these need to be understood as part of the complex system that is the UK environment.

The European Commission has published its green paper on 'Adapting to Climate Change in Europe – Options for EU Actions' (June 2007) and asks whether the EU should be including climate adaptation policy in all of its policy decisions, whether new policy responses are needed and whether adaptation actions should be incorporated into EU foreign policy objectives. It also seeks to develop the research base further, and to involve all parts of the EU in developing a comprehensive approach to adaptation.

The Royal Commission study will investigate how the UK can best adapt to living in an environment where the climate is changing, including what sorts of measures should be taken to protect and to enhance the resilience of the built and natural environments. Examples could include measures to adapt to more extreme weather, using technology to cope with the future conditions of every-day living, adjusting the way we use our land, including the management of protected areas, or making recommendations as to how societal behaviours could be modified to cope better with the emerging and changing situation.

BROAD TOPICS TO BE COVERED

Adaptation to climate change covers a huge range of scientific, technical, engineering and socio-economic areas, and there are equally as many ways of splitting up this topic for investigation. How to achieve this will be one of the first issues that the Royal Commission must address.

Broad topics that might be covered include:

- Biodiversity
- Disease, health and wellbeing
- Water management
- Sea level rise
- Agriculture
- Invasive species
- Transport
- Land use
- Socio-economic issues
- Construction and infrastructure
- Energy
- Environmental management
- Tourism

A2   INVITATION TO SUBMIT EVIDENCE

After considering the response to the original announcement, the Royal Commission wrote to more than 400 organisations and individuals in 2008 for evidence on the following questions. Around 80 responses were received.

ROYAL COMMISSION STUDY ON ADAPTING THE UK TO CLIMATE CHANGE – INVITATION TO SUBMIT EVIDENCE

The focus of the study will be on whether the UK has the institutional capacity and arrangements necessary to adapt to changes in the natural environment brought about by climate change. The scope of the study is the UK in an EU context. To help illustrate the issues, the Commission invites evidence based on three exemplar subjects:

- Biodiversity, nature conservation and protected areas;

- Sea level and coastal zones; and

- Freshwater.

The Commission believes these areas and their interconnections are particularly challenging, and will help to illustrate the complexity of adapting the UK to climate change. *These arrangements will cover a broad spectrum ranging from formal governance processes for government and large organisations through to informal and local activities.* Consideration will be given to the UK's capacity to understand how climate change is likely to impact on ecosystems and on what time scales; on the way society values the natural environment under changing circumstances; and on the mechanisms that might be employed to manage the natural environment so as to safeguard these values.

RATIONALE

The natural environment provides a 'life-support system' to society through the services it provides, and as ecosystems, habitats and species respond to climate change it is inevitable that there will be direct and indirect impacts on the human environment through the dependencies on these services. In order to adapt to these changes in the natural environment, society will need to draw on existing institutional capacity and arrangements and also generate new ones as part of the adaptation process. So a key question is 'does the UK understand what institutional capacity and arrangements it has to adapt to climate change, what are the enablers and barriers, and what institutional arrangements does it actually need?'

Climate impacts generate autonomous adaptation responses in natural systems, whereas humans will make conscious as well as autonomous responses. It will be necessary to understand both the planned and autonomous responses that society has in an attempt to minimise the adverse impacts of climate and environmental change, either as a result of events that have occurred or those that are anticipated. It is not yet clear what the likely positive and negative impacts of adaptation measures will be for both humans and the natural environment. The interactions and feedbacks between social and environmental systems will underpin the effectiveness of adaptation. The ability of individuals and society to recognise the opportunities and beneficial consequences of adaptation, as well as respond to the adverse consequences, without damaging the efforts to mitigate climate change, will be key features of success.

One of the challenges of climate change is uncertainty about the level and rate of impacts that can be expected, and consequently about the levels of risk that society is prepared to tolerate. In addition it should be recognised that the environment and society will continue to change even without climate change. Non-climate impacts will affect the range of suitable options for adaptation. Despite these complexities and uncertainties, decisions and policies will need to be made that support action now and in the future. There may be existing frameworks for decision making in the face of uncertain or incomplete information that could be relevant to making decisions about adapting to climate change, or it may be that new frameworks are required. In order to understand how best to plan adaptation actions, the institutional arrangements that enable or hinder adaptation must be explored.

The study will, therefore, draw on three exemplar issues to extract and identify the issues associated with adapting to climate change, looking at the interactions between the natural environment and society. The subjects are: biodiversity, nature conservation and protected areas; sea level rise and coastal zones and freshwater. The study will not be looking at the direct impacts of climate change on cities and urban areas generally, or the impacts on infrastructure.

Biodiversity, nature conservation and protected areas

Many species will be able to adjust to climate and environmental change; others will face extinction. Adaptation responses expected from species include changes in key stages in the life-cycle (e.g. flowering time) and migration of species and it is not clear what impact this will have on human activities. Species survivability will depend on other factors, such as the availability of suitable habitats for relocation. Successful adaptation will require a degree of coherent changes in habitats and ecosystems, which may or may not be supported by current and future institutional arrangements designed to provide protected areas for species and habitats. The situation for the natural environment is complex and difficult to predict.

Sea level and coastal zones

The most dramatic effects of climate change for the coastal environment will be the rise in sea levels combined with more severe weather events. It is likely that in parts of the UK, the current use of coastal and estuarine land both for agriculture and urban areas will have to change. In some cases, increased defences may be appropriate, whereas in others coastal realignment would be better. In all cases, successful adaptation will depend on a balance being struck between the needs of society, different types of land use, and recognition of the natural forces of the ocean and severe weather. It is in coastal zones that some of the most challenging adaptation questions for society will be highlighted, including questions of equity and livelihoods. The institutional arrangements to tackle adaptation of the coastal environment will be particularly instructive for the study.

Freshwater

Floods and droughts are headline grabbing examples of severe weather events, and projections for climate change in the UK suggest that reduced precipitation overall can be expected, albeit with periods of more intense wet weather. In times of low precipitation, there are significant pressures on human and environmental requirements for water. Adapting to these pressures will require that environmental, social and economic needs are all addressed, and this may require new institutional approaches at a variety of levels. Equally, in periods of intense rainfall, the significant environmental and social impacts of flooding are difficult to manage, and may also require new institutional arrangements. The challenge for adapting to these changes in the natural environment will be to understand the freshwater system, and to implement policies and governance arrangements that can address the competing and varied challenges of water management both in times of excess and drought.

ISSUES ON WHICH THE COMMISSION WOULD WELCOME EVIDENCE

The questions below are not intended to limit the Commission's study, but rather to highlight areas where Members believe they are most in need of input at this stage. Everyone is welcome to respond to any of the questions. It is recognised that respondents may prefer to focus on questions related to their areas of knowledge and/or interest.

The Royal Commission operates on the basis of transparency and it is our normal practice for all evidence sent to us to be made publicly available. The most likely method of such dissemination is through publication on the Commission's website. If for any reason you do not wish us to make your name, organisation (if any) or your response (in full or in part) publicly available, then please make this clear in your response so that we can take it into account.

Throughout these questions, where the term 'natural environment' is used, please provide answers referring to the three exemplars (biodiversity, nature conservation and protected areas; sea level and coastal zones; freshwater).

The questions are broadly organised into the following categories:

Adaptation – General Questions
- Definitions and terminology;

- Range of climate change;

- Awareness of adaptation to climate change;

- The relationship between adaptation and mitigation; and

- Climate change in the broader context.

The Natural Environment
- Resilience of the natural environment;

- Natural responses and thresholds;

- Institutional arrangements for environmental conservation;

- Values relating to the natural environment; and

- Opportunities presented by the changing natural environment.

Institutional Arrangements and Capacities
- Institutional adaptive capacity; and

- European, national and regional approaches.

QUESTIONS INVITING FORMAL WRITTEN EVIDENCE

Adaptation – General Questions

Definitions and terminology

Q1) The RCEP needs to have a clear view of the terms it should use for the study – is the IPCC[i] view of adaptation adequate (see below)? Are there alternative views of adaptation to climate change that the RCEP should be considering?

(The IPCC definition is "Adaptation is the adjustment in natural or human systems in response to actual or expected climatic stimuli or their effects, which moderates harm or exploits beneficial opportunities" – for a fuller definition, including anticipatory, autonomous and planned adaptation, see section on Definitions later).

---

i   IPCC: Intergovernmental Panel on Climate Change.

Range of climate change

Q2)   There are several important factors when discussing climate change, which the RCEP needs to understand for this study:

a)   Over what time period should climate change be considered for the RCEP study – 2020, 2050, 2100, or some other time period?

b)   What are the magnitude, rate and kinds of climate change impacts in the UK that the RCEP study should be considering?

Awareness of adaptation to climate change

Q3)   The Royal Commission is interested in understanding the general level of awareness about adapting to climate change. How would you describe:

a)   The level of awareness that either you or your organisation has about the need to adapt to climate change?

b)   Your awareness of what could or should be done to enable the natural environment to adapt to climate change?

c)   Your awareness of any actions (by the government or others) already planned or underway, to adapt the natural environment to climate change?

The relationship between adaptation and mitigation

Q4)   The UK is committed to significant actions to mitigate climate change – what should be the relationship between adaptation and mitigation actions for climate change?

Climate change in the broader context

Q5)   Climate change is not the only major change that will take place over the coming years, or the only issue of importance for the environment, and yet it is being used as a justification for many decisions and actions.

a)   In broad terms, what are the important non-climate changes (e.g. social, economic, demographic, technological, cultural or other) that will interact with climate change to facilitate or inhibit adaptation? *(It may be useful to cross reference your answer with your response to question 2a).*

b)   When considering wider environmental priorities, what environmental goals may suffer if a stronger climate change adaptation agenda is introduced? How can the priority of adapting to climate change be increased as part of the sustainable development agenda without detracting from other important issues?

The Natural Environment

Throughout these questions, where the term 'natural environment' is used, answers should refer to the three exemplars (biodiversity, nature conservation and protected areas; sea level and coastal zones; freshwater).

Resilience of the natural environment

Q6)   When planning what adaptive actions should be taken in order to increase the resilience of the natural environment in the UK, the RCEP is interested to know:

133

a) What form will this resilience take?

b) How resilient to climate change does the UK want the natural environment to be? How resilient does it need to be to continue providing the services upon which society depends?

c) To what extent is it possible to build in levels of resilience sufficient to deal with potentially catastrophic events induced by climate change?

Natural responses and thresholds

Q7) The natural environment will respond to climate change in the absence of any human interventions. When considering the adaptation of the natural environment, when might a 'do nothing' option be appropriate, whereby natural systems are left to respond without intervention?

Q8) In the natural world, there will be thresholds of response to climate change, which are defined by the IPCC as *"the point where stress on an exposed system or activity, if exceeded, results in a non-linear response in that system or activity"*.[ii]

a) Should thresholds of response to climate change be identified for the natural environment and, if so, how should this be done and by whom?

b) What would be an 'unacceptable' level of change to the natural environment? What are the key criteria which should underpin judgments of acceptability in this context?

Institutional arrangements for environmental conservation

Q9) How will adaptation of the natural environment interact with (either negatively or positively) adaptation responses in the major land uses (such as agriculture, water resource management, energy production, forestry, urban development, infrastructure) and what institutional arrangements, if any, are needed to facilitate changes in land use to support adaptation to climate change?

Q10) As the climate changes, so the land, aquatic and coastal environments will change, including those areas protected for biodiversity and conservation. The RCEP is interested to understand what this means for conservation policies and whether the current arrangements enable or inhibit adaptation of the natural environment.

a) If the nature of existing protected areas changes as the climate changes, what does this mean for current conservation policy?

b) With regards to site-specific conservation policies, what should be protected now and in the future, especially if the present site is bound to change? How can a range of resilient habitats be provided to conserve biodiversity?

c) How should current arrangements (such as protected areas or wildlife law) for the protection of species and habitats be adapted to ensure that the natural environment can adapt to climate change?

ii   Taken from IPCC WGII AR4 Section 2.3.1.

Values relating to the natural environment

Q11) How society perceives and interacts with the environment is different in each country, and within the different regions and sectors of that country. The values and attitudes of society will ultimately underpin its response to climate change.

   a) How will climate change affect how society perceives and values the natural environment?

   b) As the climate changes, it is likely that non-native (or alien – *see section on definitions later*) species will migrate into the UK. When and how do previously non-native species come to be regarded as part of the UK's native biodiversity, and what will this mean for the UK?

   c) Is the legal framework for species and habitat protection adequate for dealing with invasive non-native species under climate change?

Opportunities presented by the changing natural environment

Q12) Whilst much of the debate is focused on how humans can help protect the natural environment as it responds to climate change, how can the changes to the natural environment be used to help UK society adapt to climate change?

Institutional Arrangements and Capacities

When considering institutional capacities and arrangements, the Commission would be particularly grateful if the answers are framed in terms of the three exemplar issues discussed above: biodiversity, nature conservation and protected areas; sea level and coastal zones; and freshwater.

Institutional adaptive capacity

Q13) To what extent do UK institutions and organisations recognise and understand their dependence on the natural environment, and how this affects their capacity and capability to adapt? Are there examples of organisations in the UK that have quantified their level of dependence?

Q14) Does the UK have the right capacities and institutional arrangements to be able to identify the changes to which it should be adapting?

Q15) What are the relative roles of government, communities, individuals, civil society, and/or companies with regards adapting to climate change for the three exemplar issues? For example, is there too much of a focus on institutional responses and needs versus understanding of individual concerns and needs?

Q16) As society adapts to climate change, decisions will need to be made as to what is an appropriate range of adaptation objectives and responses.

   a) What should be the key objectives of climate change adaptation strategies for the three exemplars?

   b) What should be the criteria for determining appropriate adaptation objectives and the responses that would meet these objectives for the three exemplars?

   c) How should different adaptation objectives and responses be prioritised for the three exemplars?

d) Some adaptation responses could disadvantage some individuals or groups (e.g. coastal realignment could lead to individuals or communities having to move). How should the 'fairness' of different adaptation responses be considered?

European, national and regional approaches

Q17) What is the appropriate level (e.g. European, UK, regional, local) at which decisions should be made for climate change adaptation?

Q18) The regions of the UK will experience different levels of climate change impacts, and will correspondingly need to adapt in different ways. What variations in institutional capacity do we find in the different regions? What do these differences imply?

Q19) Which existing EU mechanisms (e.g. the Common Agriculture Policy or the Water Framework Directive) could play a role in delivering adaptation to climate change in the UK? What are the aspects of such mechanisms that enable or hinder adaptation?

Q20) As other countries in Europe experience climate change, they also will experience changes in the natural environment. What indirect impacts might this have on the natural environment of the UK?

And finally:

Q21) Are there any other issues which should be included within the RCEP's study?

DEFINITIONS

When discussing adaptation to climate change, there are a range of terms used with varying definitions from different sources. Some of these have been collected here to provide a ready point of reference; however, this list is not exhaustive. If there are other terms that could or should be used, please bring these to the attention of the Royal Commission on Environmental Pollution.

IPCC Definitions – taken from the Glossary to the Fourth Assessment Report of IPCC Working Group II, 2007 (unless otherwise stated)

Adaptation is the adjustment in natural or human systems in response to actual or expected climatic stimuli or their effects, which moderates harm or exploits beneficial opportunities. Various types of adaptation can be distinguished, including anticipatory, autonomous and planned adaptation:

Anticipatory adaptation – Adaptation that takes place before impacts of climate change are observed. Also referred to as proactive adaptation.

Autonomous adaptation – Adaptation that does not constitute a conscious response to climatic stimuli but is triggered by ecological changes in natural systems and by market or welfare changes in human systems. Also referred to as spontaneous adaptation. (c.f. alternative definition below.)

Planned adaptation – Adaptation that is the result of a deliberate policy decision, based on an awareness that conditions have changed or are about to change and that action is required to return to, maintain, or achieve a desired state.

Adaptive capacity (also referred to as adaptability) is the ability of a system to adjust to climate change (including climate variability and extremes) to moderate potential damages, to take advantage of opportunities, or to cope with the consequences.

Autonomous adaptation is the ongoing implementation of existing knowledge and technology in response to the changes in climate experienced. (Taken from IPCC WG II 4AR Section 5.5, c.f. alternative definition above.)

Climate change in IPCC usage refers to any change in climate over time, whether due to natural variability or as a result of human activity. This usage differs from that in the United Nations Framework Convention on Climate Change, where climate change refers to a change of climate that is attributed directly or indirectly to human activity that alters the composition of the global atmosphere and that is in addition to natural climate variability observed over comparable time periods.

Climate variability refers to variations in the mean state and other statistics (such as standard deviations, statistics of extremes etc.) of the climate on all temporal and spatial scales beyond that of individual weather events. Variability may be due to natural internal processes within the climate system (internal variability), or to variations in natural or anthropogenic external forcing (external variability).

(Climate change) impacts – the effects of climate change on natural and human systems. Depending on the consideration of adaptation, one can distinguish between potential and residual impacts:

Potential impacts – all impacts that may occur given a projected change in climate, without consideration of adaptation.

Residual impacts – the impacts of climate change that would occur after adaptation.

Aggregate impacts – total impacts integrated across sectors and/or regions. The aggregation of impacts requires knowledge (or assumptions about) the relative importance of impacts in different sectors and regions. Measures of aggregate impacts include, for example, the total number of people affected, or the total economic costs.

Market impacts – impacts that can be quantified in monetary terms, and directly affect Gross Domestic Product – e.g. changes in the price of agricultural inputs and/or goods.

Non-market impacts – impacts that affect ecosystems or human welfare, but that are not easily expressed in monetary terms, e.g., an increased risk of premature death, or increases in the number of people at risk of hunger.

Impact – a specific change in a system[iii] caused by its exposure to climate change. Impacts may be judged to be harmful or beneficial. Vulnerability to climate change is the degree to which these systems are susceptible to, and unable to cope with, adverse impacts. The concept of risk, which combines the magnitude of the impact with the probability of its occurrence, captures uncertainty in the underlying processes of climate change, exposure, impacts and adaptation. (Taken from IPCC WGII 4AR, Section 19.1.1; c.f. definition above).

---

iii   Systems are considered to be geophysical, biological and socio-economic systems.

Mitigation – an anthropogenic intervention to reduce the anthropogenic forcing of the climate system; it includes strategies to reduce greenhouse gas emissions and enhancing greenhouse gas sinks.

Invasive species and invasive alien species – a species aggressively expanding its range and population density into a region in which it is not native, often through out-competing or otherwise dominating native species. (c.f. alternative definitions below.)

Planned adaptation is the increase in adaptive capacity by mobilising institutions and policies to establish or strengthen conditions favourable for effective adaptation and investment in new technologies and infrastructure. (Taken from IPCC WGII AR4 Section 5.5, c.f. alternative definition above.)

Resilience – the ability of a social or ecological system to absorb disturbances while retaining the same basic structure and ways of functioning, the capacity for self-organisation, and the capacity to adapt to stress and change. (c.f. alternative definition below.)

Threshold – the level of magnitude of a system process at which sudden or rapid change occurs. A point or level at which new properties emerge in an ecological, economic or other system, invalidating predictions based on mathematical relationships that apply at lower levels.

Threshold – this marks the point where stress on an exposed system or activity, if exceeded, results in a non-linear response in that system or activity. (Taken from IPCC WGII AR4 Section 2.3.1, c.f. alternative definition above.)

Impact threshold – a level of change in condition, measured on a linear scale, regarded as 'unacceptable' and inviting some form of response. In the case of an impact threshold, the response is the non-linear aspect; for example, a management threshold. Exceeding a management threshold will result in a change of legal, regulatory, economic, or cultural behaviour. (Taken from IPCC WGII AR4 Section 2.3.1.)

Systemic threshold – a non-linear change in state, where a system shifts from one identifiable set of conditions to another. A systemic threshold can often be objectively measured. (Taken from IPCC WGII AR4 Section 2.3.1.)

Vulnerability is the degree to which a system is susceptible to, and unable to cope with, adverse effects of climate change, including climate variability and extremes. Vulnerability is a function of the character, magnitude, and rate of climate change and variation to which a system is exposed, its sensitivity, and its adaptive capacity. (c.f. alternative definition below.)

Definitions from sources other than the IPCC

Alien species – a species, subspecies or lower taxon, introduced outside its natural past or present distribution; includes any part, gametes, seeds, eggs, or propagules of such species that might survive and subsequently reproduce. Some international/regional/national instruments use the term 'exotic species', 'non-indigenous species' or 'non-native species' when referring to 'alien species'. (Taken from 'Developing an EU Framework for Invasive Alien Species – Discussion paper'.)

Alien species – a species, subspecies or lower taxon introduced outside of its natural range (past or present) and dispersal potential (i.e. outside the range it occupies naturally or could not occupy without direct or indirect introduction or care by humans) and includes any part, gametes or propagule of such species that might survive and subsequently reproduce. Synonyms include non-native, non-indigenous, and exotic species. (Taken from 'Biological Invasions in Europe: Drivers, Pressures, States, Impacts and Responses' by Philip E. Hulme, in *Issues in Environmental Science and Technology*, No. 25).

Adaptability is the capacity of actors in a system to influence resilience. (Taken from Holling *et al.* (2004). *Ecology and Society*, **9**(2), 5.)

Ecological resilience is a measure of the amount of change or disruption that is required to transform a system from being maintained by one set of mutually reinforcing processes and structures to a different set of processes and structures. (Taken from Garry Peterson – http://www.geog.mcgill.ca/faculty/peterson/susfut/resilience/rLandscape.html.)

Ecosystem – a dynamic complex of plant, animal and micro-organism communities and their non-living environment interacting as a functional unit. (Taken from the Convention on Biological Diversity.)

Ecosystem services are the benefits people obtain from ecosystems. These include provisioning services such as food and water; regulating services such as flood and disease control; cultural services such as spiritual, recreational, and cultural benefits; and supporting services, such as nutrient cycling, that maintain the conditions for life on Earth. (Taken from the Millennium Ecosystem Assessment.)

Habitat – the place or type of site where an organism or population naturally occurs. (Taken from the Convention on Biological Diversity.)

Habitat connectivity describes the spatial interlinkages between core areas of suitable habitat. It is often focused on the establishment or maintenance of corridors of similar habitat to link core areas, although consideration may be given to the capacity of other habitats to act as conduits for dispersal. (Taken from Secretariat of the Convention on Biological Diversity (2006). *Guidance for Promoting Synergy Among activities Addressing Biological Diversity, Desertification, Land Degradation and Climate Change.* Montreal, Technical Series no. 25.)

Inertia is the delay, slowness, or resistance in the response of the climate, biological, or human systems to factors that alter their rate of change, including continuation of change in the system after the cause of that change has been removed. (Taken from Secretariat of the Convention on Biological Diversity (2006). *Guidance for Promoting Synergy Among activities Addressing Biological Diversity, Desertification, Land Degradation and Climate Change.* Montreal, Technical Series no. 25.)

Invasive alien species – an alien species whose introduction and/or spread threaten biological diversity. (Taken from *Developing an EU Framework for Invasive Alien Species – Discussion paper.*)

Invasive alien species – a naturalised alien species which is an agent of change, and threatens human health, economy and/or native biological diversity. (Taken from *Biological Invasions in Europe: Drivers, Pressures, States, Impacts and Responses* by Philip E. Hulme, from Issues in Environmental Science and Technology, No. 25.)

Landscape permeability is the capacity for dispersal of biodiversity across the entire landscape, including the identification of potential barriers to movement. It is based on the premise that within a heterogeneous landscape species movement between areas of suitable habitat will be constrained by their varying ability to disperse across other habitats via a multitude of routes (c.f. habitat connectivity). Improving the capacity for species to disperse across marginal or unsuitable habitats enhances landscape permeability.

(Taken from Secretariat of the Convention on Biological Diversity (2006). *Guidance for Promoting Synergy Among activities Addressing Biological Diversity, Desertification, Land Degradation and Climate Change.* Montreal, Technical Series no. 25.)

Resilience is the ability of an ecosystem to maintain its functions after being perturbed. A measure of resilience is the magnitude of disturbance required to move an ecosystem irreversibly to an alternative state. Resilience decreases an ecosystem's sensitivity (c.f. alternative definition above). (Taken from Secretariat of the Convention on Biological Diversity (2006). *Guidance for Promoting Synergy Among activities Addressing Biological Diversity, Desertification, Land Degradation and Climate Change.* Montreal, Technical Series no. 25.)

Resilience is the capacity of a system to absorb disturbance and reorganise while undergoing change so as to still retain essentially the same function, structure, identity and feedbacks. (Taken from Holling *et al.* (2004) *Ecology and Society* **9**(2), 5.)

Resistance describes the capacity of an ecosystem to persist unchanged despite environmental change. Resistance decreases an ecosystem's sensitivity. (Taken from Secretariat of the Convention on Biological Diversity (2006). *Guidance for Promoting Synergy Among activities Addressing Biological Diversity, Desertification, Land Degradation and Climate Change.* Montreal, Technical Series no. 25.)

Sensitivity measures the magnitude and rate of response in proportion to the magnitude and rate of climate change. Ecosystems will be particularly sensitive to changes in climate variability and the frequency and magnitude of extreme events. (Taken from Secretariat of the Convention on Biological Diversity (2006). *Guidance for Promoting Synergy Among activities Addressing Biological Diversity, Desertification, Land Degradation and Climate Change.* Montreal, Technical Series no. 25.))

Transformability is the capacity to create a fundamentally new system when ecological, economic, or social (including political) conditions make the existing system untenable. (Taken from Holling *et al.*(2004). *Ecology and Society,* **9**(2), 5.)

Vulnerability measures an ecosystem's exposure to and sensitivity to climate change. Vulnerability is determined at specific spatial and temporal scales and is a dynamic property dependent on local conditions; for example, a forest during the dry season (c.f. alternative definition above). (Taken from Secretariat of the Convention on Biological Diversity (2006). *Guidance for Promoting Synergy Among activities Addressing Biological Diversity, Desertification, Land Degradation and Climate Change.* Montreal, Technical Series no. 25.)

Appendix B

CONDUCT OF THE STUDY

In order to carry out this study, the Royal Commission sought written and oral evidence, commissioned studies and took advice on specific topics and made a number of visits.

EVIDENCE

In parallel with the invitation to submit written evidence, which is reproduced in Appendix A, the Secretariat wrote directly to a number of organisations and individuals.

The organisations and individuals listed below either submitted evidence or provided information on request for the purposes of the study, or otherwise gave assistance. In some cases (which are indicated by an asterisk), meetings were held with Commission Members or the Secretariat so that oral evidence could be given or particular issues discussed.

GOVERNMENT DEPARTMENTS
- Civil Contingencies Secretariat (CCS)*
- Department for Children, Schools and Families
- Department for Communities and Local Government (CLG)*
- Department for Environment, Food and Rural Affairs (Defra)*
- Department of Health

DEVOLVED ADMINISTRATIONS
- Department of Environment Northern Ireland (DOENI)*
- Scottish Government*
- Welsh Assembly Government*

EUROPEAN AND INTERNATIONAL BODIES
- British Embassy in the Netherlands*
- Deltares*
- European Commission*
- Gemeente Den Haag*
- Ministry of Transport, Public Works and Water Management, the Netherlands*
- Stockholm Environment Institute
- UKREP*
- Waterschap Hollandse Delta*
- Zuid Holland Provincie*

OTHER ORGANISATIONS

- Adaptation Sub-Committee to the Committee on Climate Change*
- AEA Technology plc
- Anglian Water*
- Arts and Humanities Research Council
- Association of British Insurers*
- Audit Commission*
- Brecon Beacons National Park Authority
- British Antarctic Survey
- British Ecological Society
- British Medical Association
- British Ports Association and UK Major Ports Group Ltd.
- British Veterinary Association
- Broadland Climate Change Panel
- Broads and Norfolk Rivers Internal Drainage Boards
- Campaign for National Parks
- Campaign to Protect Rural England
- Carbon Coach
- Central Science Laboratory
- Chartered Institute of Environmental Health
- Chartered Institution of Water and Environmental Management
- Coastal Concern Action Group*
- Commission for Architecture and the Built Environment (CABE)
- Commission for Integrated Transport
- Commission for Rural Communities
- Concatenation Science Communication
- Convention of Scottish Local Authorities (COSLA)*
- Countryside Council for Wales (CCW)
- Dŵr Cymru Welsh Water
- E.ON
- East Sussex County Council
- Entec UK Ltd.
- Environment Agency (EA)*
- Environment Council
- Exmoor Mire Restoration project*
- Federation of Groundwork Trusts

- Forestry Commission
- Grantham Institute for Climate Change
- Greater London Authority
- Hampshire County Council*
- Health and Safety Commission and Executive
- Health Protection Agency
- Institute of Biological, Environmental and Rural Sciences
- Institute of Grassland and Environmental Research
- Institute of Physics
- Institution of Civil Engineers
- Institution of Civil Engineers, Wales
- Institution of Mechanical Engineers
- International Centre for the Uplands
- Joint Nature Conservation Committee (JNCC)*
- Lancashire County Council
- Landscape Institute
- Local Government Association (LGA)*
- London Borough of Barking and Dagenham
- London Climate Change Partnership
- London School of Hygiene and Tropical Medicine
- Manhood Peninsula Steering Group
- Met Office*
- National Centre for Earth Observation
- National Farmers' Union
- National Parks Wales
- National Physical Laboratory
- National Trust*
- Natural England (NE)*
- Network Rail
- Norfolk Wildlife Trust*
- North Norfolk District Council
- North West Coastal Forum
- North West England and North Wales Coastal Group
- Northamptonshire County Council
- Northern Ireland Environment Agency
- Northern Ireland Environment Link

- Northern Ireland Local Government Association (NILGA)*
- Northumbrian Water Ltd.
- Ofgem
- Ofwat*
- Oxford Institute for Sustainable Development
- Peninsula Partnership for the Rural Environment
- Plymouth City Council
- Plymouth Marine Laboratory
- Portsmouth Water Ltd.
- Proudman Oceanographic Laboratory
- Rail Safety and Standards Board
- Ramblers
- Research Councils UK
- River Glaven Conservation Group*
- Rothamsted Research
- Royal Academy of Engineering
- Royal Institution of Chartered Surveyors
- Royal Meteorological Society
- Royal Society for the Protection of Birds
- Royal Society of Chemistry
- Scotland and Northern Ireland Forum for Environmental Research (SNIFFER)
- Scottish Environment Protection Agency (SEPA)*
- Scottish Natural Heritage (SNH)*
- Scottish Water
- Somerset County Council
- South Downs Joint Committee
- South East Climate Change Partnership
- South West Climate Change Impacts Partnership
- Stody Estate Ltd.
- Stroud District Council
- Sustainability Research Institute and Institute for Climate and Atmospheric Science, University of Leeds
- Thames Barrier*
- Town and Country Planning Association (TCPA)*
- Tyndall Centre for Climate Change Research
- UK Climate Impacts Programme*

- UK Collaborative on Development Sciences
- University of East Anglia*
- Veterinary Laboratories Agency
- VisitScotland
- Water Industry Commission for Scotland (WICS)
- Water Management Alliance
- Water UK
- Waterwise
- Weatherology
- Wellcome Trust
- Welsh Local Government Association (WLGA)*
- Wildlife Trusts
- Woodland Trust
- Worcestershire County Council
- Yorkshire and Humber Climate Change Executive Group

INDIVIDUALS

- Professor Neil Adger
- Professor Jeroen Aerts
- Professor Nigel Arnell
- Andy Batchelor
- Professor Frans Berkhout
- Professor Jacquie Burgess
- Lord Chorley
- Dr Debbie Clifford*
- Dr Caroline Cowan*
- Dr Philine zu Ermgassen*
- Mr Bob Fairweather
- Mr Mark Fortune
- Professor John Gibson
- Ms Fiona Hewer
- Professor Brian Hoskins
- Dr Brian Jones
- Mr Malcolm Kerby*
- Mr Andy Lebrecht
- Professor Robert Nicholls*

- Dr Sophie Nicholson-Cole*
- Ms Ilga Nielsen
- Mr Colin Mair
- Mr Christopher McCoy
- Dr Darryn McEvoy
- Professor Tim O'Riordan*
- Mr Robert Palgrave
- My Lyn Parker, HMA
- Professor Martin Parry
- Tim Reeder*
- Mr Alan Searby
- Ms Penny Simpson
- Mr Dale Sharpe
- Professor David Stainforth
- Mr Peter Sutton
- Dr Tom Tew*
- Professor Chris Thomas
- Professor Kerry Turner*
- Professor John Twidell
- Dr Chasca Twyman
- Professor Rob Wilby*

COMMISSIONED STUDIES

A review of the legal liabilities for coastal erosion and flooding in the United Kingdom due to climate change was commissioned during 2009:

Legal liabilities for coastal erosion and flooding in the United Kingdom due to climate change. Dr John Gibson, Faculty of Law, University of Cape Town.

In addition, other reports were commissioned as follows:

Helping to deliver Climate Change Adaptation through the Planning System. Town and Country Planning Association (TCPA).

The River InVertebrate Prediction And Classification System (RIVPACS) and the Water Framework Directive under Climate Change. Dr P. zu Ermgassen.

Saline intrusion, groundwater and coastal habitat: Impacts of sea level rise. Dr D. Clifford.

The Commissioned studies are available on the Royal Commission on Environmental Pollution website at: http://www.rcep.org.uk.

VISITS

During the course of the study, Members of the Commission and its Secretariat made a series of evidence-gathering visits. The Secretariat is particularly indebted to the National Trust for organising the Gower visit, the United Kingdom Permanent Representation to the European Union (UKREP) for the organisation of the visit to Brussels and the Netherlands, the Norfolk Wildlife Trust and Anglian Water for their efforts in organising the visit to Hickling Broad, and Malcolm Kerby and colleagues at the Coastal Concern Action Group for a very informative visit to Happisburgh.

December 2008, Cardiff and the Gower Peninsula. Members met representatives from the Welsh Assembly Government, and staff from the National Trust, who escorted groups around the Gower Peninsula. The National Trust was able to demonstrate its approach to adapting to the problems caused by a changing climate on the Gower.

January 2009, Brussels and the Netherlands. In Brussels, Members met with representatives of UKREP hosted by Peter Green (Counsellor for Social, Environmental and Regional Affairs) to be briefed on adaptation in the EU. Members also attended a meeting with European Commission DG Environment officials hosted by Peter Gammletoft (Head of Unit, Protection of Water & Marine Environment). In the Netherlands, meetings were organised with Provincie Zuid Holland, Waterschap Hollandse Delta and Geemente Den Haag. Members also met with representatives of the private organisation Deltares. Members discussed water management and matters pertaining to strategic flood and coastal defence in Holland. Members also met with Professors Frans Berkhout and Jeroen Aerts of the Free University of Amsterdam to discuss matters of spatial planning and compensation.

January 2009, Thames Barrier. Members visited the Thames Barrier to learn about the Thames Estuary 2100 project. Discussions were had with Tim Reeder of the Environment Agency and colleagues to understand the development and operation of the project.

February 2009, Norfolk. Members visited the River Glaven catchment, courtesy of the Environment Agency and Anglian Water. Discussions were centred on how the two organisations work together to solve problems associated with water management and abstraction issues in the face of climate change. The application of the European Water Framework Directive was also discussed. Members also visited Happisburgh to witness first hand a village threatened by coastal erosion. Members met with Environment Agency representatives as well as representatives of the local community. To learn more about how sea level rise might impact on biodiversity and the provision of freshwater, Members visited Hickling Broads.

February 2009, the Met Office and the south west. Members travelled to Devon to learn more about climate change modelling and to discover what is being done in the south west to address the challenges of adapting to climate change. Members first met with representatives of the Environment Agency for detailed discussions about the climate-related problems facing the south west region. Members also attended a day of discussions about the modelling of climate with scientists at the Met Office Hadley Centre and other experts in the field. Arrangements were also made for Members to visit the Exmoor Mire Restoration project in Exmoor National Park. Although the weather did not permit a visit onto the moor, Members were able to discuss how initiatives such as the peat restoration project helped to link issues of mitigation and adaptation.

Appendix C

SEMINARS AND WORKSHOPS HELD IN SUPPORT OF THE STUDY

SEMINAR IN EDINBURGH: INSTITUTIONAL CAPACITY FOR ADAPTATION TO CLIMATE CHANGE – SYNERGIES, GAPS, CONFLICTS AND INCENTIVES

On 5 September 2008 the Royal Commission hosted a seminar at the BMA Scotland Offices, in support of the adaptation study. The seminar was attended by over 30 participants including Members of the Commission and Secretariat, and officials from both the Northern Ireland and Scottish Governments, as well as non-governmental organisations and industry.

Participants discussed a wide range of topics, including the differences between adaptation in Scotland, England and Northern Ireland, and the need to make adaptation relevant to people both as individuals and as part of institutions.

A report of the seminar is available on the Commission's website at http://www.rcep.org.uk.

In addition to Members of the Commission and Secretariat, participants included:

- Dr Christine Butler   Department of Agriculture and Rural Development (Northern Ireland)
- Hugh Clayden   Forestry Commission Scotland
- Madeleine Cusack   Scottish Government
- Jonnie Hall   NFU Scotland
- Julian Holbrook   Scotland and Northern Ireland Forum for Environmental Research (SNIFFER)
- Dr Andy Kerr   University of Edinburgh/Scottish Government
- Diane Keys   Conservation Volunteers
- Professor Colin Moffat   Fisheries Research Services (FRS) Marine Laboratory
- Janet Moxley   Scottish Environment Protection Agency (SEPA)
- Fiona Mulholland   Northern Ireland Environment Agency
- Marion Mulholland   Scottish Government
- Simon Pepper
- Maf Smith   Sustainable Development Commission
- Pat Snowdon   Forestry Commission
- Professor Sharon Turner   Queen's University Belfast
- Rebecca Walker   SEPA

- Mark Williams   Scottish Water
- Ruth Wolstenholme   SNIFFER

Seminar in Reading: Institutional capacity for adaptation to climate change – Synergies, gaps, conflicts and incentives

On 18 November 2008 the Royal Commission hosted a seminar at the Innovation Centre in Reading to gather views from interested parties relevant to deciding the scope of the adaptation study. The seminar involved around 50 participants, including officials from UK governments, academics and researchers, and representatives from non-governmental organisations and industry.

Participants worked in small groups to identify a range of issues relating to the three chosen exemplar areas (biodiversity, nature conservation and protected areas; sea level and coastal zones; freshwater) and then explored the roles of institutional actors within these areas in greater detail.

A report of the seminar is available on the Commission's website at http://www.rcep.org.uk.

In addition to Members of the Commission and Secretariat, participants included:

- Dr Pam Berry   Environmental Change Institute, University of Oxford
- Bryan Boult   Hampshire County Council
- Paul Bowtell   Audit Commission
- Nicola Britton   Welsh Assembly Government
- Robin Buxton   Oxfordshire Nature Conservation Forum
- Caroline Cowan   Natural England
- Mark Ellis-Jones   Environment Agency
- Amir Ghani   Department for Environment, Food and Rural Affairs (Defra)
- Andrew Gouldson   Leeds University
- Emily Hay   Department for Communities and Local Government
- Clifford Henry   Northern Ireland Environment Agency
- Steve Hill   Severn Trent Water
- Nikki Hodgson   AEA
- Ceris Jones   National Farmers' Union
- Elaine Kendall   Defra
- Professor Dan Laffoley   Natural England and International Union for Conservation & Nature (IUCN)
- John Laverty   Institution of Civil Engineers
- Rosie Manise   Natural England
- Mike Morecroft   Centre for Ecology and Hydrology
- Dr Sophie Nicholson-Cole Tyndall Centre for Climate Change Research
- Alex Nickson   Greater London Authority

149

- Rachel Newton   Royal Society
- Denis Peach   British Geological Survey
- Deborah Procter   Joint Nature Conservation Committee
- Russell Reefer   Local Government Association
- Chris Thomas   University of York
- Emma Tompkins   Sustainability Research Institute, University of Leeds
- Carol Turley   Plymouth Marine Laboratory
- Clive Walmsley   Countryside Council for Wales
- Chris West   UK Climate Impacts Programme
- Rob Wilby   Lancaster University
- Michael Woods   Environment Group, Stephenson Harwood

WORKSHOP IN LONDON: HELPING TO DELIVER CLIMATE CHANGE ADAPTATION THROUGH THE UK PLANNING SYSTEM

On the 28 July 2009 the Town and Country Planning Association (TCPA) organised a joint workshop with the Commission. The workshop was held to inform the TCPA study on the delivery of climate change adaptation through the UK planning system. This study was commissioned by the Royal Commission to inform this report on adapting institutions to climate change.

The workshop was attended by more than 40 people including Members of the Commission, Secretariat and TCPA staff. Guests were invited from the built environment and environmental sectors, with a particular focus on planning professionals and those with experience and knowledge of the planning process. Participants represented government departments, agencies, local authorities, non-governmental organisations, community groups, universities, consultancies and professional bodies and industries from England, Wales, Scotland and Northern Ireland.

A report of the seminar and the TCPA's report *Helping to Deliver Climate Change Adaptation through the UK Planning System* are available on the Commission's website at http://www.rcep.org.uk.

Appendix D

MEMBERS OF THE ROYAL COMMISSION ON ENVIRONMENTAL POLLUTION

CHAIRMAN

PROFESSOR SIR JOHN LAWTON CBE FRS

- President, Council of the British Ecological Society, 2005-2007

- Chief Executive, Natural Environment Research Council, 1999-2005

- Director (and founder), Natural Environment Research Council Centre for Population Biology at Imperial College, Silwood Park, 1989-1999

- Member, Royal Commission on Environmental Pollution, 1996-1999

- Lecturer, Senior Lecturer, Reader, Professor of Biology, University of York, 1972-1989

- Demonstrator in Animal Ecology, Department of Zoology, University of Oxford, 1968-1971

- Chairman, Royal Society for the Protection of Birds, 1993-1998

- Vice-President, Royal Society for the Protection of Birds, 1999-

- Past Vice-President, British Trust for Ornithology, 1999-2007

- Trustee, WWF-UK, 2002–2008; Fellow of WWF-UK, 2008-

- Chairman, Yorkshire Wildlife Trust, 2009-

- Foreign Associate, US National Academy of Sciences, 2008-

- Foreign Honorary Member, American Academy of Arts and Sciences, 2008-

MEMBERS

PROFESSOR NICHOLAS CUMPSTY

- Professor of Mechanical Engineering, Imperial College, 2005-2008

- Emeritus Professor of Mechanical Engineering, Imperial College, 2008-

- Member, Defence Science Advisory Council, 2005-

- Visiting Professor, Department of Aeronautics and Astronautics, Massachusetts Institute of Technology, 2005-

- Chief Technologist, Rolls-Royce plc, 2000-2005

- Lecturer, Reader, Professor, University of Cambridge, 1972-1999

- Director of the Whittle Laboratory, University of Cambridge, 1989-1999

PROFESSOR MICHAEL H. DEPLEDGE

- Professor of Environment and Human Health, Peninsula Medical School, Universities of Exeter and Plymouth

- Honorary Visiting Professor, Department of Zoology, University of Oxford

- Former Keeley Visiting Fellow, Wadham College, University of Oxford, 2006-2007

- Chief Scientific Adviser, Environment Agency of England and Wales, 2002-2006

- Senior Science Adviser, Plymouth Marine Laboratory, 2005-2007

- Chairman, Science Advisory Committee, European Commission, DG-Research, 2006-

- Founding Board Member, Natural England, 2006-2009

- Council Member, Natural Environment Research Council, 2003-2006

- Honorary Professor, School of Earth Sciences and Engineering, Imperial College, 2002-

- Honorary Visiting Scientist, School of Public Health, Harvard University, USA, 2000-2003

DR IAN GRAHAM-BRYCE CBE

- Principal Emeritus, University of Dundee

- Chairman, East Malling Trust for Horticultural Research

- Principal and Vice-Chancellor, University of Dundee, 1994-2000

- Convener, Committee of Scottish Higher Education Principals, 1998-2000

- President, Scottish Association for Marine Science, 2000-2004; and currently Honorary Vice-President

- President, British Crop Protection Council, 1996-2000

- Council Member, Natural Environment Research Council, 1989-1996

- Head, Environmental Affairs Division, Shell International, 1986-1994

- President, Association of Applied Biologists, 1988-1989

- Director, East Malling Research Station, 1979-1986

- President, Society of Chemical Industry, 1982-1984

PROFESSOR JEFFREY JOWELL QC

- Professor of Law, University College London

- UK's Member on the Council of Europe's Commission for Democracy Through Law ('The Venice Commission')

- Chair, British Waterways Ombudsman Committee

- Former non-executive Director of the Office of Rail Regulation

- Practising barrister at Blackstone Chambers

PROFESSOR MARIA LEE

- Professor of Law at University College London

- Member, London Sustainable Development Commission

- Member of the academic panel of the barristers' chambers Francis Taylor Buildings

PROFESSOR PETER LISS CBE FRS

- Professor of Environmental Sciences, University of East Anglia, 1985-

- Chair, Scientific Committee of the International Geosphere-Biosphere Programme (IGBP), 1993-1997

- Chair, International Scientific Steering Committee for Surface Ocean – Lower Atmosphere Study (SOLAS), 2002-2007

- Council Member, Natural Environment Research Council, 1990–1995

- Independent Member, Inter-Agency Committee on Marine Science and Technology, 2000-2008

- Chair, Royal Society Global Environmental Research Committee, 2007-

- Council Member, Marine Biological Association of the UK

- Chair, Higher Education Funding Council's Research Assessment Exercise Panel in Earth and Environmental Sciences, 2001

- Guest Professor, Ocean University of Qingdao, China

- President, Challenger Society for Marine Science, 2006-2008

- Chair, European Research Council Advanced Grants Panel in Earth System Science, 2008-

PROFESSOR PETER MATTHEWS OBE

- Board Member, Port of London Authority, 2006-

- Chair, Northern Ireland Authority for Utility Regulation, 2007-

- Chair, Northern Ireland Authority for Energy Regulation, 2006-2007

- Board of the Environment Agency and Chair of its Audit Committee, 2000-2006

- Deputy Managing Director, Anglian Water International, 1997-1998

- President of the European Water Association, 1997-1998

- President of Chartered Institution of Water and Environmental Management, 1998–1999

- Chair, Society for the Environment, 2005-

- Governor and Chair of Audit Committee, Anglia Ruskin University, 1998-2007

- Visiting Professor, Imperial College, 1991-2004

- Member, Worshipful Company of Water Conservators

PROFESSOR JUDITH PETTS

- Pro-Vice-Chancellor (Research and Knowledge Transfer), University of Birmingham, 2008-

- Head, School of Geography, Earth and Environmental Sciences, University of Birmingham, 2002-2007

- Chair, Environmental Risk Management, University of Birmingham, 1999-

- Member, Engineering and Physical Sciences Research Council Societal Issues Panel, 2007-

- Council Member, National Environment Research Council, 2000-2006

- Member, Environmental Advisory Board, Veolia Environmental, 1999-

- Member, Royal Society Science in Society Group, 2005-2008

- Member, Higher Education Funding Council's Research Assessment Exercise Panel in Geography and Environmental Studies, 2005-2008

- Member, Office of Science and Innovation Sciencewise Strategy Group, 2004-2008

- Former Specialist Advisor House of Commons Environment, Transport and Regional Affairs Committee and House of Lords Sub-Committee

- Member, Council of the Institute of Environmental Assessment, 1990-2000

PROFESSOR STEVE RAYNER

- James Martin Professor of Science and Civilization, Director of the Institute for Science, Innovation and Society, University of Oxford and Professorial Fellow of Keble College

- Honorary Professor of Climate Change and Society, University of Copenhagen

- Professor of Environment and Public Affairs, Columbia University, USA, 1999-2003

- Chief Scientist, Pacific Northwest National Laboratory, USA, 1996-1999

- Director, Economic and Social Research Council Science in Society Programme, 2001-2007

- Lead Author, Working Group III, Intergovernmental Panel on Climate Change Third and Fourth Assessment Reports

- Past President of the Sociology and Social Policy Section of the British Association

DR MICHAEL ROBERTS CBE

- Ministerial appointee to the Veterinary Residues Committee, 2008-

- Non-Executive Director, National Non-Food Crops Centre (NNFCC), 2008-

- Chief Executive of the Department for Environment Food and Rural Affairs (Defra) Central Science Laboratory, 2001-2008

- Director, Centre for Ecology and Hydrology, 1999-2001

- Director, Institute of Terrestrial Ecology, 1989-1999

- Member, Yorkshire and Humber Science and Innovation Council, 2005-2008

Professor Joanne Scott

- Professor of European Law, and Vice-Dean for International Links, at the Faculty of Laws, University College London

- Member of the editorial boards of the Journal of Environmental Law and the Journal of International Economic Law

- Visiting Professor, Columbia Law School (2002-2003; Spring 2004, 2005, 2007) and Harvard Law School (2005-2006)

Professor Lynda Warren

- Emeritus Professor of Environmental Law, University of Aberystwyth

- Deputy Chair, Joint Nature Conservation Committee

- Chair, Wildlife Trust of South and West Wales

- Chair, Wales Coastal and Maritime Partnership

- Member, Committee on Radioactive Waste Management

- Board Member, British Geological Survey

- Board Member, Environment Agency, 2000-2006

- Chair, Salmon and Freshwater Fisheries Review, 1998-2000

- Member, Radioactive Waste Management Advisory Committee, 1994-2003

- Member, Countryside Council for Wales, 1991-2003

- Trustee, Field Studies Council 2006-2009

- Trustee, WWF-UK, 2002-2005

- Visiting Professor, Birmingham Central University

Economic Advisor to the RCEP

Professor Gordon MacKerron

- Director, SPRU (Science and Technology Policy Research), University of Sussex, 2008-

- Director, Sussex Energy Group, SPRU, University of Sussex, 2005-2008

- Chair of the Committee on Radioactive Waste Management, 2003-2007

- Deputy leader of the UK Government's Energy Review team, PIU, Cabinet Office, June-December 2001

- Chair, The Energy Panel, DTI/OST Technology Foresight Programme, 1995-1998

- Visiting Professor, Imperial College

MEMBERS WHO RETIRED FROM THE COMMISSION BEFORE THE REPORT WAS PUBLISHED:

- Professor Paul Ekins
- Professor Stephen Holgate
- Professor Susan Owens OBE
- Mr John Speirs CBE LVO
- Professor Janet Sprent OBE
- In addition, the former Secretary to the Commission, Tom Eddy CBE, retired during production of the report.

Abbreviations

ACC	Adapting to Climate Change Programme (a cross-departmental co-ordination programme)
ASC	Adaptation Sub-Committee of the Committee on Climate Change (established by the Climate Change Act 2008)
ASSI	Area of Special Scientific Interest (Northern Ireland)
BES	British Ecological Society
Branch	**B**iodiversity **R**equires **A**daptation in **N**orthwest Europe under a **Ch**anging Climate project
CAP	Common Agricultural Policy
CBA	cost–benefit analysis
CBD	Convention on Biological Diversity
CCW	Countryside Council for Wales
CEH	Centre for Ecology & Hydrology
CFP	Common Fisheries Policy
CLG	Department for Communities and Local Government
CSF	catchment sensitive farming
DASH Board	Climate Change and Energy **D**elivery **a**nd **S**trategy **H**igh-level Board (responsible for delivery of Government's climate change and energy objectives)
Defra	Department for Environment, Food and Rural Affairs
DECC	Department of Energy and Climate Change
EA	Environment Agency
ED(EE)	Cabinet Sub-Committee on Environment and Energy
ESPACE	European Spatial Planning: Adapting to Climate Events
EU	European Union
GCM	Global Circulation Model
GHG	greenhouse gas
GLA	Greater London Authority
GMT	Greenwich Mean Time
HCC	Hampshire County Council
ICZM	integrated coastal zone management
IPC	Infrastructure Planning Commission
IPCC	Intergovernmental Panel on Climate Change

JNCC	Joint Nature Conservation Committee
LAAs	local area agreements
LGA	Local Government Association
LRAP	Local and Regional Adaptation Partnership Board
LSP	local strategic partnership
LWEC	Living With Environmental Change
NAO	National Audit Office
NDPB	non-departmental public body
NE	Natural England
NGO	non-governmental organisation
NI	national indicator or Northern Ireland, depending on context
NI188	national indicator 188 on planning to adapt to climate change
NICCIP	Northern Ireland Climate Change Impacts Partnership
NNDC	North Norfolk District Council
NPF	National Planning Framework (Scotland)
Ofcom	Office of Communications
Ofgem	Office of the Gas and Electricity Markets
Ofsted	Office for Standards in Education
Ofwat	Office of Water Supplies, the Water Services Regulation Authority
ORR	Office of Rail Regulation
OSPAR	Convention for the Protection of the Marine Environment
PACT	Performance Acceleration Capacity-building Tool
ppm	parts per million
PPS	Planning Policy Statement
RCEP	Royal Commission on Environmental Pollution
RIVPACS	River InVertebrate Prediction And Classification System
RSPB	Royal Society for the Protection of Birds
SAC	Special Area of Conservation
SCCIP	Scottish Climate Change Impacts Partnership
SEPA	Scottish Environment Protection Agency
SMP	Shoreline Management Plan
SNH	Scottish Natural Heritage
SNIFFER	Scotland and Northern Ireland Forum for Environmental Research

SPA	Special Protection Area
SSSI	Site of Special Scientific Interest
TAN	Technical Advice Note
TCPA	Town and Country Planning Association
TE2100	Thames Estuary 2100 project
TUC	Trades Union Congress
UK	United Kingdom
UKCIP	UK Climate Impacts Programme
UKCIP02	UK Climate Projections preceding UKCP09
UKCP09	UK Climate Projections (updated in 2009)
WAG	Welsh Assembly Government
WCA	Wildlife and Countryside Act
WFD	EU Water Framework Directive

Index

Locators referring to definitions are in **bold** type. In subheadings, climate change is abbreviated as cc.

adaptability **Appendix A2**
adaptation 1.8–1.10, **Appendix A2**
  across Government departments 3.13
  business management approaches 4.46–4.48
  challenges to *see* challenges to adaptation
  difficulties in 1.18–1.20
  dynamism of 2.36
  local aspect of 1.13, 3.3
  and mitigation 1.11–1.13, 3.3, 3.65
  RCEP questions to organisations Box 5A
  test 5.13–5.14, 5.19
  urgency of 1.14
  see also adaptive capacity
Adaptation Sub-Committee (ASC) of the
  Committee on Climate Change 3.8
  RCEP recommendations to 5.11, 5.80–5.81
  role of 3.19, 3.109, Box 3A
Adapting to Climate Change (ACC) Programme
  3.9, 3.11, 4.108, 4.112, 5.31, 5.51
  governance structure of 3.10, Figure 3–I
  work streams 3.12, Figure 3–II
Adapting to climate change (European
  Commission) 2.102, 3.6
Adapting to climate change (National Audit
  Office) 3.14
adaptive capacity 1.4, 4.119, Figure 4–III, 5.1–
  5.11, 5.82–5.85, **Appendix A2,**
  Adaptation Sub-Committee *see* Adaptation
    Sub-Committee (ASC) of the Committee on
    Climate Change
  equity 5.60–5.69
  and institutional arrangements 1.6
    land use planning system 5.33–5.37
    shortcomings of current system 5.38–5.46
  policy framework 5.12
    adaptation duty 5.19–5.21
    indicators 5.25–5.28
    investment appraisal 5.15–5.18

    policy appraisal 5.13–5.14
    reporting/monitoring 5.22–5.24
  public engagement 5.71–5.79
  RCEP questions to organisations Box 5A
  resources for 5.47
    commitment of 5.58–5.59
    knowledge and skills 5.53–5.57
    leadership and cultural change 5.48–5.52
aggregate impacts **Appendix A2**
agriculture 2.45, 2.54, 2.57, 4.89
algae 2.50, 2.52
alien species 2.92–2.94, **Appendix A2**
Anglian Coastal Authorities Group 3.86–3.88
anticipatory adaptation 1.4, 1.22–1.23, **Box 1A**,
  Appendix A2
aquatic ecosystems 2.52, 2.59, 2.92, Box 3C
Areas of Special Scientific Interest (ASSIs) 3.99
Audit Commission 3.24, 3.25, 3.27, 4.108–4.109
autonomous adaptation **Box 1A**, Appendix A1,
  Appendix A2

Barroso, José Manuel 3.6
Bayesian probabilities 2.22
biodiversity 2.103, 4.68, 4.84, Box 4D,
  Appendix A1
  alien species, introduction of 2.92–2.94
  aquatic 2.55, 2.59, 2.61
  climate envelopes and responses to cc
    2.83–2.91
  ecosystem services 2.102
  habitat change/loss 2.99–2.101
  institutional arrangements for 3.95–3.108
  life cycle timing 2.95–2.96
  RCEP recommendations for 5.42, 5.44
  species assemblages 2.97–2.98
  uncertainties about 4.14, 4.55
  see also nature conservation
Biodiversity Action Partnership 2.99

Biodiversity Action Plan 2.99

Birds Directive (EU) 1979 3.46, 3.99, 3.101–3.102, 4.55, Box 4D, 5.42

Brundtland Report 4.19

Cabinet Office Civil Contingencies Secretariat 3.18

carbon dioxide levels 2.12

catchment sensitive farming Box 3D

challenges to adaptation 4.2–4.3, 4.5

  addressing 4.43–4.49, Figure 4–II

    framing *see* framing challenge/response

    implementing *see* implementing adaptation

    learning *see* learning about adaptation

  complexities 4.15–4.17

  efficiency 4.28, 4.36–4.42

  equity 4.28–4.35

  path dependencies 4.18–4.27, Box 4A

  scale of 1.3, 1.14–1.23

  uncertainties 4.6–4.14, Figure 4–I

changes, social/technical 4.12

climate change **Appendix A2**

  dangerous **1.12**

  global 2.8–2.15, Figure 2–I

  speed of current 2.29

  see also UK climate change

Climate Change Act 2008 3.8, Box 3A

  RCEP recommendations for amendment 5.21, 5.23

  reporting authorities 3.20, 3.22, Figure 3–IV, 5.23–5.24, 5.32

Climate change adaptation principles (Defra) 2.99

Climate Change Risk Assessment 3.8, Box 3A, 5.59

Climate Change (Scotland) Act 2009 3.8, 3.16, Box 3A, 5.20, 5.22

  planning regimes 3.33, 3.35

climate data tools 2.8, 2.21, Box 2B, Box 2C

climate envelopes 2.83–2.91

climate models, uncertainties in Box 2C, 4.6–4.7

climate variability **Appendix A2**

coastal areas 2.68

  defences 2.73, 2.79, 2.81, 3.78, 4.29, 4.93

  development 2.74, 3.37, 3.38, 3.79, 3.84, 3.89

dynamism of 2.71–2.72

erosion *see* coastal erosion

factors affecting character/shape of Box 2D

flooding 1.16, 2.77–2.79, 2.80–2.82, 3.85, 4.33–4.34

  costs, distribution of 4.92–4.97, 5.69

  Future flooding (Office of Science and Technology) 3.77

  legal aspects of Box 4G

  Making space for water strategy (Defra) 3.64, 3.77–3.79

  Netherlands example Box 4F

  Thames Estuary 2100 project 3.70–3.71, Box 3E, 4.13, 4.25

governance of 2.69

infrastructure of 2.73

ingress of salt water upstream 2.55

institutions managing 3.72–3.81, 3.89–3.94

  SMPs 3.82–3.88

integrated coastal zone management 2.69

protection of, legal aspects of Box 4G

threats to 2.80

  responses to 2.81–2.82

coastal change pathfinder programme 3.94

Coastal Concern Action Group 3.88

coastal defences 2.73, 2.79, 2.81, 3.78, 4.29, 4.93

coastal erosion 2.72, 2.75–2.76, Figure 3–VII

  and adaptive capacity 5.60–5.69

  financial compensation 5.62–5.63

  Future flooding (Office of Science and Technology) 3.77

  institutions managing 3.72–3.81, 3.89–3.94

    SMPs 3.82–3.88

  insurance 4.96–4.98

  legal aspects of Box 4G

  Making space for water strategy (Defra) 3.64, 3.77–3.79

  RCEP recommendations regarding 5.64, 5.69

  uneven burden distribution 1.20, 4.29, 4.34, 4.92–4.93, 4.95

coastal realignment 2.82, Figure 2–V

coastal squeeze 2.74

Committee on Climate Change Box 3A

  see also Adaptation Sub-Committee (ASC) of the Committee on Climate Change

Common Agricultural Policy (EU) 3.107
complexities of adaptation 4.15–4.17
cost-benefit analysis (CBA) 4.36–4.38, 4.93
    limitations of 4.39–4.42, 5.15
cost-effective analysis 4.36

data, global warming 2.9, Box 2C, Figure 2–I
Defra *see* Department for Environment, Food
    and Rural Affairs (Defra)
deliberative engagement 4.11
Department for Communities and Local
  Government (CLG) 3.34, 3.73, 5.16
    ESPACE Project Box 3B
    planning policies 3.40, 3.93
Department for Environment, Food and Rural
  Affairs (Defra) 3.18
    adaptation to coastal changes 3.93
    Adapting to Climate Change (ACC)
      Programme 3.10, 5.31
    catchment sensitive farming Box 3D
    coastal change pathfinder programme 3.94
    departmental adaptation plans 5.27, 5.48, 5.50
    ecosystem services 4.69, 5.16
    England, adaptation in 3.13
    England Biodiversity Strategy 2.99,
      Appendix A1
    flood/coastal erosion management 3.64, 3.73,
      3.77–3.79, 3.82
        adaptation to change 3.93–3.94
        public engagement 4.83
    Local and Regional Adaptation Partnership
      (LRAP) Board 5.31
    planning 3.37
    publications
        Climate change adaptation principles 2.99
        Consultation on coastal change policy 4.83
        Future water 3.59
        Making space for water 3.37, 3.64, 3.77–3.79
    RCEP recommendations to 5.31, 5.73
    reporting authorities 3.20–3.22, Figure 3–IV,
      5.23–5.24
    'Securing Biodiversity' framework 3.104
    valuing ecosystems 5.16
    water management 3.59, Figure 3–V

Department of Energy and Climate Change
  Box 2B, 3.44
development
    coastal areas 2.74, 3.37, 3.38, 3.79, 3.84, 3.89
    and flood risk 3.79, 3.89, 4.116
    see also planning regimes
disruption from weather events 2.6–2.7, 4.34,
    5.64
drainage systems 2.62, 3.48, 3.69
    natural 2.66, 3.108, Box 4E
drought 2.58–2.60, 2.101
duty, adaptation 5.19–5.21, 5.22, 5.34

ecological resilience **Appendix A2**
ecosystem **Appendix A2**
ecosystem services 2.102, 3.103, 4.69, 5.44,
    Appendix A2
efficiency 4.28, 4.36–4.42
    and equity 4.37, 4.40
El Niño 2.10
emissions reductions
    and mitigation 1.11, 3.3
    UK goals for 1.2
England
    coastal defences 2.73
    coastal erosion 2.76, 3.77
    coastal management 3.72–3.73, 3.80, 4.94
    coastal vulnerability 2.78
    conservation management 3.95, 3.104, 3.108,
      Figure 3–VIII
    flood management 3.37, 3.61, 3.66–3.67, 3.80,
      4.94
    Future water (Defra) 3.59
    information generation/sharing 4.111–4.112,
      5.31
    local authorities' action 3.24
    NI188, response to 4.107–4.109
    planning regimes 3.32, 3.34, 3.37, 3.42, 4.110
    precipitation 2.17
    water
        demand forecast 2.46
        management of 3.59, Figure 3–V
        quality of 3.50
        regulation of companies 3.57
        resources strategy 3.49, 3.56, 3.58

supply and treatment of 3.55
England Biodiversity Strategy 2.99,
    Appendix A1
Environment Agency
    catchment sensitive farming Box 3D
    coastal realignment of Hesketh Out
        Marsh Figure 2–V
    floods/coastal erosion management 3.37, 3.67,
        3.73, 3.80, 4.93, 4.116
        in England 3.61, 3.66, 3.80, 4.94
    Local and Regional Adaptation Partnership
        (LRAP) Board 5.31
    NI188 3.25
    Thames Estuary 2100 project 3.70–3.71,
        Box 3E
    water management 2.46, 3.49, 3.56
    water quality 3.50
Environment (NI) Order 2002 3.99
environmental assessments 3.40
equity 4.28–4.30
    and adaptive capacity 5.60–5.69
    and efficiency 4.37, 4.40
    uneven burden distribution 1.20, 4.31, 4.92
        social 4.33–4.34
        spatial 4.32
        temporal 4.35
erosion *see* coastal erosion
EU directives 5.42
    Birds Directive 1979 3.46, 3.99, 3.101–3.102,
        4.55, Box 4D, 5.42
    Floods Directive 2007 3.66
    Habitats Directive 1992 1.10, 2.100, 3.46,
        3.100–3.102, 4.55, Box 4D, 5.42
    Water Framework Directive 2000 2.50, 3.46,
        3.50, 3.53, Box 3C, 4.21, Box 4A, 5.41
European Spatial Planning : Adapting to Climate
    Events (ESPACE) Project 3.41, Box 3B, Box 4C
Exmoor Mire Restoration Project 4.73, 4.117,
    Box 4E
extinction of species 2.90, 2.97
extreme weather events 2.5–2.7, 2.18, 2.37, 5.1

fairness *see* equity
Financial inclusion 4.98

flexibility
    of EU directives Box 3C, 4.20–4.22, Box 4D,
        5.42
        inflexibility interpretations of Box 4A
    importance of 1.16, 1.22, 3.105, 4.13, 5.4
    in institutional arrangements 2.37
    of policy 4.25–4.26, 5.41, 5.43
    RCEP recommendations about 5.17, 5.42
Flood and Water Management Bill 2009
    3.67–3.69, 3.80, 3.92, 4.76, 4.78, 4.94
Flood Risk Management (Scotland) Act
    2009 3.66
Flood Risk Regulations 2009 3.66
flooding 2.14, 3.37
    and adaptive capacity 5.60–5.69
    floods of 1953 2.78
    floods of 2007 2.64, 3.65
    floods of 2009 2.6, 2.64
    institutions managing risk 3.61–3.71
    insurance 4.96–4.98
    legal aspects of Box 4G
    and planning policies 4.76
    RCEP recommendations about 5.69
    responses to 2.66
        Exmoor Mire Restoration Project 4.73,
            4.117, Box 4E
        Netherlands water management Box 4F
        Thames Barrier 3.70, Figure 3–VI
        Thames Estuary 2100 project 3.70–3.71,
            Box 3E, 4.13, 4.25
    and strategic memory 4.116
    in summer 2.61–2.63
    uneven burden distribution 4.32–4.34,
        4.92–4.99
    in winter 2.64–2.65
    see also coastal areas, flooding; drainage
        systems
Floods Directive (EU) 2007 3.66
framing challenge/response 4.43–4.45, 4.50–
    4.53, Box 4B, Figure 4–II
    differing values/interests 4.66–4.70
    goals, competition between 4.59–4.63
    key missions and cc response 4.54–4.55,
        Box 4C, Box 4D
    roles in partnerships 4.56–4.58

framing challenge/response *continued*
　'short-termism' 4.64–4.65
frost, days of Box 2A
Future flooding (Office of Science and
　Technology) 3.77
Future water (Defra) 3.59

GHG *see* greenhouse gas (GHG) emissions
Global Circulation Models (GCMs) 2.8, 2.21,
　Box 2C
global warming
　average near-surface temperatures
　　1850–2006 Figure 2–I
　current rate of 1.11, 2.10
　data on 2.9
　man-made causes of 2.10
　predictions about 2.12, 2.30
　see also temperatures
Government, defined **3.4**
government(s), defined **3.4**
Greater London Authority Act 2007 3.7, 5.21
greenhouse gas (GHG) emissions 1.11, 2.10,
　2.15, 2.18, Box 2B, Box 2C

habitats **Appendix A2**
　change/loss of 2.63, 2.99–2.101
　　coastal areas 2.74, 2.82, 2.100, Figure 2–V
　　wetlands 2.101
　climate envelopes 2.83–2.91
　connectivity of **Appendix A2**
　vs. livelihoods 3.90
　see also biodiversity; Habitats Directive (EU)
　　1992; nature conservation
Habitats Directive (EU) 1992 1.10, 2.100, 3.46,
　3.100–3.102, 4.55, Box 4D, 5.42
Hampshire County Council Box 3B, Box 4C, 5.73
Happisburgh, coastal erosion at 2.76, 3.88,
　Figure 3–VII, 4.29–4.30
Heat-Health Watch system 2.13
heatwaves 2.12–2.13
　of 2003 2.6, 2.37
Hesketh Out Marsh Figure 2–V
Human Rights Act 1998 Box 4G
hydrological cycle 2.14, 2.41–2.42, 2.101
impact threshold **Appendix A2**

impacts Box 4B, **Appendix A2**
　of current UK weather 2.5–2.7
　by Government department Figure 3–III
implementing adaptation 4.43–4.44, 4.71–4.99,
　Figure 4–II
　co-ordination of actors 4.86–4.89, Box 4F
　costs, distribution of 4.92–4.99, Box 4G
　enabling mechanisms 4.75–4.78
　public engagement 4.79–4.85
　resources 4.90–4.91
　up-scaling initiatives 4.73–4.74, Box 4E
indicators, adaptive capacity 5.25–5.28
inertia **Appendix A2**
information
　generating/sharing 4.106–4.112, 5.52, 5.57,
　　5.75
　using 4.113–4.114, 5.56
　see also knowledge
infrastructure 1.5
　coastal 2.73, 2.76, 2.100
　energy 3.44
　flaws in current 1.14, 2.7
　investment 5.17
　lock-in 4.27
　nationally significant 3.42–3.44
　resiliency required 2.37
　time frames 4.65
Infrastructure Planning Commission
　(IPC) 3.18, 3.43–3.44, 5.37
innovation 4.117–4.118, Box 4E
institutional arrangements **1.10**, 2.37, 3.45–3.47
　coastal erosion/inundation
　　management 3.72–3.94
　complexity of 4.16–4.17, 5.30
　cooperative initiatives 5.32, 5.44–5.46
　flood management 3.61–3.71, Box 3E
　key missions and cc response 4.54–4.55
　land use planning system 5.33–5.37
　missions/objectives 5.39–5.40
　nature conservation and biodiversity
　　3.95–3.108, Figure 3–VIII
　shortcomings of current system 5.38–5.46
　water management 3.48–3.49
　water quality 3.50–3.54, Box 3C, Box 3D

water supply and wastewater treatment 3.55–3.60, Figure 3–V
see also path dependencies
institutions **1.10**
integrated coastal zone management (ICZM) 2.69
Intergovernmental Panel on Climate Change (IPCC) 1.3, 1.9, Box1A, 2.10, 2.12
International Scientific Congress on Climate Change (Copenhagen, 2009) 1.3
invasive alien species **Appendix A2**
invasive species **Appendix A2**
investment appraisal 5.15–5.18
IPCC *see* Intergovernmental Panel on Climate Change (IPCC)

knowledge
    developing 5.53–5.57
    and risk management 4.9–4.11, Figure 4–I
    using 4.113–4.114
        accredited practitioners scheme 5.56
    see also information; learning about adaptation

landscape permeability **Appendix A2**
leadership 3.109, 5.48–5.52
learning about adaptation 4.43–4.44, 4.100–4.105, Figure 4–II
    continuing professional development 5.55
    information
        generating/sharing 4.106–4.112, 5.52, 5.57, 5.75
        using 4.113–4.114, 5.56
    innovation 4.117–4.118
    strategic memory and social learning 4.115–4.116
    see also knowledge
'Legal liabilities for coastal erosion and flooding in the United Kingdom due to climate change' (RCEP) Box 4G
Living Landscapes initiative 3.107
Living with Environmental Change (LWEC) 3.17, 5.57
Local and Regional Adaptation Partnership (LRAP) Board 3.11, 5.31
local area agreements (LAAs) 3.24

local authorities
    coastal protection 3.73, 3.76, 3.81
    flood management 3.61, 3.66, 3.67, 3.69
    NI188 4.107–4.109
    planning regimes 3.35, 4.77–4.78, 4.91
    RCEP recommendations to 5.33, 5.73
    reporting on progress 3.23–3.28
Local Democracy, Economic Development and Construction Act 2009 3.32
Local Government and Public Involvement in Health Act 2007 3.23–3.24
Local Government Association (LGA) 3.25, 5.51
Local Government White Paper 2006 3.23
Local Strategic Partnerships (LSPs) 3.24–3.25
London Assembly 3.7, 5.20
London, Mayor of 3.7, 5.20

Making space for water strategy (Defra) 3.37, 3.64, 3.77–3.79
Manhood Peninsula 4.29–4.30
Marine and Coastal Access Act 2009 2.69, 3.102
Marine (Scotland) Bill 3.102
market impacts **Appendix A2**
Met Office Hadley Centre 2.19, 2.30, Box 2B
migration of species 2.87–2.91, 5.9
mitigation 1.11–1.13, 3.3, **Appendix A2**
monitoring/reporting 3.20–3.27, 5.22–5.24

national indicators (NIs) 3.24–3.25
    NI188 3.25–3.27, 4.107–4.109, Box 4C
National Parks and Access to Countryside Act 1949 3.98
National Policy Statements 3.40, 3.42, 3.43, 3.44, 5.37
National Risk Assessment 3.18, 5.46
National Risk Register 3.18
Natura 2000 network 3.101, Box 4D, 5.42
Natural England 2.102, 3.108, Box 3D, 5.45
nature conservation
    framing of 4.66–4.70
    institutions managing 3.95–3.108, Figure 3–VIII, 4.14
    see also biodiversity
nature reserves 2.91, 2.98, 3.98, Box 4D

nature's responses 2.103, 4.14
   alien species, introduction of 2.92–2.94
   climate envelopes 2.83–2.91
   ecosystem services 2.102
   habitat change/loss 2.99–2.101
   life cycle timing 2.95–2.96
   species assemblages 2.97–2.98
Netherlands water management Box 4F
nitrates in water 2.54
nitrogen compounds in water 2.53
non-market impacts **Appendix A2**
North Norfolk District Council 3.88
Northern Ireland
   coastal management 3.73
   conservation management 3.96, 3.99, 3.100
   flood management 3.61
   information gathering/sharing 4.111
   Northern Ireland Environment Agency 3.50
   water
      management of 4.88
      regulation of companies 3.57
      supply and treatment of 3.55
Northern Ireland Environment Agency 3.50

Office of Science and Technology 3.77
Ofwat (Water Services Regulation
  Authority) 3.57, 4.55
'organisation', defined **1.10**

path dependencies 4.18–4.19
   infrastructure lock-in 4.27
   overcoming
      flexibility, importance of 4.25
      planning system, use of 4.26
   regulations and monitoring tools 4.21–4.22,
     Box 4A
   responsibilities, statutory 4.24
   responsibility/accountability, fragmentation
     of 4.23
phenology 2.95–2.96
Pitt Review 2.64, 3.18, 3.65, 3.67
planned adaptation **Box 1A, Appendix A2**
Planning Act 2008 3.40, 3.42, 5.37
Planning Policy Statements (PPSs) 3.34

cc revisions 3.38, 4.110
   PPS25 3.37, 3.79
planning regimes 3.29, 4.77–4.78
   addressing cc via 3.38
   and cc adaptation 3.39–3.40, 5.33–5.37
   in England 3.34
   ESPACE Project Box 3B
   path dependencies, avoiding 4.26
   planning permission 3.31
   planning vs. control 3.30
   in Scotland 3.33–3.34, 3.35
   specific policies, use of 3.36
   statutory obligations in respect of cc 3.32
   and strategies 3.37
   in Wales 3.34
policies/programmes for climate change
   3.5–3.19, Box 3A, Figure 3–I, Figure 3–II
   see also adaptive capacity, policy framework
potential impacts **Appendix A2**
precipitation 2.14, 2.17, 2.27, 2.40, Box 2A,
  Figure 2–III
'predict and provide' approach 4.8
probabilities, Bayesian 2.22
projections for UK 2.23–2.28, Table 2.1
   rainfall 2.27, Figure 2–III
   temperatures 2.26, 2.29–2.30, Figure 2–II
   variability and uncertainty in 2.25
   see also Global Circulation Models (GCMs);
    UK Climate Impacts Programme (UKCIP)
public engagement 4.79–4.85, 5.71–5.79
   adaptation assessments 4.11, 4.42, Figure 4–II
   Climate Change (Scotland) Act 2009 3.16
   flooding/coastal erosion 3.79, 3.80, 3.87
   RCEP recommendations for 5.74
   Thames Estuary 2100 project Box 3E

questions, indicative, on adaptation Box 5A

rainfall 2.14, 2.17, 2.27, 2.40, 2.46, Box 2A,
  Figure 2–III
recommendations, RCEP
   Adaptation Sub-Committee, to the 5.80–5.81
   equity
      addressing losses due to cc 5.64
      political/public debates 5.69

institutional arrangements
  adaptation duty, imposition of 5.34
  adaptation test 5.34
  cross-sectoral approach 5.46
  flexibility, use of 5.42
  Infrastructure Planning Commission (IPC)
    activities 5.37
  LRAP Board, extension of 5.31
  missions/objectives 5.40
  planning departments, support of 5.33
  planning policy guidelines 5.37
  water management models 5.43
policy framework
  accountability, systems of 5.22
  adaptation duty, imposition of 5.21
  adaptation test 5.13
  Climate Change Act 2008, amendment
    to 5.21
  discount rates for appraising
    investments 5.18
  reporting authorities 5.23–5.24
  Treasury Green Book, use of 5.17
public engagement
  earlier use of 5.74
  presenting narratives/stories to public 5.73
resources for adaptive capacity
  accredited practitioners scheme 5.56
  capability to produce/interpret cc
    projections 5.54
  commitment to 5.59
  continuing professional development 5.55
  information sharing 5.57
  leadership 5.50
reporting/monitoring 3.20–3.27, 5.22–5.24
residual impacts **Appendix A2**
resilience 3.18, **Appendix A2**
resistance **Appendix A2**
risk management 4.9–4.11
river basin management 3.50–3.51, Box 3C,
  Box 3D
River basin management in a changing climate
  (EU) Box 3C
River Glaven case study 2.56, 3.51, Box 3D, 4.74
River Invertebrate Prediction and Classification
  System (RIVPACS) 4.22, Box 4A

Royal Commission on Environmental Pollution
  announcement of study Appendix A1
  commissioned studies Appendix B
  conduct of study Appendix B
  evidence, invitation to submit Appendix A2
  'Legal liabilities for coastal erosion and
    flooding in the United Kingdom due to
    climate change' Box 4G
  members Appendix D
  organisations/individuals giving
    evidence Appendix B
  questions to organisations Box 5A
  recommendations of *see* recommendations,
    RCEP
  seminars/workshops held Appendix C
  visits Appendix B
Royal Society for the Protection of Birds
  (RSPB) Figure 2–V, 3.74, Box 4D

Scotland
  Climate Change (Scotland) Act 2009 *see*
    Climate Change (Scotland) Act 2009
  coastal erosion 3.81
  coastal management 3.73
  conservation management 3.96, 3.102
  flood management 3.61, 3.66, 4.23
  information gathering/sharing 4.111
  local authorities' action 3.28
  planning regimes 3.33–3.34, 3.35
  Scotland and Northern Ireland Forum for
    Environmental Research 4.111
  Scotland's climate change adaptation framework 3.15
  Scotland's Climate Change Declaration 3.28
  Scottish Environment Protection
    Agency 3.50
  Scottish Environment Protection Agency
    (SEPA) 3.50, 4.23
  Scottish National Planning Framework
    3.34–3.35
  water
    regulation of companies 3.57
    supply and treatment of 3.55
Scotland and Northern Ireland Forum for
  Environmental Research 4.111
Scotland's climate change adaptation framework 3.15

Scotland's Climate Change Declaration 3.28

Scottish Environment Protection Agency
  (SEPA) 3.50, 4.23

Scottish National Planning Framework 3.34–3.35

sea levels
    global averages 2.11, 2.15
    rise of
        affect on coastal erosion 2.76
        affect on coastal flooding 2.77
        affect on habitats 2.100
    UK changes 2.17

Secretary of State 3.20, 3.37, 3.42, Box 3A

'Securing Biodiversity' framework 3.104

sediments in water 2.56, 2.59, 2.61, Box 3D,
  Box 4E

sensitivity **Appendix A2**

shoreline management plans (SMPs) 3.82–3.85
    draft for Kelling to Lowestoft coastline
      3.86–3.88

'short-termism' 1.19, 4.64–4.65

Sites of Special Scientific Interest (SSSIs) 3.98,
  3.99, 3.101

skills 4.90, 4.101, 4.105, 5.53–5.57

snow cover 2.11, Box 2A, Box 2C
    see also precipitation

Special Areas of Conservation (SACs) 2.100,
  3.101, Box 4D

Special Protection Areas (SPAs) 3.101, Box 4D

storm sewage 2.62–2.63, 2.65

storm surges 2.78, 4.59

strategic memory 4.115–4.116

sunshine levels Box 2A

sustainability appraisal 3.40

systemic threshold **Appendix A2**

Technical Advice Notes (TANs) 3.34
    TAN15 3.37

temperatures
    changes over Western Europe 1900-
      2100 Figure 2–IV
    impact of increased 2.29–2.30
    UK changes/trends 2.16–17, 2.26, 2.29–2.30,
      Box 2A, Figure 2–II
    water quality, affect on 2.51–2.52
    see also global warming

Thames Barrier 3.70, Figure 3–VI

Thames Estuary 2100 project 3.70–3.71,
  Box 3E, 4.13, 4.25

thresholds **Appendix A2**

Trades Union Congress (TUC) 4.108

transformability **Appendix A2**

Treasury Green Book 4.37, 5.16–5.17

Tyndall Centre for Climate Change
  Research 2.19

UK climate change 1.5
    biodiversity 2.85, 2.103
        alien species 2.92–2.94
        change/loss of habitats 2.99–2.101
        ecosystem services 2.102
        extinction of species 2.90
        life cycle timing 2.95–2.96
        nature reserves 2.91
        range shifts 2.88–2.91
    changes/trends Box 2A
    coastal areas 2.68–2.73
        addressing threats to 2.80–2.82
        coastal squeeze 2.74
        erosion and flooding 2.75–2.79
        factors affecting character/shape
          of Box 2D
    effects, examples of 2.35
    fresh water 2.39–2.43
    impacts/risks by Government
      departments Figure 3–III
    opportunities from 2.34
    precipitation 2.17
    projections 2.23–2.28, Table 2.1
        rainfall 2.27, Figure 2–III
        temperatures 2.26, 2.29–2.30, Figure 2–II
        variability and uncertainty in 2.25
    research offices 2.19
    temperatures 2.16–17
    water
        demand for 2.44–2.48
        flooding 2.61–2.66
        lack of (drought) 2.58–2.60
        management planning 2.67
        quality of 2.49–2.57
        seasonal precipitation distributions 2.40

UK Climate Impacts Programme
 (UKCIP) 2.19–2.20, 3.11, 3.25, 5.31
  continuing professional development
  5.54–5.55
  framing adaptation Box 4B
  UKCP09 1.8, 2.23–2.28, Box 2B, Table 2.1,
  5.54
   uncertainties, dealing with 2.31
uncertainties 4.6–4.7, Figure 4–I
 in climate predictions 2.31–2.33, Box 2C
 institutional responses to 4.8–4.14
 nature's response to cc 4.14
United Nations Framework Convention on
 Climate Change 1992 3.6

vulnerability 3.21, Box 4B, 5.2, 5.10, 5.45,
 Appendix A2

Wales 4.94
 coastal defences 2.73
 coastal erosion 2.76, 3.77, 4.94
 coastal management 3.73, 3.80
 conservation management Figure 3–VIII
 flood risk management 3.61, 3.66, 3.67, 3.80,
  4.56, 4.94
 information generation/sharing 4.111
 local authorities' action 3.28
 planning regimes 3.32, 3.34, 3.37, 3.42
 precipitation 2.17
 water
  demand forecast 2.46
  management of Figure 3–V
  quality of 3.50

regulation of companies 3.57
 resources strategy 3.56, 3.59
 supply and treatment of 3.55
Welsh Climate Change Commission 4.111
Welsh Ministers 3.67, 3.80, Box 3A, 4.94, 5.23
water
 availability, factors affecting 2.47
 centrality to life 2.39
 demand for 2.44–2.48
 drought 2.58–2.60
 flooding 2.61–2.66
 hydrological cycle 2.41–2.42
 institutions managing 3.48–3.49, Figure 3–V
  EU Water Framework Directive Box 3C
  flood strategies 3.61–3.71, Box 3E,
   Figure 3–VI
  supply and treatment 3.55–3.60
  water quality 3.50–3.54, Box 3D
 management planning 2.67, Box 4F, 5.43
 quality of 2.49–2.57, 5.43
Water Framework Directive (EU) 2000 2.50,
 3.46, 3.50, 3.53, Box 3C, 4.21, Box 4A, 5.41
Water Resources Strategy for England 2008 3.49
Water Services Regulation Authority
 (Ofwat) 4.55
Watson, Professor Robert 2.30
weather, extreme 2.5–2.7, 2.18, 2.37, 5.1
Welsh Climate Change Commission 4.111
Welsh Ministers 3.67, 3.80, Box 3A, 4.94, 5.23
wetland habitats 2.101
Wildlife and Countryside Act 1981 3.99
Wildlife (NI) Order 1985 3.99
Wildlife Trusts 3.107